# Experiment Central

*Understanding Scientific Principles*
*Through Projects*

# Experiment Central

*Understanding Scientific Principles*
*Through Projects*
## Second Edition

VOLUME 3: F-K

M. Rae Nelson

*Kristine Krapp, editor*

U·X·L
*A part of Gale, Cengage Learning*

GALE
CENGAGE Learning

Detroit • New York • San Francisco • New Haven, Conn • Waterville, Maine • London

# GALE
## CENGAGE Learning™

**Experiment Central**
**Understanding Scientific**
**Principles Through Projects**
**Second Edition**
**M. Rae Nelson**

Project Editor: Kristine Krapp

Managing Editor: Debra Kirby

Rights Acquisition and Management:
Margaret Abendroth, Robyn Young

Composition: Evi Abou-El-Seoud, Mary
Beth Trimper

Manufacturing: Wendy Blurton

Product Manager: Julia Furtaw

Product Design: Jennifer Wahi

© 2010 Gale, Cengage Learning

For product information and technology assistance, contact us at
**Gale Customer Support, 1-800-877-4253.**
For permission to use material from this text or product,
submit all requests online at **www.cengage.com/permissions.**
Further permissions questions can be e-mailed to
**permissionrequest@cengage.com**

Cover photographs: Images courtesy of Dreamstime, Photos.com, and
iStockPhoto.

**Library of Congress Cataloging-in-Publication Data**

Experiment central : understanding scientific principles through projects. --
2nd ed. / M. Rae Nelson, Kristine Krapp, editors.    p. cm. --
   Includes bibliographical references and index.
   ISBN 978-1-4144-7613-1 (set) -- ISBN 978-1-4144-7614-8 (vol. 1) --
ISBN 978-1-4144-7615-5 (vol. 2) -- ISBN 978-1-4144-7616-2 (vol. 3) --
ISBN 978-1-4144-7617-9 (vol. 4) -- ISBN 978-1-4144-7618-6 (vol. 5) --
ISBN 978-1-4144-7619-3 (vol. 6)
   1. Science--Experiments--Juvenile literature. I. Nelson, M. Rae. II. Krapp,
Kristine M.

Q164.E96 2010
507.8--dc22                                                    2009050304

Gale
27500 Drake Rd.
Farmington Hills, MI, 48331-3535

978-1-4144-7613-1 (set)          1-4144-7613-2 (set)
978-1-4144-7614-8 (vol. 1)       1-4144-7614-0 (vol. 1)
978-1-4144-7615-5 (vol. 2)       1-4144-7615-9 (vol. 2)
978-1-4144-7616-2 (vol. 3)       1-4144-7616-7 (vol. 3)
978-1-4144-7617-9 (vol. 4)       1-4144-7617-5 (vol. 4)
978-1-4144-7618-6 (vol. 5)       1-4144-7618-3 (vol. 5)
978-1-4144-7619-3 (vol. 6)       1-4144-7619-1 (vol. 6)

This title is also available as an e-book.
ISBN-13: 978-1-4144-7620-9 (set)
ISBN-10: 1-4144-7620-5 (set)
Contact your Gale sales representative for ordering information.

Printed by China Translation & Printing Services Limited,
Guangdong Province, China. 1st printing. 05/2010
1 2 3 4 5 6 7 14 13 12 11 10

# Table of Contents

*Experiment Central, 2nd edition*

*Experiment Central, 2nd edition*

*Experiment Central, 2nd edition*

# Reader's Guide

*Experiment Central: Understanding Scientific Principles Through Projects* provides in one resource a wide variety of science experiments covering nine key science curriculum fields—astronomy, biology, botany, chemistry, ecology, food science, geology, meteorology, and physics—spanning the earth sciences, life sciences, and physical sciences.

*Experiment Central, 2nd edition* combines, expands, and updates the original four-volume and two-volume UXL sets. This new edition includes 20 new chapters, 60 new experiments, and more than 35 enhanced experiments. Each chapter explores a scientific subject and offers experiments or projects that utilize or reinforce the topic studied. Chapters are alphabetically arranged according to scientific concept, including: Air and Water Pollution, Color, Eclipses, Forensic Science, Genetics, Magnetism, Mountains, Periodic Table, Renewable Energy, Storms and Water Cycle. Two to three experiments or projects are included in each chapter.

## Entry format

Chapters are presented in a standard, easy-to-follow format. All chapters open with an explanatory overview section designed to introduce students to the scientific concept and provide the background behind a concept s discovery or important figures who helped advance the study of the field.

Each experiment is divided into eight standard sections to help students follow the experimental process clearly from beginning to end. Sections are:

- Purpose/Hypothesis
- Level of Difficulty

- Materials Needed
- Approximate Budget
- Timetable
- Step-by-Step Instructions
- Summary of Results
- Change the Variables

Chapters also include a "Design Your Own Experiment" section that allows students to apply what they have learned about a particular concept and to create their own experiments. This section is divided into:

- How to Select a Topic Relating to this Concept
- Steps in the Scientific Method
- Recording Data and Summarizing the Results
- Related Projects

## Special Features

A "Words to Know" sidebar provides definitions of terms used in each chapter. A cumulative glossary collected from all the "Words to Know" sections is included in the beginning of each volume.

The "Experiments by Scientific Field" section categorizes experiments by scientific curriculum area. This section cumulates all experiments across the six-volume series.

The Parent's and Teacher's Guide recommends that a responsible adult always oversee a student's experiment and provides several safety guidelines for all students to follow.

Standard sidebars accompany experiments and projects.

- "What Are the Variables?" explains the factors that may have an impact on the outcome of a particular experiment.
- "How to Experiment Safely" clearly explains any risks involved with the experiment and how to avoid them.
- "Troubleshooter's Guide" presents problems that a student might encounter with an experiment, possible causes of the problem, and ways to remedy the problem.

Over 450 photos enhance the text; approximately 450 custom illustrations show the steps in the experiments.

Four indexes cumulate information from all the experiments in this six-volume set, including:

- Budget Index categorizes the experiments by approximate cost.
- Level of Difficulty Index lists experiments according to "easy," "moderate," or "difficult," or a combination thereof.
- Timetable Index categorizes each experiment by the amount of time needed to complete it, including setup and follow-through time.
- General Subject Index provides access to all major terms, people, places, and topics covered in the set.

## Acknowledgments

The author wishes to acknowledge and thank Laurie Curtis, teacher/researcher; Cindy O'Neill, science educator; and Joyce Nelson, chemist, for their contributions to this edition as consultants.

## Comments and Suggestions

We welcome your comments on *Experiment Central*. Please write: Editors, *Experiment Central*, U*X*L, 27500 Drake Rd. Farmington Hills, MI 48331-3535; call toll-free: 1-800-347-4253; or visit us at www.gale.cengage.com.

# Parent's and Teacher's Guide

The experiments and projects in *Experiment Central* have been carefully constructed with issues of safety in mind, but your guidance and supervision are still required. Following the safety guidelines that accompany each experiment and project (found in the "How to Experiment Safely" sidebar box), as well as putting to work the safe practices listed below, will help your child or student avoid accidents. Oversee your child or student during experiments, and make sure he or she follows these safety guidelines:

- Always wear safety goggle is there is any possiblity of sharp objects, small particles, splashes of liquid, or gas fumes getting in someone's eyes.
- Always wear protective gloves when handling materials that could irritate the skin.
- Never leave an open flame, such as a lit candle, unattended. Never wear loose clothing around an open flame.
- Follow instructions carefully when using electrical equipment, including batteries, to avoid getting shocked.
- Be cautious when handling sharp objects or glass equipment that might break. Point scissors away from you and use them carefully.
- Always ask for help in cleaning up spills, broken glass, or other hazardous materials.
- Always use protective gloves when handling hot objects. Set them down only on a protected surface that will not be damaged by heat.

- Always wash your hands thoroughly after handling material that might contain harmful microorganisms, such as soil and pond water.

- Do not substitute materials in an experiment without asking a knowledgeable adult about possible reactions.

- Do not use or mix unidentified liquids or powders. The result might be an explosion or poisonous fumes.

- Never taste or eat any substances being used in an experiment.

- Always wear old clothing or a protective apron to avoid staining your clothes.

# Experiments by Scientific Field

Chapter name in brackets, followed by experiment name. The numeral before the colon indicates volume; numbers after the colon indicate page number.

## BIOLOGY

*Experiment Central, 2nd edition*

## CHEMISTRY

## ECOLOGY

## FOOD SCIENCE

## GEOLOGY

# Words to Know

### A

**Abdomen:** The third segment of an insect body.

**Abscission:** Barrier of special cells created at the base of leaves in autumn.

**Absolute dating:** The age of an object correlated to a specific fixed time, as established by some precise dating method.

**Acceleration:** The rate at which the velocity and/or direction of an object is changing with respect to time.

**Acid:** Substance that when dissolved in water is capable of reacting with a base to form salts and release hydrogen ions.

**Acid rain:** A form of precipitation that is significantly more acidic than neutral water, often produced as the result of industrial processes and pollution.

**Acoustics:** The science concerned with the production, properties, and propagation of sound waves.

**Acronym:** A word or phrase formed from the first letter of other words.

**Active solar energy system:** A solar energy system that uses pumps or fans to circulate heat captured from the Sun.

**Additive:** A chemical compound that is added to foods to give them some desirable quality, such as preventing them from spoiling.

**Adhesion:** Attraction between two different substances.

**Adhesive:** A substance that bonds or adheres two substances together.

**Aeration:** Mixing a gas, like oxygen, with a liquid, like water.

**Aerobic:** A process that requires oxygen.

**Aerodynamics:** The study of the motion of gases (particularly air) and the motion and control of objects in the air.

**Agar:** A nutrient rich, gelatinous substance that is used to grow bacteria.

**Air:** Gaseous mixture that covers Earth, composed mainly of nitrogen (about 78%) and oxygen (about 21%) with lesser amounts of argon, carbon dioxide, and other gases.

**Air density:** The ratio of the mass of a substance to the volume it occupies.

**Air mass:** A large body of air that has similar characteristics.

**Air pressure:** The force exerted by the weight of the atmosphere above a point on or above Earth's surface.

**Alga/Algae:** Single-celled or multicellular plants or plant-like organisms that contain chlorophyll, thus making their own food by photosynthesis. Algae grow mainly in water.

**Alignment:** Adjustment in a certain direction or orientation.

**Alkali metals:** The first group of elements in the periodic table, these metals have a single electron in the outermost shell.

**Alkaline:** Having a pH of more than 7.

**Alleles:** One version of the same gene.

**Alloy:** A mixture of two or more metals with properties different from those metals of which it is made.

**Amine:** An organic compound derived from ammonia.

**Amino acid:** One of a group of organic compounds that make up proteins.

**Amnesia:** Partial or total memory loss.

**Amperage:** A measurement of current. The common unit of measure is the ampere or amp.

**Amphibians:** Animals that live on land and breathe air but return to the water to reproduce.

**Amplitude:** The maximum displacement (difference between an original position and a later position) of the material that is vibrating. Amplitude can be thought of visually as the highest and lowest point of a wave.

**Anaerobic:** A process that does not require oxygen.

**Anal fin:**  Fin on the belly of a fish, used for balance.

**Anatomy:**  The study of the structure of living things.

**Anemometer:**  A device that measures wind speed.

**Angiosperm:**  A flowering plant that has its seeds produced within an ovary.

**Animalcules:**  Life forms that Anton van Leeuwenhoek named when he first saw them under his microscope; they later became known as protozoa and bacteria.

**Anther:**  The male reproductive organs of the plant, located on the tip of a flower's stamen.

**Anthocyanin:**  Red pigment found in leaves, petals, stems, and other parts of a plant.

**Antibiotic:**  A substance produced by or derived from certain fungi and other organisms, that can destroy or inhibit the growth of other microorganisms.

**Antibiotic resistance:**  The ability of microorganisms to change so that they are not killed by antibiotics.

**Antibody:**  A protein produced by certain cells of the body as an immune (disease-fighting) response to a specific foreign antigen.

**Antigen:**  A substance that causes the production of an antibody when injected directly into the body.

**Antioxidants:**  Used as a food additive, these substances can prevent food spoilage by reducing the food's exposure to air.

**Aquifer:**  Underground layer of sand, gravel, or spongy rock that collects water.

**Arch:**  A curved structure that spans an opening and supports a weight above the opening.

**Artesian well:**  A well in which water is forced out under pressure.

**Asexual reproduction:**  A reproductive process that does not involve the union of two individuals in the exchange of genetic material.

**Astronomers:**  Scientists who study the positions, motions, and composition of stars and other objects in the sky.

**Astronomy:**  The study of the physical properties of objects and matter outside Earth's atmosphere.

**Atmosphere:**  Layers of air that surround Earth.

**Atmospheric pressure:** The pressure exerted by the atmosphere at Earth's surface due to the weight of the air.

**Atom:** The smallest unit of an element, made up of protons and neutrons in a central nucleus surrounded by moving electrons.

**Atomic mass:** Also known as atomic weight, the average mass of the atoms in an element; the number that appears under the element symbol in the periodic table.

**Atomic number:** The number of protons (or electrons) in an atom; the number that appears over the element symbol in the periodic table.

**Atomic symbol:** The one- or two-letter abbreviation for a chemical element.

**Autotroph:** An organism that can build all the food and produce all the energy it needs with its own resources.

**Auxins:** A group of plant hormones responsible for patterns of plant growth.

**Axis:** An imaginary straight line around which an object, like a planet, spins or turns. Earth's axis is a line that goes through the North and South Poles.

**B**

**Bacteria:** Single-celled microorganisms that live in soil, water, plants, and animals that play a key role in the decay of organic matter and the cycling of nutrients. Some are agents of disease.

**Bacteriology:** The scientific study of bacteria, their characteristics, and their activities as related to medicine, industry, and agriculture.

**Barometer:** An instrument for measuring atmospheric pressure, used especially in weather forecasting.

**Base:** Substance that when dissolved in water is capable of reacting with an acid to form salts and release hydrogen ions; has a pH of more than 7.

**Base pairs:** In DNA, the pairing of two nucleotides with each other: adenine (A) with thymine (T), and guanine (G) with cytosine (C).

**Beam:** A straight, horizontal structure that spans an opening and supports a weight above the opening.

**Bedrock:** Solid layer of rock lying beneath the soil and other loose material.

**Beriberi:** A disease caused by a deficiency of thiamine and characterized by nerve and gastrointestinal disorders.

**Biochemical oxygen demand (BOD5):** The amount of oxygen micro-organisms use over a five-day period in 68°F (20°C) water to decay organic matter.

**Biodegradable:** Capable of being decomposed by biological agents.

**Biological variables:** Living factors such as bacteria, fungi, and animals that can affect the processes that occur in nature and in an experiment.

**Bioluminescence:** The chemical phenomenon in which an organism can produce its own light.

**Biomass:** Organic materials that are used to produce usable energy.

**Biomes:** Large geographical areas with specific climates and soils, as well as distinct plant and animal communities that are interdependent.

**Biomimetics:** The development of materials that are found in nature.

**Biopesticide:** Pesticide produced from substances found in nature.

**Bivalve:** Bivalves are characterized by shells that are divided into two parts or valves that completely enclose the mollusk like the clam or scallop.

**Blanching:** A cooking technique in which the food, usually vegetables and fruits, are briefly cooked in boiling water and then plunged into cold water.

**Blood pattern analysis:** The study of the shape, location, and pattern of blood in order to understand how it got there.

**Blueshift:** The shortening of the frequency of light waves toward the blue end of the visible light spectrum as they travel towards an observer; most commonly used to describe movement of stars towards Earth.

**Boiling point:** The temperature at which a substance changes from a liquid to a gas or vapor.

**Bond:** The force that holds two atoms together.

**Bone joint:** A place in the body where two or more bones are connected.

**Bone marrow:** The spongy center of many bones in which blood cells are manufactured.

**Bone tissue:** A group of similar cells in the bone with a common function.

**Bony fish:** The largest group of fish, whose skeleton is made of bone.

**Boreal:** Northern.

**Botany:** The branch of biology involving the scientific study of plant life.

**Braided rivers:** Wide, shallow rivers with multiple channels and pebbly islands in the middle.

**Buoyancy:** The tendency of a liquid to exert a lifting effect on a body immersed in it.

**By-product:** A secondary substance produced as the result of a physical or chemical process, in addition to the main product.


## C

**Calcium carbonate:** A substance that is secreted by a mollusk to create the shell it lives in.

**Calibration:** To standardize or adjust a measuring instrument so its measurements are correct.

**Cambium:** The tissue below the bark that produces new cells, which become wood and bark.

**Camouflage:** Markings or coloring that help hide an animal by making it blend into the surrounding environment.

**Cancellous bone:** Also called spongy bone, the inner layer of a bone that has cells with large spaces in between them filled with marrow.

**Canning:** A method of preserving food using airtight, vacuum-sealed containers and heat processing.

**Capillary action:** The tendency of water to rise through a narrow tube by the force of adhesion between the water and the walls of the tube.

**Caramelization:** The process of heating sugars to the point at which they break down and lead to the formation of new compounds.

**Carbohydrate:** A compound consisting of carbon, hydrogen, and oxygen found in plants and used as a food by humans and other animals.

**Carbonic acid:** A weak acid that forms from the mixture of water and carbon dioxide.

**Carnivore:** A meat-eating organism.

**Carotene:** Yellow-orange pigment in plants.

**Cartilage:** The connective tissue that covers and protects the bones.

**Cartilaginous fish:** The second largest group of fish whose skeleton is made of cartilage

**Cast:** In paleontology, the fossil formed when a mold is later filled in by mud or mineral matter.

**Catalase:** An enzyme found in animal liver tissue that breaks down hydrogen peroxide into oxygen and water.

**Catalyst:** A compound that starts or speeds up the rate of a chemical reaction without undergoing any change in its own composition.

**Caudal fin:** Tail fin of a fish used for fast swimming.

**Cave:** Also called cavern, a hollow or natural passage under or into the ground large enough for a person to enter.

**Celestial bodies:** Describing planets or other objects in space.

**Cell membrane:** The layer that surrounds the cell, but is inside the cell wall, allowing some molecules to enter and keeping others out of the cell.

**Cell theory:** All living things have one or more similar cells that carry out the same functions for the living process.

**Cell wall:** A tough outer covering over the cell membrane of bacteria and plant cells.

**Cells:** The basic unit for living organisms; cells are structured to perform highly specialized functions.

**Centrifugal force:** The apparent force pushing a rotating body away from the center of rotation.

**Centrifuge:** A device that rapidly spins a solution so that the heavier components will separate from the lighter ones.

**Centripetal force:** Rotating force that moves towards the center or axis.

**Cerebral cortex:** The outer layer of the brain.

**Channel:** A shallow trench carved into the ground by the pressure and movement of a river.

**Chemical change:** The change of one or more substances into other substances.

**Chemical energy:** Energy stored in chemical bonds.

**Chemical property:** A characteristic of a substance that allows it to undergo a chemical change. Chemical properties include flammability and sensitivity to light.

**Chemical reaction:** Any chemical change in which at least one new substance is formed.

**Chemosense:** A sense stimulated by specific chemicals that cause the sensory cell to transmit a signal to the brain.

**Chitin:** Substance that makes up the exoskeleton of crustaceans.

**Chlorophyll:** A green pigment found in plants that absorbs sunlight, providing the energy used in photosynthesis, or the conversion of carbon dioxide and water to complex carbohydrates.

**Chloroplasts:** Small structures in plant cells that contain chlorophyll and in which the process of photosynthesis takes place.

**Chromatography:** A method for identifying the components of a substance based on their characteristic colors.

**Chromosome:** A structure of DNA found in the cell nucleus.

**Cilia:** Hairlike structures on olfactory receptor cells that sense odor molecules.

**Circuit:** The complete path of an electric current including the source of electric energy.

**Circumference:** The distance around a circle.

**Clay:** Type of soil comprising the smallest soil particles.

**Cleavage:** The tendency of a mineral to split along certain planes.

**Climate:** The average weather that a region experiences over a long period.

**Coagulation:** The clumping together of particles in a mixture, often because the repelling force separating them is disrupted.

**Cohesion:** Attraction between like substances.

**Cold blooded:** When an animals body temperature rises or falls to match the environment.

**Collagen:** A protein in bone that gives the bone elasticity.

**Colloid:** A mixture containing particles suspended in, but not dissolved in, a dispersing medium.

**Colony:** A mass of microorganisms that have been bred in a medium.

**Colorfast:** The ability of a material to keep its dye and not fade or change color.

**Coma:** Glowing cloud of gas surrounding the nucleus of a comet.

**Combustion:** Any chemical reaction in which heat, and usually light, is produced. It is commonly the burning of organic substances during which oxygen from the air is used to form carbon dioxide and water vapor.

**Comet:** An icy body orbiting in the solar system, which partially vaporizes when it nears the Sun and develops a diffuse envelope of dust and gas as well as one or more tails.

**Comet head:** The nucleus and the coma of a comet.

**Comet nucleus:** The core or center of a comet. (Plural: Comet nuclei.)

**Comet tail:** The most distinctive feature of comets; comets can display two basic types of tails: one gaseous and the other largely composed of dust.

**Compact bone:** The outer, hard layer of the bone.

**Complete metamorphosis:** Metamorphosis in which a larva becomes a pupa before changing into an adult form.

**Composting:** The process in which organic compounds break down and become dark, fertile soil called humus.

**Compression:** A type of force on an object where the object is pushed or squeezed from each end.

**Concave:** Hollowed or rounded inward, like the inside of a bowl.

**Concave lens:** A lens that is thinner in the middle than at the edges.

**Concentration:** The amount of a substance present in a given volume, such as the number of molecules in a liter.

**Condensation:** The process by which a gas changes into a liquid.

**Conduction:** The flow of heat through a solid.

**Conductivity:** The ability of a material to carry an electrical current.

**Conductor:** A substance able to carry an electrical current.

**Cones:** Cells in the retina that can perceive color.

**Confined aquifer:** An aquifer with a layer of impermeable rock above it where the water is held under pressure.

**Coniferous:** Refers to trees, such as pines and firs, that bear cones and have needle-like leaves that are not shed all at once.

**Conservation of energy:** The law of physics that states that energy can be transformed from one form to another, but can be neither created nor destroyed.

**Constellations:** Patterns of stars in the night sky. There are eighty-eight known constellations.

**Continental drift:** The theory that continents move apart slowly at a predictable rate.

**Contract:** To shorten, pull together.

**Control experiment:** A set-up that is identical to the experiment but is not affected by the variable that will be changed during the experiment.

**Convection:** The circulatory motion that occurs in a gas or liquid at a nonuniform temperature owing to the variation of its density and the action of gravity.

**Convection current:** A circular movement of a fluid in response to alternating heating and cooling.

**Convex:** Curved or rounded outward, like the outside of a ball.

**Convex lens:** A lens that is thicker in the middle than at the edges.

**Coprolites:** The fossilized droppings of animals.

**Coriolis force:** A force that makes a moving object appear to travel in a curved path over the surface of a spinning body.

**Corona:** The outermost atmospheric layer of the Sun.

**Corrosion:** An oxidation-reduction reaction in which a metal is oxidized (reacted with oxygen) and oxygen is reduced, usually in the presence of moisture.

**Cotyledon:** Seed leaves, which contain the stored source of food for the embryo.

**Crater:** An indentation caused by an object hitting the surface of a planet or moon.

**Crest:** The highest point reached by a wave.

**Cross-pollination:** The process by which pollen from one plant pollinates another plant of the same species.

**Crust:** The hard outer shell of Earth that floats upon the softer, denser mantle.

**Crustacean:** A type of arthropod characterized by hard and thick skin, and having shells that are jointed. This group includes the lobster, crab, and crayfish.

**Crystal:** Naturally occurring solid composed of atoms or molecules arranged in an orderly pattern that repeats at regular intervals.

**Crystal faces:** The flat, smooth surfaces of a crystal.

**Crystal lattice:** The regular and repeating pattern of the atoms in a crystal.

**Cultures:** Microorganisms growing in prepared nutrients.

**Cumulonimbus cloud:** The parent cloud of a thunderstorm; a tall, vertically developed cloud capable of producing heavy rain, high winds, and lightning.

**Current:** The flow of electrical charge from one point to another.

**Currents:** The horizontal and vertical circulation of ocean waters.

**Cyanobacteria:** Oxygen-producing, aquatic bacteria capable of manufacturing its own food; resembles algae.

**Cycles:** Occurrence of events that take place on a regular, repeating basis.

**Cytology:** The branch of biology concerned with the study of cells.

**Cytoplasm:** The semifluid substance inside a cell that surrounds the nucleus and other membrane-enclosed organelles.

**D**

**Decanting:** The process of separating a suspension by waiting for its heavier components to settle out and then pouring off the lighter ones.

**Decibel (dB):** A unit of measurement for the amplitude of sound.

**Deciduous:** Plants that lose their leaves during some season of the year, and then grow them back during another season.

**Decompose:** To break down into two or more simpler substances.

**Decomposition:** The breakdown of complex molecules of dead organisms into simple nutrients that can be reutilized by living organisms.

**Decomposition reaction:** A chemical reaction in which one substance is broken down into two or more substances.

**Deficiency disease:** A disease marked by a lack of an essential nutrient in the diet.

**Degrade:** Break down.

**Dehydration:** The removal of water from a material.

**Denaturization:** Altering an enzyme so it no longer works.

**Density:** The mass of a substance divided by its volume.

**Density ball:** A ball with the fixed standard of 1.0 gram per milliliter, which is the exact density of pure water.

**Deoxyribonucleic acid (DNA):** Large, complex molecules found in the nuclei of cells that carry genetic information for an organism's development; double helix. (Pronounced DEE-ox-see-rye-bo-noo-klay-ick acid)

**Dependent variable:** The variable in an experiment whose value depends on the value of another variable in the experiment.

**Deposition:** Dropping of sediments that occurs when a river loses its energy of motion.

**Desert:** A biome with a hot-to-cool climate and dry weather.

**Desertification:** Transformation of arid or semiarid productive land into desert.

**Dewpoint:** The point at which water vapor begins to condense.

**Dicot:** Plants with a pair of embryonic seeds that appear at germination.

**Diffraction:** The bending of light or another form of electromagnetic radiation as it passes through a tiny hole or around a sharp edge.

**Diffraction grating:** A device consisting of a surface into which are etched very fine, closely spaced grooves that cause different wavelengths of light to reflect or refract (bend) by different amounts.

**Diffusion:** Random movement of molecules that leads to a net movement of molecules from a region of high concentration to a region of low concentration.

**Disinfection:** Using chemicals to kill harmful organisms.

**Dissolved oxygen:** Oxygen molecules that have dissolved in water.

**Distillation:** The process of separating liquids from solids or from other liquids with different boiling points by a method of evaporation and condensation, so that each component in a mixture can be collected separately in its pure form.

**DNA fingerprinting:** A technique that uses DNA fragments to identify the unique DNA sequences of an individual.

**DNA replication:** The process by which one DNA strand unwinds and duplicates all its information, creating two new DNA strands that are identical to each other and to the original strand.

**DNA (deoxyribonucleic acid):** Large, complex molecules found in nuclei of cells that carry genetic information for an organism's development.

**Domain:** Small regions in iron that possess their own magnetic charges.

**Dominant gene:** A gene that passes on a certain characteristic, even when there is only one copy (allele) of the gene.

**Doppler effect:** The change in wavelength and frequency (number of vibrations per second) of either light or sound as the source is moving either towards or away from the observer.

**Dormant:** A state of inactivity in an organism.

**Dorsal fin:** The fin located on the back of a fish, used for balance.

**Double helix:** The shape taken by DNA (deoxyribonucleic acid) molecules in a nucleus.

**Drought:** A prolonged period of dry weather that damages crops or prevents their growth.

**Dry cell:** A source of electricity that uses a non-liquid electrolyte.

**Dust tail:** One of two types of tails a comet may have, it is composed mainly of dust and it points away from the Sun.

**Dye:** A colored substance that is used to give color to a material.

**Dynamic equilibrium:** A situation in which substances are moving into and out of cell walls at an equal rate.

### E

**Earthquake:** An unpredictable event in which masses of rock suddenly shift or rupture below Earth's surface, releasing enormous amounts of energy and sending out shockwaves that sometimes cause the ground to shake dramatically.

**Eclipse:** A phenomenon in which the light from a celestial body is temporarily cut off by the presence of another.

**Ecologists:** Scientists who study the interrelationship of organisms and their environments.

**Ecosystem:** An ecological community, including plants, animals and microorganisms, considered together with their environment.

**Efficiency:** The amount of power output divided by the amount of power input. It is a measure of how well a device converts one form of power into another.

**Effort:** The force applied to move a load using a simple machine.

**Elastomers:** Any of various polymers having rubbery properties.

**Electric charge repulsion:** Repulsion of particles caused by a layer of negative ions surrounding each particle. The repulsion prevents coagulation and promotes the even dispersion of such particles through a mixtures.

**Electrical energy:** Kinetic energy resulting from the motion of electrons within any object that conducts electricity.

**Electricity:** A form of energy caused by the presence of electrical charges in matter.

**Electrode:** A material that will conduct an electrical current, usually a metal; used to carry electrons into or out of a battery.

**Electrolyte:** Any substance that, when dissolved in water, conducts an electric current.

**Electromagnetic spectrum:** The complete array of electromagnetic radiation, including radio waves (at the longest-wavelength end), microwaves, infrared radiation, visible light, ultraviolet radiation, X rays, and gamma rays (at the shortest-wavelength end).

**Electromagnetism:** A form of magnetic energy produced by the flow of an electric current through a metal core. Also, the study of electric and magnetic fields and their interaction with charges and currents.

**Electron:** A subatomic particle with a single negative electrical change that orbits the nucleus of an atom.

**Electroplating:** The process of coating one metal with another metal by means of an electrical current.

**Electroscope:** A device that determines whether an object is electrically charged.

**Element:** A pure substance composed of just one type of atom that cannot be broken down into anything simpler by ordinary chemical means.

**Elevation:** Height above sea level.

**Elliptical:** An orbital path which is egg-shaped or resembles an elongated circle.

**Elongation:** The percentage increase in length that occurs before a material breaks under tension.

**Embryo:** The seed of a plant, which through germination can develop into a new plant.

**Embryonic:** The earliest stages of development.

**Endothermic reaction:** A chemical reaction that absorbs heat or light energy, such as photosynthesis, the production of food by plant cells.

**Energy:** The ability to cause an action or to perform work.

**Entomology:** The study of insects.

**Environmental variables:** Nonliving factors such as air temperature, water, pollution, and pH that can affect processes that occur in nature and in an experiment.

**Enzyme:** Any of numerous complex proteins produced by living cells that act as catalysts, speeding up the rate of chemical reactions in living organisms.

**Enzymology:** The science of studying enzymes.

**Ephemerals:** Plants that lie dormant in dry soil for years until major rainstorms occur.

**Epicenter:** The location where the seismic waves of an earthquake first appear on the surface, usually almost directly above the focus.

**Equilibrium:** A balancing or canceling out of opposing forces, so that an object will remain at rest.

**Erosion:** The process by which topsoil is carried away by water, wind, or ice action.

**Ethnobotany:** The study of how cultures use plants in everyday life.

**Eukaryotic:** Multicellular organism whose cells contain distinct nuclei, which contain the genetic material. (Pronounced yoo-KAR-ee-ah-tic)

**Euphotic zone:** The upper part of the ocean where sunlight penetrates, supporting plant life, such as phytoplankton.

**Eutrophication:** The process by which high nutrient concentrations in a body of water eventually cause the natural wildlife to die.

**Evaporation:** The process by which liquid changes into a gas.

**Exoskeleton:** A hard outer covering on animals, which provide protection and structure.

**Exothermic reaction:** A chemical reaction that releases heat or light energy, such as the burning of fuel.

**Experiment:** A controlled observation.

**Extremophiles:** Bacteria that thrive in environments too harsh to support most life forms.

F

**False memory:** A memory of an event that never happened or an altered memory from what happened.

**Family:** A group of elements in the same column of the periodic table or in closely related columns of the table. A family of chemical compounds share similar structures and properties.

**Fat:** A type of lipid, or chemical compound used as a source of energy, to provide insulation and to protect organs in an animal body.

**Fat-soluble vitamins:** Vitamins such as A, D, E, and K that can be dissolved in the fat of plants and animals.

**Fault:** A crack running through rock as the result of tectonic forces.

**Fault blocks:** Pieces of rock from Earth's crust that press against each other and cause earthquakes when they suddenly shift or rupture from the pressure.

**Fault mountain:** A mountain that is formed when Earth's plates come together and cause rocks to break and move upwards.

**Fermentation:** A chemical reaction in which enzymes break down complex organic compounds (for example, carbohydrates and sugars) into simpler ones (for example, ethyl alcohol).

**Filament:** In a flower, stalk of the stamen that bears the anther.

**Filtration:** The mechanical separation of a liquid from the undissolved particles floating in it.

**Fireball:** Meteors that create an intense, bright light and, sometimes, an explosion.

**First law of motion (Newton's):** An object at rest or moving in a certain direction and speed will remain at rest or moving in the same motion and speed unless acted upon by a force.

**Fish:** Animals that live in water who have gills, fins, and are cold blooded.

**Fixative:** A substance that mixes with the dye to hold it to the material.

**Flagella:** Whiplike structures used by some organisms for movement. (Singular: flagellum.)

**Flammability:** The ability of a material to ignite and burn.

**Flower:** The reproductive part of a flowering plant.

**Fluid:** A substance that flows; a liquid or gas.

**Fluorescence:** The emission of visible light from an object when the object is bombarded with electromagnetic radiation, such as ultraviolet rays. The emission of visible light stops after the radiation source has been removed.

**Focal length:** The distance from the lens to the point where the light rays come together to a focus.

**Focal point:** The point at which rays of light converge or from which they diverge.

**Focus:** The point within Earth where a sudden shift or rupture occurs.

**Fold mountain:** A mountain that is formed when Earth's plates come together and push rocks up into folds.

**Food webs:** Interconnected sets of food chains, which are a sequence of organisms directly dependent on one another for food.

**Force:** A physical interaction (pushing or pulling) tending to change the state of motion (velocity) of an object.

**Forensic science:** The application of science to the law and justice system.

**Fortified:** The addition of nutrients, such as vitamins or minerals, to food.

**Fossil:** The remains, trace, or impressions of a living organism that inhabited Earth more than ten thousand years ago.

**Fossil fuel:** A fuel such as coal, oil, or natural gas that is formed over millions of years from the remains of plants and animals.

**Fossil record:** The documentation of fossils placed in relationship to one another; a key source to understand the evolution of life on Earth.

**Fracture:** A mineral's tendency to break into curved, rough, or jagged surfaces.

**Frequency:** The rate at which vibrations take place (number of times per second the motion is repeated), given in cycles per second or in hertz (Hz). Also, the number of waves that pass a given point in a given period of time.

**Friction:** A force that resists the motion of an object, resulting when two objects rub against one another.

**Front:** The area between air masses of different temperatures or densities.

**Fuel cell:** A device that uses hydrogen as the fuel to produce electricity and heat with water as a byproduct.

**Fulcrum:** The point at which a lever arm pivots.

**Fungi:** Kingdom of various single-celled or multicellular organisms, including mushrooms, molds, yeasts, and mildews, that do not contain chlorophyll.

**Funnel cloud:** A fully developed tornado vortex before it has touched the ground.

**Fusion:** Combining of nuclei of two or more lighter elements into one nucleus of a heavier element; the process stars use to produce energy to produce light and support themselves against their own gravity.

**G**

**Galaxy:** A large collection of stars and clusters of stars containing anywhere from a few million to a few trillion stars.

**Gastropod:** The largest group of mollusks; characterized by a single shell that is often coiled in a spiral. Snails are gastropods.

**Gene:** A segment of a DNA (deoxyribonucleic acid) molecule contained in the nucleus of a cell that acts as a kind of code for the production of some specific protein. Genes carry instructions for the formation, functioning, and transmission of specific traits from one generation to another.

**Generator:** A device that converts mechanical energy into electrical energy,

**Genetic engineering:** A technique that modifies the DNA of living cells in order to make them change its characteristics. Also called genetic modification.

**Genetic material:** Material that transfers characteristics from a parent to its offspring.

**Geology:** The study of the origin, history and structure of Earth.

**Geothermal energy:** Energy from deep within Earth.

**Geotropism:** The tendency of roots to bend toward Earth.

**Germ theory of disease:** The theory that disease is caused by micro-organisms or germs, and not by spontaneous generation.

**Germination:** First stage in development of a plant seed.

**Gibbous moon:** A phase of the Moon when more than half of its surface is lighted.

**Gills:** Special organ located behind the head of a fish that takes in oxygen from the water.

**Glacier:** A large mass of ice formed from snow that has packed together and which moves slowly down a slope under its own weight.

**Global warming:** Warming of Earth's atmosphere as a result of an increase in the concentration of gases that store heat, such as carbon dioxide.

**Glucose:** A simple sugar broken down in cells to produce energy.

**Gnomon:** The perpendicular piece of the sundial that casts the shadow.

**Golgi body:** An organelles that sorts, modifies, and packages molecules.

**Gravity:** Force of attraction between objects, the strength of which depends on the mass of each object and the distance between them.

**Greenhouse effect:** The warming of Earth's atmosphere due to water vapor, carbon dioxide, and other gases in the atmosphere that trap heat radiated from Earth's surface.

**Greenhouse gases:** Gases that absorb infrared radiation and warm the air before the heat energy escapes into space.

**Greenwich Mean Time (GMT):** The time at an imaginary line that runs north and south through Greenwich, England, used as the standard for time throughout the world.

**Groundwater:** Water that soaks into the ground and is stored in the small spaces between the rocks and soil.

**Group:** A vertical column of the periodic table that contains elements possessing similar chemical characteristics.

**H**

**Hardwood:** Wood from angiosperm, mostly deciduous, trees.

**Heartwood:** The inner layers of wood that provide structure and have no living cells.

**Heat:** A form of energy produced by the motion of molecules that make up a substance.

**Heat capacity:** The measure of how well a substance stores heat.

**Heat energy:** The energy produced when two substances that have different temperatures are combined.

**Heliotropism:** The tendency of plants to turn towards the Sun throughout the day.

**Herbivore:** A plant-eating organism.

**Hertz (Hz):** The unit of measurement of frequency; a measure of the number of waves that pass a given point per second of time.

**Heterogeneous:** Different throughout.

**Heterotrophs:** Organisms that cannot make their own food and that must, therefore, obtain their food from other organisms.

**High air pressure:** An area where the air is cooler and more dense, and the air pressure is higher than normal.

**Hippocampus:** A part of the brain associated with learning and memory.

**Homogenous:** The same throughout.

**Hormones:** Chemicals produced in the cells of plants and animals that control bodily functions.

**Hue:** The color or shade.

**Humidity:** The amount of water vapor (moisture) contained in the air.

**Humus:** Fragrant, spongy, nutrient-rich decayed plant or animal matter.

**Hydrologic cycle:** Continual movement of water from the atmosphere to Earth's surface through precipitation and back to the atmosphere through evaporation and transpiration.

**Hydrologists:** Scientists who study water and its cycle.

**Hydrology:** The study of water and its cycle.

**Hydrometer:** An instrument that determines the specific gravity of a liquid.

**Hydrophilic:** A substance that is attracted to and readily mixes with water.

**Hydrophobic:** A substance that is repelled by and does not mix with water.

**Hydropower:** Energy produced from capturing moving water.

**Hydrotropism:** The tendency of roots to grow toward a water source.

**Hypertonic solution:** A solution with a higher concentration of materials than a cell immersed in the solution.

**Hypha:** Slender, cottony filaments making up the body of multicellular fungi. (Plural: hyphae)

**Hypothesis:** An idea in the form of a statement that can be tested by observation and/or experiment.

**Hypotonic solution:** A solution with a lower concentration of materials than a cell immersed in the solution.

**I**

**Igneous rock:** Rock formed from the cooling and hardening of magma.

**Immiscible:** Incapable of being mixed.

**Imperfect flower:** Flowers that have only the male reproductive organ (stamen) or the female reproductive organs (pistil).

**Impermeable:** Not allowing substances to pass through.

**Impurities:** Chemicals or other pollutants in water.

**Inclined plane:** A simple machine with no moving parts; a slanted surface.

**Incomplete metamorphosis:** Metamorphosis in which a nymph form gradually becomes an adult through molting.

**Independent variable:** The variable in an experiment that determines the final result of the experiment.

**Indicator:** Pigments that change color when they come into contact with acidic or basic solutions.

**Inertia:** The tendency of an object to continue in its state of motion.

**Infrared radiation:** Electromagnetic radiation of a wavelength shorter than radio waves but longer than visible light that takes the form of heat.

**Inner core:**  Very dense, solid center of Earth.

**Inorganic:**  Not containing carbon; not derived from a living organism.

**Insect:**  A six-legged invertebrate whose body has three segments.

**Insoluble:**  A substance that cannot be dissolved in some other substance.

**Insulated wire:**  Electrical wire coated with a non-conducting material such as plastic.

**Insulation:**  A material that is a poor conductor of heat or electricity.

**Insulator:**  A material through which little or no electrical current or heat energy will flow.

**Interference fringes:**  Bands of color that fan out around an object.

**Internal skeleton:**  An animal that has a backbone.

**Invertebrate:**  An animal that lacks a backbone or internal skeleton.

**Ion:**  An atom or groups of atoms that carry an electrical charge—either positive or negative—as a result of losing or gaining one or more electrons.

**Ion tail:**  One of two types of tails a comet may have, it is composed mainly of charged particles and it points away from the Sun.

**Ionic conduction:**  The flow of an electrical current by the movement of charged particles, or ions.

**Isobars:**  Continuous lines that connect areas with the same air pressure.

**Isotonic solutions:**  Two solutions that have the same concentration of solute particles and therefore the same osmotic pressure.

**J**

**Jawless fish:**  The smallest group of fishes, who lacks a jaw.

**K**

**Kinetic energy:**  The energy of an object or system due to its motion.

**Kingdom:**  One of the five classifications in the widely accepted classification system that designates all living organisms into animals, plants, fungi, protists, and monerans.

### L

**Labyrinth:** A lung-like organ located above the gills that allows the fish to breathe in oxygen from the air.

**Lactobacilli:** A strain of bacteria.

**Landfill:** A method of disposing of waste materials by placing them in a depression in the ground or piling them in a mound. In a sanitary landfill, the daily deposits of waste materials are covered with a layer of soil.

**Larva:** Immature form (wormlike in insects; fishlike in amphibians) of an organism capable of surviving on its own. A larva does not resemble the parent and must go through metamorphosis, or change, to reach its adult stage.

**Lava:** Molten rock that occurs at the surface of Earth, usually through volcanic eruptions.

**Lava cave:** A cave formed from the flow of lava streaming over solid matter.

**Leach:** The movement of dissolved minerals or chemicals with water as it percolates, or oozes, downward through the soil.

**Leaching:** The movement of dissolved chemicals with water that is percolating, or oozing, downward through the soil.

**Leavening agent:** A substance used to make foods like dough and batter to rise.

**Leeward:** The side away from the wind or flow direction.

**Lens:** A piece of transparent material with two curved surfaces that bend rays of light passing through it.

**Lichen:** An organism composed of a fungus and a photosynthetic organism in a symbiotic relationship.

**Lift:** Upward force on the wings of an aircraft created by differences in air pressure on top of and underneath the wings.

**Ligaments:** Tough, fibrous tissue connecting bones.

**Light:** A form of energy that travels in waves.

**Light-year:** Distance light travels in one year in the vacuum of space, roughly 5.9 trillion miles (9.5 trillion kilometers).

**The Local Group:** A cluster of thirty galaxies, including the Milky Way, pulled together by gravity.

**Long-term memory:** The last category of memory in which memories are stored away and can last for years.

**Low air pressure:** An area where the air is warmer and less dense, and the air pressure is lower than normal.

**Luminescent:** Producing light through a chemical process.

**Luminol:** A compound used to detect blood.

**Lunar eclipse:** An eclipse that occurs when Earth passes between the Sun and the Moon, casting a shadow on the Moon.

**Luster:** A glow of reflected light; a sheen.

## M

**Machine:** Any device that makes work easier by providing a mechanical advantage.

**Macrominerals:** Minerals needed in relatively large quantities.

**Macroorganisms:** Visible organisms that aid in breaking down organic matter.

**Magma:** Molten rock deep within Earth that consists of liquids, gases, and particles of rocks and crystals. Magma underlies areas of volcanic activity and at Earth's surface is called lava.

**Magma chambers:** Pools of bubbling liquid rock that are the source of energy causing volcanoes to be active.

**Magma surge:** A swell or rising wave of magma caused by the movement and friction of tectonic plates, which heats and melts rock, adding to the magma and its force.

**Magnet:** A material that attracts other like materials, especially metals.

**Magnetic circuit:** A series of magnetic domains aligned in the same direction.

**Magnetic field:** The space around an electric current or a magnet in which a magnetic force can be observed.

**Magnetism:** A fundamental force in nature caused by the motion of electrons in an atom.

**Maillard reaction:** A reaction caused by heat and sugars and resulting in foods browning and flavors.

**Mammals:** Animals that have a backbone, are warm blooded, have mammary glands to feed their young and have or are born with hair.

**Mantle:** Thick dense layer of rock that underlies Earth's crust and overlies the core; also soft tissue that is located between the shell and an animal's inner organs. The mantle produces the calcium carbonate substance that create the shell of the animal.

**Manure:** The waste matter of animals.

**Mass:** Measure of the total amount of matter in an object. Also, an object's quantity of matter as shown by its gravitational pull on another object.

**Matter:** Anything that has mass and takes up space.

**Meandering river:** A lowland river that twists and turns along its route to the sea.

**Medium:** A material that contains the nutrients required for a particular microorganism to grow.

**Melting point:** The temperature at which a substance changes from a solid to a liquid.

**Memory:** The process of retaining and recalling past events and experiences.

**Meniscus:** The curved surface of a column of liquid.

**Metabolism:** The process by which living organisms convert food into energy and waste products.

**Metamorphic rock:** Rock formed by transformation of pre-existing rock through changes in temperature and pressure.

**Metamorphosis:** Transformation of an immature animal into an adult.

**Meteor:** An object from space that becomes glowing hot when it passes into Earth's atmosphere; also called shooting star.

**Meteor shower:** A group of meteors that occurs when Earth's orbit intersects the orbit of a meteor stream.

**Meteorites:** A meteor that is large enough to survive its passage through the atmosphere and hit the ground.

**Meteoroid:** A piece of debris that is traveling in space.

**Meteorologist:** Scientist who studies the weather and the atmosphere.

**Microbiology:** Branch of biology dealing with microscopic forms of life.

**Microclimate:** A unique climate that exists only in a small, localized area.

**Microorganisms:** Living organisms so small that they can be seen only with the aid of a microscope.

**Micropyle:** Seed opening that enables water to enter easily.

**Microvilli:** The extension of each taste cell that pokes through the taste pore and first senses the chemicals.

**Milky Way:** The galaxy in which our solar system is located.

**Mimicry:** A characteristic in which an animal is protected against predators by resembling another, more distasteful animal.

**Mineral:** An inorganic substance found in nature with a definite chemical composition and structure. As a nutrient, it helps build bones and soft tissues and regulates body functions.

**Mixture:** A combination of two or more substances that are not chemically combined with each other and that can exist in any proportion.

**Mnemonics:** Techniques to improve memory.

**Mold:** In paleontology, the fossil formed when acidic water dissolves a shell or bone around which sand or mud has already hardened.

**Molecule:** The smallest particle of a substance that retains all the properties of the substance and is composed of one or more atoms.

**Mollusk:** An invertebrate animal usually enclosed in a shell, the largest group of shelled animals.

**Molting:** A process by which an animal sheds its skin or shell.

**Monocot:** Plants with a single embryonic leaf at germination.

**Monomer:** A small molecule that can be combined with itself many times over to make a large molecule, the polymer.

**Moraine:** Mass of boulders, stones, and other rock debris carried along and deposited by a glacier.

**Mordant:** A substance that fixes the dye to the material.

**Mountain:** A landform that stands well above its surroundings; higher than a hill.

**Mucus:** A thick, slippery substance that serves as a protective lubricant coating in passages of the body that communicate with the air.

**Multicellular:** Living things with many cells joined together.

**Muscle fibers:** Stacks of long, thin cells that make up muscle; there are three types of muscle fiber: skeletal, cardiac, and smooth.

**Mycelium:** In fungi, the mass of threadlike, branching hyphae.

*Experiment Central, 2nd edition*

**N**

**Nanobots:** A nanoscale robot.

**Nanometer:** A unit of length; this measurement is equal to one-billionth of a meter.

**Nanotechnology:** Technology that involves working and developing technologies on the nanometer (atomic and molecular) scale.

**Nansen bottles:** Self-closing containers with thermometers that draw in water at different depths.

**Nebula:** Bright or dark cloud, often composed of gases and dust, hovering in the space between the stars.

**Nectar:** A sweet liquid, found inside a flower, that attracts pollinators.

**Neutralization:** A chemical reaction in which the mixing of an acidic solution with a basic (alkaline) solution results in a solution that has the properties of neither an acid nor a base.

**Neutron:** A subatomic particle with a mass of about one atomic mass unit and no electrical charge that is found in the nucleus of an atom.

**Newtonian fluid:** A fluid that follows certain properties, such as the viscosity remains constant at a given temperature.

**Niche:** The specific location and place in the food chain that an organism occupies in its environment.

**Noble gases:** Also known as inert or rare gases; the elements argon, helium, krypton, neon, radon, and xenon, which are nonreactive gases and form few compounds with other elements.

**Non-Newtonian fluid:** A fluid whose property do not follow Newtonian properties, such as viscosity can vary based on the stress.

**Nonpoint source:** An unidentified source of pollution, which may actually be a number of sources.

**Nucleation:** The process by which crystals start growing.

**Nucleotide:** The basic unit of a nucleic acid. It consists of a simple sugar, a phosphate group, and a nitrogen-containing base. (Pronounced noo-KLEE-uh-tide.)

**Nucleus:** The central part of the cell that contains the DNA; the central core of an atom, consisting of protons and (usually) neutrons.

**Nutrient:** A substance needed by an organism in order for it to survive, grow, and develop.

**Nutrition:** The study of the food nutrients an organism needs in order to maintain well-being.

**Nymph:** An immature form in the life cycle of insects that go through an incomplete metamorphosis.

**O**

**Objective lens:** In a refracting telescope, the lens farthest away from the eye that collects the light.

**Oceanographer:** A person who studies the chemistry of the oceans, as well as their currents, marine life, and the ocean floor.

**Oceanography:** The study of the chemistry of the oceans, as well as their currents, marine life, and the ocean bed.

**Olfactory:** Relating to the sense of smell.

**Olfactory bulb:** The part of the brain that processes olfactory (smell) information.

**Olfactory epithelium:** The patch of mucous membrane at the top of the nasal cavity that contains the olfactory (smell) nerve cells.

**Olfactory receptor cells:** Nerve cells in the olfactory epithelium that detect odors and transmit the information to the brain.

**Oort cloud:** Region of space beyond our solar system that theoretically contains about one trillion inactive comets.

**Optics:** The study of the nature of light and its properties.

**Orbit:** The path followed by a body (such as a planet) in its travel around another body (such as the Sun).

**Organelle:** A membrane-enclosed structure that performs a specific function within a cell.

**Organic:** Containing carbon; also referring to materials that are derived from living organisms.

**Oscillation:** A repeated back-and-forth movement.

**Osmosis:** The movement of fluids and substances dissolved in liquids across a semipermeable membrane from an area of its greater concentration to an area of its lesser concentration until all substances involved reach a balance.

**Outer core:** A liquid core that surrounds Earth's solid inner core; made mostly of iron.

**Ovary:** In a plant, the base part of the pistil that bears ovules and develops into a fruit.

**Ovule:** Structure within the ovary that develops into a seed after fertilization.

**Oxidation:** A chemical reaction in which oxygen reacts with some other substance and in which ions, atoms, or molecules lose electrons.

**Oxidation state:** The sum of an atom's positive and negative charges.

**Oxidation-reduction reaction:** A chemical reaction in which one substance loses one or more electrons and the other substance gains one or more electrons.

**Oxidizing agent:** A chemical substance that gives up oxygen or takes on electrons from another substance.

**P**

**Paleontologist:** Scientist who studies the life of past geological periods as known from fossil remains.

**Papain:** An enzyme obtained from the fruit of the papaya used as a meat tenderizer, as a drug to clean cuts and wounds, and as a digestive aid for stomach disorders.

**Papillae:** The raised bumps on the tongue that contain the taste buds.

**Parent material:** The underlying rock from which soil forms.

**Partial solar/lunar eclipse:** An eclipse in which our view of the Sun/ Moon is only partially blocked.

**Particulate matter:** Solid matter in the form of tiny particles in the atmosphere. (Pronounced par-TIK-you-let.)

**Passive solar energy system:** A solar energy system in which the heat of the Sun is captured, used, and stored by means of the design of a building and the materials from which it is made.

**Pasteurization:** The process of slow heating that kills bacteria and other microorganisms.

**Peaks:** The points at which the energy in a wave is maximum.

**Pectin:** A natural carbohydrate found in fruits and vegetables.

**Pectoral fin:** Pair of fins located on the side of a fish, used for steering.

**Pedigree:** A diagram that illustrates the pattern of inheritance of a genetic trait in a family.

**Pelvic fin:** Pair of fins located toward the belly of a fish, used for stability.

**Pendulum:** A free-swinging weight, usually consisting of a heavy object attached to the end of a long rod or string, suspended from a fixed point.

**Penicillin:** A mold from the fungi group of microorganisms; used as an antibiotic.

**Pepsin:** Digestive enzyme that breaks down protein.

**Percolate:** To pass through a permeable substance.

**Perfect flower:** Flowers that have both male and female reproductive organs.

**Period:** A horizontal row in the periodic table.

**Periodic table:** A chart organizing elements by atomic number and chemical properties into groups and periods.

**Permeable:** Having pores that permit a liquid or a gas to pass through.

**Permineralization:** A form of preservation in which mineral matter has filled in the inner and outer spaces of the cell.

**Pest:** Any living thing that is unwanted by humans or causes injury and disease to crops and other growth.

**Pesticide:** Substance used to reduce the abundance of pests.

**Petal:** Leafy structure of a flower just inside the sepals; they are often brightly colored and have many different shapes.

**Petrifaction:** Process of turning organic material into rock by the replacement of that material with minerals.

**pH:** A measure of the acidity or alkalinity of a solution referring to the concentration of hydrogen ions present in a liter of a given fluid. The pH scale ranges from 0 (greatest concentration of hydrogen ions and therefore most acidic) to 14 (least concentration of hydrogen ions and therefore most alkaline), with 7 representing a neutral solution, such as pure water.

**Pharmacology:** The science dealing with the properties, reactions, and therapeutic values of drugs.

**Phases:** Changes in the portion of the Moon's surface that is illuminated by light from the Sun as the Moon revolves around Earth.

**Phloem:** The plant tissue that carries dissolved nutrients through the plant.

**Phosphorescence:** The emission of visible light from an object when the object is bombarded with electromagnetic radiation, such as ultraviolet rays. The object stores part of the radiation energy and the emission of visible light continues for a period ranging from a fraction of a second to several days after the radiation source has been removed.

**Photoelectric effect:** The phenomenon in which light falling upon certain metals stimulates the emission of electrons and changes light into electricity.

**Photosynthesis:** Chemical process by which plants containing chlorophyll use sunlight to manufacture their own food by converting carbon dioxide and water to carbohydrates, releasing oxygen as a by-product.

**Phototropism:** The tendency of a plant to grow toward a source of light.

**Photovoltaic cells:** A device made of silicon that converts sunlight into electricity.

**Physical change:** A change in which the substance keeps its molecular identity, such as a piece of chalk that has been ground up.

**Physical property:** A characteristic that you can detect with your senses, such as color and shape.

**Physiologist:** A scientist who studies the functions and processes of living organisms.

**Phytoplankton:** Microscopic aquatic plants that live suspended in the water.

**Pigment:** A substance that displays a color because of the wavelengths of light that it reflects.

**Pili:** Short projections that assist bacteria in attaching to tissues.

**Pistil:** Female reproductive organ of flowers that is composed of the stigma, style, and ovary.

**Pitch:** A property of a sound, determined by its frequency; the highness or lowness of a sound.

**Plant extract:** The juice or liquid essence obtained from a plant by squeezing or mashing it.

**Plasmolysis:** Occurs in walled cells in which cytoplasm, the semifluid substance inside a cell, shrivels and the membrane pulls away from the cell wall when the vacuole loses water.

**Plates:** Large regions of Earth's surface, composed of the crust and uppermost mantle, which move about, forming many of Earth's major geologic surface features.

**Platform:** The horizontal surface of a bridge on which traffic travels.

**Pnematocysts:** Stinging cells.

**Point source:** An identified source of pollution.

**Pollen:** Dust-like grains or particles produced by a plant that contain male sex cells.

**Pollinate:** The transfer of pollen from the male reproductive organs to the female reproductive organs of plants.

**Pollination:** Transfer of pollen from the male reproductive organs to the female reproductive organs of plants.

**Pollinator:** Any animal, such as an insect or bird, that transfers the pollen from one flower to another.

**Pollution:** The contamination of the natural environment, usually through human activity.

**Polymer:** Chemical compound formed of simple molecules (known as monomers) linked with themselves many times over.

**Polymerization:** The bonding of two or more monomers to form a polymer.

**Polyvinyl acetate:** A type of polymer that is the main ingredient of white glues.

**Pore:** An opening or space.

**Potential energy:** The energy of an object or system due to its position.

**Precipitation:** Any form of water that falls to Earth, such as rain, snow, or sleet.

**Predator:** An animal that hunts another animal for food.

**Preservative:** An additive used to keep food from spoiling.

**Primary colors:** The three colors red, green, and blue; when combined evenly they produce white light and by combining varying amounts can produce the range of colors.

**Prism:** A piece of transparent material with a triangular cross-section. When light passes through it, it causes different colors to bend different amounts, thus separating them into a rainbow of colors.

**Probe:** The terminal of a voltmeter, used to connect the voltmeter to a circuit.

**Producer:** An organism that can manufacture its own food from nonliving materials and an external energy source, usually by photosynthesis.

**Product:** A compound that is formed as a result of a chemical reaction.

**Prokaryote:** A cell without a true nucleus, such as a bacterium.

**Prominences:** Masses of glowing gas, mainly hydrogen, that rise from the Sun's surface like flames.

**Propeller:** Radiating blades mounted on a rapidly rotating shaft, which moves aircraft forward.

**Protein:** A complex chemical compound consisting of many amino acids attached to each other that are essential to the structure and functioning of all living cells.

**Protists:** Members of the kingdom Protista, primarily single-celled organisms that are not plants or animals.

**Proton:** A subatomic particle with a single positive charge that is found in the nucleus of an atom.

**Protozoa:** Single-celled animal-like microscopic organisms that live by taking in food rather than making it by photosynthesis. They must live in the presence of water.

**Pulley:** A simple machine made of a cord wrapped around a wheel.

**Pupa:** The insect stage of development between the larva and adult in insects that go through complete metamorphosis.

**R**

**Radiation:** Energy transmitted in the form of electromagnetic waves or subatomic particles.

**Radicule:** Seed's root system.

**Radio wave:** Longest form of electromagnetic radiation, measuring up to 6 miles (9.6 kilometers) from peak to peak.

**Radioisotope dating:** A technique used to date fossils, based on the decay rate of known radioactive elements.

**Radiosonde balloons:** Instruments for collecting data in the atmosphere and then transmitting that data back to Earth by means of radio waves.

**Radon:** A radioactive gas located in the ground; invisible and odorless, radon is a health hazard when it accumulates to high levels inside homes and other structures where it is breathed.

**Rain shadow:** Region on the side of the mountain that receives less rainfall than the area windward of the mountain.

**Rancidity:** Having the condition when food has a disagreeable odor or taste from decomposing oils or fats.

**Reactant:** A compound present at the beginning of a chemical reaction.

**Reaction:** Response to an action prompted by stimulus.

**Recessive gene:** A gene that produces a certain characteristic only two both copies (alleles) of the gene are present.

**Recycling:** The use of waste materials, also known as secondary materials or recyclables, to produce new products.

**Redshift:** The lengthening of the frequency of light waves toward the red end of the visible light spectrum as they travel away from an observer; most commonly used to describe movement of stars away from Earth.

**Reduction:** A process in which a chemical substance gives off oxygen or takes on electrons.

**Reed:** A tall woody perennial grass that has a hollow stem.

**Reflection:** The bouncing of light rays in a regular pattern off the surface of an object.

**Reflector telescope:** A telescope that directs light from an opening at one end to a concave mirror at the far end, which reflects the light back to a smaller mirror that directs it to an eyepiece on the side of the tube.

**Refraction:** The bending of light rays as they pass at an angle from one transparent or clear medium into a second one of different density.

**Refractor telescope:** A telescope that directs light through a glass lens, which bends the light waves and brings them to a focus at an eyepiece that acts as a magnifying glass.

**Relative age:** The age of an object expressed in relation to another like object, such as earlier or later.

**Relative density:** The density of one material compared to another.

**Rennin:** Enzyme used in making cheese.

**Resistance:** A partial or complete limiting of the flow of electrical current through a material. The common unit of measure is the ohm.

**Respiration:** The physical process that supplies oxygen to living cells and the chemical reactions that take place inside the cells.

**Resultant:** A force that results from the combined action of two other forces.

**Retina:** The light-sensitive part of the eyeball that receives images and transmits visual impulses through the optic nerve to the brain.

**Ribosome:** A protein composed of two subunits that functions in protein synthesis (creation).

**Rigidity:** The amount an object will deflect when supporting a weight. The less it deflects for a given amount of weight, the greater its rigidity.

**River:** A main course of water into which many other smaller bodies of water flow.

**Rock:** Naturally occurring solid mixture of minerals.

**Rods:** Cells in the retina that are sensitive to degrees of light and movement.

**Root hairs:** Fine, hair-like extensions from the plant's root.

**Rotate:** To turn around on an axis or center.

**Runoff:** Water that does not soak into the ground or evaporate, but flows across the surface of the ground.

**S**

**Salinity:** The amount of salts dissolved in water.

**Saliva:** Watery mixture with chemicals that lubricates chewed food.

**Sand:** Granular portion of soil composed of the largest soil particles.

**Sapwood:** The outer wood in a tree, which is usually a lighter color.

**Saturated:** In referring to solutions, a solution that contains the maximum amount of solute for a given amount of solvent at a given temperature.

**Saturation:** The intensity of a color.

**Scanning tunneling microscope:** A microscope that can show images of surfaces at the atomic level by scanning a probe over a surface.

**Scientific method:** Collecting evidence and arriving at a conclusion under carefully controlled conditions.

**Screw:** A simple machine; an inclined plane wrapped around a cylinder.

**Scurvy:** A disease caused by a deficiency of vitamin C, which causes a weakening of connective tissue in bone and muscle.

**Sea cave:** A cave in sea cliffs, formed most commonly by waves eroding the rock.

**Second law of motion (Newton's):** The force exerted on an object is proportional to the mass of the object times the acceleration produced by the force.

**Sediment:** Sand, silt, clay, rock, gravel, mud, or other matter that has been transported by flowing water.

**Sedimentary rock:** Rock formed from compressed and solidified layers of organic or inorganic matter.

**Sedimentation:** A process during which gravity pulls particles out of a liquid.

**Seed crystal:** Small form of a crystalline structure that has all the facets of a complete new crystal contained in it.

**Seedling:** A small plant just starting to grow into its mature form.

**Seismic belt:** Boundaries where Earth's plates meet.

**Seismic waves:** Vibrations in rock and soil that transfer the force of an earthquake from the focus into the surrounding area.

**Seismograph:** A device that detects and records vibrations of the ground.

**Seismology:** The study and measurement of earthquakes.

**Seismometer:** A seismograph that measures the movement of the ground.

**Self-pollination:** The process in which pollen from one part of a plant fertilizes ovules on another part of the same plant.

**Semipermeable membrane:** A thin barrier between two solutions that permits only certain components of the solutions, usually the solvent, to pass through.

**Sensory memory:** Memory that the brain retains for a few seconds.

**Sepal:** The outermost part of a flower; typically leaflike and green.

**Sexual reproduction:** A reproductive process that involves the union of two individuals in the exchange of genetic material.

**Shear stress:** An applied force to a give area.

**Shell:** A region of space around the center of the atom in which electrons are located; also, a hard outer covering that protects an animal living inside.

**Short-term memory:** Also known as working memory, this memory was transferred here from sensory memory.

**Sidereal day:** The time it takes for a particular star to travel around and reach the same position in the sky; about four minutes shorter than the average solar day.

**Silt:** Medium-sized soil particles.

**Simple machine:** Any of the basic structures that provide a mechanical advantage and have no or few moving parts.

**Smog:** A form of air pollution produced when moisture in the air combines and reacts with the products of fossil fuel combustion. Smog is characterized by hazy skies and a tendency to cause respiratory problems among humans.

**Softwood:** Wood from coniferous trees, which usually remain green all year.

**Soil:** The upper layer of Earth that contains nutrients for plants and organisms; a mixture of mineral matter, organic matter, air, and water.

**Soil horizon:** An identifiable soil layer due to color, structure, and/or texture.

**Soil profile:** Combined soil horizons or layers.

**Solar collector:** A device that absorbs sunlight and collects solar heat.

**Solar day:** Called a day, the time between each arrival of the Sun at its highest point.

**Solar eclipse:** An eclipse that occurs when the Moon passes between Earth and the Sun, casting a shadow on Earth.

**Solar energy:** Any form of electromagnetic radiation that is emitted by the Sun.

**Solubility:** The tendency of a substance to dissolve in some other substance.

**Soluble:**  A substance that can be dissolved in some other substance.

**Solute:**  The substance that is dissolved to make a solution and exists in the least amount in a solution, for example sugar in sugar water.

**Solution:**  A mixture of two or more substances that appears to be uniform throughout except on a molecular level.

**Solvent:**  The major component of a solution or the liquid in which some other component is dissolved, for example water in sugar water.

**Specific gravity:**  The ratio of the density of a substance to the density of pure water.

**Specific heat capacity:**  The energy required to raise the temperature of 1 kilogram of the substance by 1 degree Celsius.

**Speleologist:**  One who studies caves.

**Speleology:**  Scientific study of caves and their plant and animal life.

**Spelunkers:**  Also called cavers, people who explore caves for a hobby.

**Spiracles:**  The openings on an insects side where air enters.

**Spoilage:**  The condition when food has taken on an undesirable color, odor, or texture.

**Spore:**  A small, usually one-celled, reproductive body that is capable of growing into a new organism.

**Stalactite:**  Cylindrical or icicle-shaped mineral deposit projecting downward from the roof of a cave. (Pronounced sta-LACK-tite.)

**Stalagmite:**  Cylindrical or icicle-shaped mineral deposit projecting upward from the floor of a cave. (Pronounced sta-LAG-mite.)

**Stamen:**  Male reproductive organ of flowers that is composed of the anther and filament.

**Standard:**  A base for comparison.

**Star:**  A vast clump of hydrogen gas and dust that produces great energy through fusion reactions at its core.

**Static electricity:**  A form of electricity produced by friction in which the electric charge does not flow in a current but stays in one place.

**Stigma:**  Top part of the pistil upon which pollen lands and receives the male pollen grains during fertilization.

**Stomata:**  Pores in the epidermis (surface) of leaves.

**Storm:** An extreme atmospheric disturbance, associated with strong damaging winds, and often with thunder and lightning.

**Storm chasers:** People who track and seek out storms, often tornadoes.

**Stratification:** Layers according to density; applies to fluids.

**Streak:** The color of the dust left when a mineral is rubbed across a rough surface.

**Style:** Stalk of the pistil that connects the stigma to the ovary.

**Subatomic:** Smaller than an atom. It usually refers to particles that make up an atom, such as protons, neutrons, and electrons.

**Sublime:** The process of changing a solid into a vapor without passing through the liquid phase.

**Substrate:** The substance on which an enzyme operates in a chemical reaction.

**Succulent:** Plants that live in dry environments and have water storage tissue.

**Sundial:** A device that uses the position of the Sun to indicate time.

**Supersaturated:** Solution that is more highly concentrated than is normally possible under given conditions of temperature and pressure.

**Supertaster:** A person who is extremely sensitive to specific tastes due to a greater number of taste buds.

**Supplements:** A substance intended to enhance the diet.

**Surface area:** The total area of the outside of an object; the area of a body of water that is exposed to the air.

**Surface tension:** The attractive force of molecules to each other on the surface of a liquid.

**Surface water:** Water in lakes, rivers, ponds, and streams.

**Suspension:** A temporary mixture of a solid in a gas or liquid from which the solid will eventually settle out.

**Swim bladder:** Located above the stomach, takes in air when the fish wants to move upwards and releases air when the fish wants to move downwards.

**Symbiosis:** A pattern in which two or more organisms live in close connection with each other, often to the benefit of both or all organisms.

**Synthesis reaction:** A chemical reaction in which two or more substances combine to form a new substance.

**Synthesize:** To make something artificially, in a laboratory or chemical plant, that is generally not found in nature.

**Synthetic:** A substance that is synthesized, or manufactured, in a laboratory; not naturally occurring.

**Synthetic crystals:** Artificial or manmade crystals.

**T**

**Taiga:** A large land biome mostly dominated by coniferous trees.

**Taste buds:** Groups of taste cells located on the papillae that recognize the different tastes.

**Taste pore:** The opening at the top of the taste bud from which chemicals reach the taste cells.

**Tectonic:** Relating to the forces and structures of the outer shell of Earth.

**Tectonic plates:** Huge flat rocks that form Earth's crust.

**Telescope:** A tube with lenses or mirrors that collect, transmit, and focus light.

**Temperate:** Mild or moderate weather conditions.

**Temperature:** The measure of the average energy of the molecules in a substance.

**Tendon:** Tough, fibrous connective tissue that attaches muscle to bone.

**Tensile strength:** The force needed to stretch a material until it breaks.

**Terminal:** A connection in an electric circuit; usually a connection on a source of electric energy such as a battery.

**Terracing:** A series of horizontal ridges made in a hillside to reduce erosion.

**Testa:** A tough outer layer that protects the embryo and endosperm of a seed from damage.

**Theory of special relativity:** Theory put forth by Albert Einstein that time is not absolute, but it is relative according to the speed of the observer's frame of reference.

**Thermal conductivity:** A number representing a material's ability to conduct heat.

**Thermal energy:** Kinetic energy caused by the movement of molecules due to temperature.

**Thermal inversion:** A region in which the warmer air lies above the colder air; can cause smog to worsen.

**Thermal pollution:** The discharge of heated water from industrial processes that can kill or injure water life.

**Thiamine:** A vitamin of the B complex that is essential to normal metabolism and nerve function.

**Thigmotropism:** The tendency for a plant to grow toward a surface it touches.

**Third law of motion (Newton's):** For every action there is an equal and opposite reaction.

**Thorax:** The middle segment of an insect body; the legs and wings are connected to the thorax.

**Tides:** The cyclic rise and fall of seawater.

**Titration:** A procedure in which an acid and a base are slowly mixed to achieve a neutral substance.

**Topsoil:** The uppermost layers of soil containing an abundant supply of decomposed organic material to supply plants with nutrients.

**Tornado:** A violently rotating, narrow column of air in contact with the ground and usually extending from a cumulonimbus cloud.

**Total solar/lunar eclipse:** An eclipse in which our view of the Sun/Moon is totally blocked.

**Toxic:** Poisonous.

**Trace element:** A chemical element present in minute quantities.

**Trace minerals:** Minerals needed in relatively small quantities.

**Translucent:** Permits the passage of light.

**Transpiration:** Evaporation of water in the form of water vapor from the stomata on the surfaces of leaves and stems of plants.

**Troglobite:** An animal that lives in a cave and is unable to live outside of one.

**Troglophile:** An animal that lives the majority of its life cycle in a cave but is also able to live outside of the cave.

**Trogloxene:** An animal that spends only part of its life cycle in a cave and returns periodically to the cave.

**Tropism:** The growth or movement of a plant toward or away from a stimulus.

**Troposphere:** The lowest layer of Earth's atmosphere, ranging to an altitude of about 9 miles (15 km) above Earth's surface.

**Trough:** The lowest point of a wave. (Pronounced trawf.)

**Tsunami:** A large wave of water caused by an underwater earthquake.

**Tuber:** An underground, starch-storing stem, such as a potato.

**Tundra:** A treeless, frozen biome with low-lying plants.

**Turbine:** A spinning device used to transform mechanical power from energy into electrical energy.

**Turbulence:** Air disturbance that affects an aircraft's flight.

**Turgor pressure:** The force that is exerted on a plant's cell wall by the water within the cell.

**Tyndall effect:** The effect achieved when colloidal particles reflect a beam of light, making it visible when shined through such a mixture.

## U

**Ultraviolet:** Electromagnetic radiation (energy) of a wavelength just shorter than the violet (shortest wavelength) end of the visible light spectrum and thus with higher energy than the visible light.

**Unconfined aquifer:** An aquifer under a layer of permeable rock and soil.

**Unicellular:** Living things that have one cell. Protozoans are unicellular, for example.

**Unit cell:** The basic unit of the crystalline structure.

**Universal law of gravity:** The law of physics that defines the constancy of the force of gravity between two bodies.

**Updraft:** Warm, moist air that moves away from the ground.

**Upwelling:** The process by which lower-level, nutrient-rich waters rise upward to the ocean's surface.

## V

**Vacuole:** An enclosed, space-filling sac within plant cells containing mostly water and providing structural support for the cell.

**Van der Waals' force:** An attractive force between two molecules based on the positive and negative side of the molecule.

**Variable:** Something that can affect the results of an experiment.

**Vegetative propagation:** A form of asexual reproduction in which plants are produced that are genetically identical to the parent.

**Velocity:** The rate at which the position of an object changes with time, including both the speed and the direction.

**Veneer:** Thin slices of wood.

**Viable:** The capability of developing or growing under favorable conditions.

**Vibration:** A regular, back-and-forth motion of molecules in the air.

**Viscosity:** The measure of a fluid's resistance to flow; its flowability.

**Visible spectrum:** The range of individual wavelengths of radiation visible to the human eye when white light is broken into its component colors as it passes through a prism or by some other means.

**Vitamin:** A complex organic compound found naturally in plants and animals that the body needs in small amounts for normal growth and activity.

**Volatilization:** The process by which a liquid changes (volatilizes) to a gas.

**Volcano:** A conical mountain or dome of lava, ash, and cinders that forms around a vent leading to molten rock deep within Earth.

**Voltage:** Also called potential difference; a measurement of the amount of electric energy stored in a mass of electric charges compared to the energy stored in some other mass of charges. The common unit of measure is the volt.

**Voltmeter:** An instrument for measuring the amperage, voltage, or resistance in an electrical circuit.

**Volume:** The amount of space occupied by a three-dimensional object; the amplitude or loudness of a sound.

**Vortex:** A rotating column of a fluid such as air or water.

**Waste stream:** The waste materials generated by the population of an area, or by a specific industrial process, and removed for disposal.

**Water (hydrologic) cycle:** The constant movement of water molecules on Earth as they rise into the atmosphere as water vapor, condense into droplets and fall to land or bodies of water, evaporate, and rise again.

**Water clock:** A device that uses the flow of water to measure time.

**Water table:** The level of the upper surface of groundwater.

**Water vapor:** Water in its gaseous state.

**Water-soluble vitamins:** Vitamins such as C and the B-complex vitamins that dissolve in the watery parts of plant and animal tissues.

**Waterline:** The highest point to which water rises on the hull of a ship. The portion of the hull below the waterline is under water.

**Wave:** A means of transmitting energy in which the peak energy occurs at a regular interval; the rise and fall of the ocean water.

**Wavelength:** The distance between the peak of a wave of light, heat, or other form of energy and the next corresponding peak.

**Weather:** The state of the troposphere at a particular time and place.

**Weather forecasting:** The scientific predictions of future weather patterns.

**Weathered:** Natural process that breaks down rocks and minerals at Earth's surface into simpler materials by physical (mechanical) or chemical means.

**Wedge:** A simple machine; a form of inclined plane.

**Weight:** The gravitational attraction of Earth on an object; the measure of the heaviness of an object.

**Wet cell:** A source of electricity that uses a liquid electrolyte.

**Wetlands:** Areas that are wet or covered with water for at least part of the year.

**Wheel and axle:** A simple machine; a larger wheel(s) fastened to a smaller cylinder, an axle, so that they turn together.

**Work:** The result of a force moving a mass a given distance. The greater the mass or the greater the distance, the greater the work involved.

**X**

**Xanthophyll:** Yellow pigment in plants.

**Xerophytes:** Plants that require little water to survive.

**Xylem:** Plant tissue consisting of elongated, thick-walled cells that transport water and mineral nutrients. (Pronounced ZY-lem.)

**Yeast:** A single-celled fungi that can be used to as a leavening agent.

# 31

# Fish

Fish are animals that live in water and have gills. There are more than 25,000 types of fish identified, and new species are discovered every year. There are fish that span 45 feet (13.7 meters) long to species that are the size of your nail. They come in a wide variety of colors and shapes. Fish are an important food source and livelihood to many cultures throughout the world. People also enjoy them for their beauty and recreation. These animals play a vital role in the ecosystem, both in the waters and on land.

*What makes a fish a fish* Fish are a diverse group, but they have certain characteristics that set them apart from land dwellers. Fish have backbones made out of bone or cartilage (a strong and flexible tissue). Most fish have scales on their bodies that cover and protect the skin. Scales come in all sizes and shapes. Fish are also cold blooded, meaning the internal temperature matches the temperature of its environment.

There are three main groups of fish:

- The jawless fish: The smallest group, jawless fish have a round mouth with small sharp teeth in place of a jaw. The fish use their mouth to suck in food. Lampreys and hagfish are examples of jawless fish.
- Cartilaginous fish: This group has skeletons made of cartilage. A skeleton that is light and flexible allows this group of fish to move easily and quickly through the water. Sharks, rays and skates belong to this group.
- Bony fish: The bony fish, the largest group of fish, are fish whose skeleton is made of bone. The goldfish and guppy are common bony fish.

Where a fish lives shapes its characteristics. There are fish that live the majority of their life in freshwater. Freshwater fish need special gills that help them regulate the salt in their bodies. Most ocean fish live in the top

*The lamprey is a type of jawless fish. Fossil records trace the lamprey as far back as any fish, including the prehistoric sturgeon.* AP PHOTO/THE COLUMBIAN, DAVE OLSON.

*The goldfish is a type of bony fish.* AP PHOTO/THE ALBU-QUERQUE JOURNAL, JAELYN DEMARIA.

layers of the sea where sunlight reaches and plants thrive. The relatively few species of fish that live in the deep sea have adapted to the dark, cold environment. Some deep sea fish produce their own light by a chemical process similar to fireflies. Others have huge mouths to gather food and dagger-like teeth.

*Breathing underwater* Like humans, fish need oxygen to live. Unlike humans, fish do not have lungs to take oxygen out of the air. They have gills that take oxygen out of the water. Gills are specialized organs located behind the mouth. A fish takes in water through its mouth and as it passes over the gills the oxygen from the water moves into the blood in the gills. This process is similar to how your lungs take oxygen from the air and move it into your bloodstream. Just as humans release carbon dioxide into the air as a by-product of the air we breathe, fish also release carbon dioxide through their gills into the water.

Some fish have both gills and lungs to breathe in oxygen from the water and air. These fish are called lungfish and are found in Africa, Australia, and South America. This allows the fish to survive in environments when lakes or marshes become dry in the summer or during a drought (an extended period of dry weather).

Whales and dolphins are mammals and therefore do not have gills but lungs. They can stay underwater for a long time but eventually they need to return to the surface of to breathe.

*Moving through water* Ever wonder why fish don't sink in the water? Most bony fish have an organ called a swim bladder that allows them to control their upward and downward movements. The swim bladder, located above the stomach, takes in air when the fish wants to move up and releases air when the fish wants to move down. Not all fish have swim bladders. A shark, for example, does not have a swim bladder but has an oily liver that keeps the shark from sinking because oil is lighter than water.

Fins help fish move, turn, stop and control speed. Fins vary in shape, size and location, depending upon the fish and its way of life. Each fin has a specific function and name. Fins can be located on the fish's back (dorsal fin), sides (pectoral fins), belly (anal fin and pelvic fins), and tail (caudal fin). Some fins come in pairs, such as the pectoral and pelvic fins.

The shape of the body helps determine how speedy a fish moves. A fish with a narrow body is more aerodynamic and is therefore a faster swimmer compared to a fish that is wider.

Fish have powerful body muscles along the sides of their body and in the tail that allow them to move quickly and with force. When a fish wants to move it uses the muscles on the side of its body, bending back and forth in an "S" shape. The salmon is an example of a fish that uses its powerful muscles on its sides and in its tail to propel itself out of the water.

*Sensing the surroundings* Fish eyes are similar to human eyes, but with a few differences. Fish cannot see as clearly as humans because their lens (the part of the eye that makes an image sharp) is a different shape. For most fish their eyes are located on the sides of their head enabling them to see in every direction except directly behind themselves. The pupil, a part of the eye that expands and contracts in relation to light in the human eye, does not change size in a fish's eye. Fish need to adjust their depth in the water to make adjustments for more and less light.

Fish have ears hidden on both sides of its head. A fish senses sound the same way as humans: through vibrations. Vibrations created by a sound travel through the water into its ear. In many fish the swim bladder and the ears are connected by a series of small bones or tubes. The swim bladder vibrates when a sound is made and this vibration is carried along the bones or tubes to the ear.

Many fish have a developed sense of smell and taste. Fish have small holes in their head called nares that act as nostrils. The nares connect to an area lined with sensory pads. When water is pumped over the sensory pads, fish are able to detect chemical signals in the water. The signals are transmitted to the brain where it is interpreted as food or danger. Taste buds on a

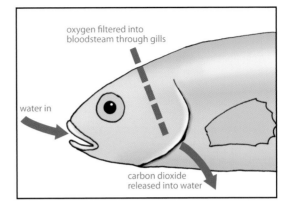

*A fish takes in water through its mouth and as it passes over the gills, the oxygen from the water moves into the blood in the gills.* ILLUSTRATION BY TEMAH NELSON.

*Most bony fish have an organ called a swim bladder that allows them to control their upward and downward movements.* ILLUSTRATION BY TEMAH NELSON.

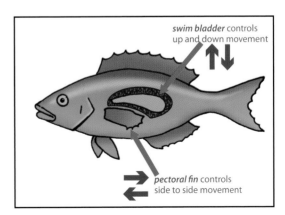

## WORDS TO KNOW

**Anal fin:** Fin on the belly of a fish, used for balance.

**Bony fish:** The largest group of fish, whose skeleton is made of bone.

**Cartilaginous fish:** The second largest group of fish whose skeleton is made of cartilage

**Caudal fin:** Tail fin of a fish used for fast swimming.

**Cold blooded:** When an animals body temperature rises or falls to match the environment.

**Dorsal fin:** The fin located on the back of a fish, used for balance.

**Fish:** Animals that live in water who have gills, fins, and are cold blooded.

**Gills:** Special organ located behind the head of a fish that takes in oxygen from the water.

**Hypothesis:** An idea in the form of a statement that can be tested by observation and/or experiment.

**Jawless fish:** The smallest group of fish, who lacks a jaw.

**Labyrinth:** A lung-like organ located above the gills that allows the fish to breathe in oxygen from the air.

**Mammals:** Animals that have a backbone, are warm blooded, have mammary glands to feed their young and have or are born with hair.

**Pectoral fin:** Pair of fins located on the side of a fish, used for steering.

**Pelvic fin:** Pair of fins located toward the belly of a fish, used for stability.

**Swim bladder:** Located above the stomach, takes in air when the fish wants to move upwards and releases air when the fish wants to move downwards.

**Variable:** Something that can affect the results of an experiment.

fish are found on the lips, head and fins. There are some fish like the cod and catfish that have long feelers around their mouths with taste buds at the ends and are used for detecting food in murky and muddy waters.

In the experiments that follow, you will care for your own fish to observe some of their unique characteristics. In Experiment 1 you will measure how two different types of fish breathe. In the second experiment you will observe how body shape and fins affect the way fish move in the water.

## EXPERIMENT 1

## Fish Breathing: How do different fish take in oxygen?

Purpose/Hypothesis In this experiment, you will create an environment to nurture and maintain two different types of fish to observe the way they breathe. Most fish use their gills to breathe in oxygen from the water. There are some fish who have gills and a lung-like organ called a labyrinth. This lets fish take in oxygen from the air and live in low oxygenated water. The labyrinth is located in the head of the fish just above the gills. The fish takes in air through its mouth and as it passes over the labyrinth the oxygen flows into the bloodstream and the carbon dioxide is released out of the body through the gills.

The Betta has both gills and a labyrinth. The guppy has gills. By creating a comfortable living environment for each of these fish you can measure the differences in how the two fish breathe.

## How to Experiment Safely

Ask for assistance when carrying and lifting the fish tank. Before you begin the experiment, ask an adult if you can care for the fish when the experiment is finished. If you do not want to or cannot care for the fish, find a suitable home for the fish before you begin.

**Level of Difficulty** Moderate. (This project requires continuous care and attention to maintaining a healthy environment for the fish.)

## Materials Needed

- 2, 2–5 gallon fish tank (plastic tanks work well). Size depends on space available and number of fish in the tank. If you only have one fish tank, you could place the fish in the same tank. However, male Betta fish can be aggressive to other fish, although they usually are not harmful to guppies. If you use one tank and find that your Betta becomes aggressive to the guppy, separate them and make your observations separately.
- 2 thermometers for aquarium
- gravel
- male Betta fish (males have more distinct fins)
- guppy (danio or barb fish work well also)
- food for both types of fish (usually different)
- several aquatic plants
- filter (optional)

*Steps 7 and 8: Record the number of times you see the Betta rising to the surface of the tank for air and the number of times you see the guppy opening and closing its mouth.*
ILLUSTRATION BY
TEMAH NELSON.

**Approximate Budget** $25. (Try to use an old fish tank or container if possible.)

## Troubleshooter's Guide

When you are creating a fish tank, many forces of nature can affect the project. These include the health of the fish and water quality. Here are some common problems and a few tips to maintain the best environment:

- Fish when bought at a pet store are usually healthy and will remain healthy if cared for properly. However, a fish could have an illness that is undetectable when purchased and cannot be treated, or even with treatment may not live.

- Clean water without a lot of chemicals is the best environment for fish. Adding plants to the tank enhances the water quality.

- Monitor the tank temperature. If the tank gets too cold or hot it can affect the fish. If you have trouble maintaining an optimal temperature (68–75°Fahrenheit) you may consider adding a heater to the tank.

- If you continue your observations, it is important to change the water in the tank every two weeks, perhaps more frequently if you do not have a filter or plants.

Timetable 1 hour for set up and 10–15 minutes observation time.

Step-by-Step Instructions

1. Place a 1-inch (2.5-centimeter) layer of gravel on the bottom of the fish tanks.

2. Fill the tanks with tap water and let it stand overnight. This will allow the water to reach room temperature and water additives, such as chlorine, to evaporate. (Some pet stores have special products that you can add to the water to ready it for the fish.)

3. Place the thermometer in each tank where it is visible. Bettas and guppies do well in water that is 68–75° Fahrenheit (20–24° Celsius) (room temperature). Be careful to keep the tank out of direct sunlight.

4. Plant one or two aquatic plants in the gravel. The plants provide hiding places for the fish, take in the carbon dioxide that the fish release into the water, and can act as a filtration system for the tank.

5. If you have a filter place it in the tank.

6. Gently transfer the Betta and guppy into the fish tank. Feed according to the instructions on their food containers.

7. Over a period of five minutes, record the number of times you see the Betta rising to the surface of the tank for air.

8. For five minutes, record the number of times you see the guppy opening and closing its mouth

9. Wait overnight or 24 hours and repeat Steps 7 and 8.

Summary of Results How long can the betta stay underwater before he rises to the surface? How often does the guppy breathe? Was there a major difference between the two different times you observed the breathing? Consider the benefits and challenges to the two different forms of breathing. Write a paragraph summarizing the results and your conclusions.

## EXPERIMENT 2

## Fish Movement: How do fins and body shape affect the movement of fish?

In this experiment, you will create an environment to nurture and maintain two types of fish to determine how each moves in the water. Fish use their bodies and fins to move in the water. The tetra and angel fish are two common types of fish that have different body and fin shapes. A tetra fish has a sleek body and small fins as compared to an angel fish, who has a triangular body and large, flowing fins.

Before you begin, make an educated guess about the outcome of this experiment based upon your knowledge of fish. This educated guess, or prediction, is your hypothesis. A hypothesis should explain these things:

- the topic of the experiment
- the variable you will change
- the variable you will measure
- hat you expect to happen

A hypothesis should be brief, specific, and measurable. It must be something you can test through observation. Your experiment will prove or disprove whether your hypothesis is correct. Here is one possible hypothesis for this experiment: "Due to its shape and fins, the tetra fish will move faster through the water than the betta."

**What are the variables?** Variables are anything that might affect the results of an experiment. Here are the main variables in this experiment:

- the type of fish
- the water temperature
- the water environment

In other words, the variables in this experiment are everything that might affect the movement of the fish.

**Level of Difficulty** Moderate. (This project requires continuous care and attention to maintaining a healthy environment for fish.)

**Materials Needed**

- 2–5 gallon fish tank (plastic tanks work well). Size depends on space available and number of fish in the tank
- thermometer for aquarium
- gravel

- heater
- angel fish (male Betta fish also work well)
- tetra fish (guppys also work well)
- food for both types of fish (usually different)
- 1 to 3 aquatic plants, depending upon the size of the tank
- LED light (small LEDs found on keychains work well)
- filter (optional)

Some fish can be aggressive to other fish. Although these fish are usually compatible with each other, if you find that one of your fish becomes aggressive to the other you may want to separate them and make your observations separately.

Approximate Budget $25. (Try to find a used fish tank or other container.)

Timetable 60–75 minutes, several hours apart, depending upon the observation time.

Step-by-Step Instructions

1. Place a 1-inch (2.5-centimeter) layer of gravel on the bottom of the fish tank.
2. Fill the tank with tap water and let it stand overnight. This allows the water to reach room temperature and for additives such as chlorine, to evaporate. Some pet stores have special liquids that you can add to the water to ready it for the fish.
3. Place the heater in the tank; this will help regulate the water temperature.
4. Place the thermometer in the tank where it is visible. Angel and tetra fish do well in water that is 75 degrees Fahrenheit (24 degrees Celsius). Be careful to keep the tank out of direct sunlight.
5. Plant one or two aquatic plants into the gravel. The plants provide hiding places for the fish, take in the carbon dioxide from the water, and act as a filtration system for the tank.
6. If you have a filter, place it in tank.
7. Gently place the angel and tetra into the tank. Feed according to the instructions on their food containers.

8. Make a drawing of both fish. Note their different body shapes and coloring.

9. Observe the behavior of both fish for several minutes.

10. Using the LED light, shine the light at a point just ahead and slightly down from the tetra. Be careful not to shine the light directly into its eyes. Move the LED back and forth across the tank two times and watch how it follows the light. Make a note of the fins' movement they are using to move forward, stop, and turn.

11. Again, move the LED back and forth across the tank two times, having the tetra start at one end of the tank. As you move the light across the tank, have a helper use the stopwatch to time how long it takes for the fish complete its movements. Make a note of the time. Repeat for a second trial.

12. Repeat Step 11 with the angel fish.

13. Wait at least two hours and then repeat Step 11 for both fish, making sure to conduct two trials.

*Step 7: Gently place the angel and tetra into the tank.*
ILLUSTRATION BY TEMAH NELSON.

**Summary of Results** Average the four trials for each fish. Was one fish faster that the other? How do the fins and body shape relate to the speed of the fish. How do the fins and body shape relate to the way each fish moves in general. Summarize the findings of your results, using drawings or pictures. You may want to label the parts of the fins on your drawings. If you keep the fish, it is important to change the water in the tank every two weeks, or more frequently if you do not have a filter or plants.

*Steps 11 and 13: Move the LED back and forth across the tank two times and watch how the fish follow the light.*
ILLUSTRATION BY TEMAH NELSON.

## Design Your Own Experiment

**How to Select a Topic Relating to this Concept** In the fish investigations, you observed two fish that exhibited characteristics common to fish. Many fish have specific adaptations that are suited to the environment in which they live. Consider what types of fish you are curious

## Troubleshooter's Guide

Experiments do not always work out as planned. When you are conducting an experiment with live animals, many forces of nature can affect the project. Here are some common problems and a few tips to maintain the best environment for the fish.

- **Problem:** The fish was never moving much.
- **Possible cause:** Fish when bought at a pet store are usually healthy and will remain healthy if cared for properly. However, sometimes fish have illnesses that are undetectable when purchased. Try purchasing another fish and repeating. Remember to handle the fish gently and not place stress on it.
- **Problem:** The fish is not following the LED.
- **Possible cause:** There can be many possible reasons your fish is not following the LED. Try again the next day. If the fish still does not follow the LED, simply observe the fish movements. You can also try to purchase another fish and repeat the experiment.
- **Problem:** The fish was not acting well once it went into the tank.
- **Possible cause:** It may be the water quality. It is important for the tap water, if not specifically treated for the fish, to rest overnight so that substances such as chlorine and ammonia evaporate. Make sure the water sat for at least 24 hours, and try adding more water plants to the tank, then repeat.
- **Possible cause:** The temperature of the tank may be too warm or cold. Make sure your thermometer is working and take the tank temperature. Angel fish and tetra fish do well at 75 degrees Fahrenheit (24 degrees Celsius). You may consider adding a heater to the tank.

about? You may want to research the types of fish common to your area.

Check the Further Readings section and talk with your science teacher or school or community media specialist to start gathering information on fish questions that interest you.

**Steps in the Scientific Method** To do an original experiment, you need to plan carefully and think things through. Otherwise, you might not be sure what question you are answering, what you are or should be measuring, or what your findings prove or disprove.

Here are the steps in designing an experiment:

- State the purpose of—and the underlying question behind—the experiment you propose to do.
- Recognize the variables involved, and select one that will help you answer the question at hand.
- State a testable hypothesis, an educated guess about the answer to your question.
- Decide how to change the variable you selected.
- Decide how to measure your results.

**Recording Data and Summarizing the Results** It is important to document as much information as possible about your experiment. Part of your presentation should be visual, using charts and graphs. Remember, whether or not your experiment is successful, your conclusions and experiences can benefit others.

**Related Projects** More specific projects can be performed to explore detailed information about fish. For instance, scientists are finding that some fish are in danger of becoming extinct due to pollution and from overfishing. Both pollution and over fishing are impacting the shark population along the Great Barrier Reef in Australia. Learn more about pollution and over fishing and what can be done to prevent this.

You can also look at fish survival. How do fish defend themselves against predators? What sights and sounds do different types of fish respond to? You can examine why fish travel in schools and how they keep from bumping into one another. There are many experiments you could design to further observe the characteristics of fish.

## For More Information

"Animals: Fish." *National Geographic.* http://animals. nationalgeographic.com/ animals/fish.html (accessed on April 9, 2008). Video and images of fish, along with fish-related news and information.

"Fish: Setting Up Your Fish Tank." *American Humane Association.* http://www. americanhumane.org/kids/aquarium.htm (accessed on April 10, 2008). Provides information on how to set up and maintain a fish tank.

Kalman, Bobbie. *Animals called Fish.* New York: Crabtree publishing, 2005. Describes fish, their breathing, reproduction, and defenses.

Sneeden, Robert. *What is a fish?* Great Britain: Belitha Press Limited, 1993. Describes different types of fish, their breathing, movement senses, food, defenses and birth.

Stewart, Melissa. *How Do Fish Breathe Underwater?* New York: Marshall Cavendish Corporation, 2007. An examination of the phenomena of scientific principles behind the ability of fish to extract oxygen from water.

U.S. Fish and Wildlife Service. *Kid's Corner.* http://www.fws.gov/endangered/ kids (accessed April 9, 2008). Provides information on the fish and wildlife conservation.

# Flight

# 32

For birds, flight is moving through the air with wings; but for humans, flight is traveling through the air in an airplane. It is surprising that applying the dynamics of flight did not get off the ground earlier than the twentieth century, because the first human attempts to glide through the sky took place about 3,000 years ago in China using kites. It is recorded that in 196 B.C.E., General Han Hsin used kites to measure the distance to an enemy stronghold. Kites would later provide the key to wing performance principles used in the twentieth century airplane.

*It's a bird, it's a man, it crashed ...* In the eleventh century, an English inventor named Eilmer fastened wing mechanisms to his hands and feet and launched himself off a tower. Although Eilmer actually glided for a while before crashing, he broke both his legs and regretted forgetting to put a tail device on his back end. In the fifteenth century, Leonardo da Vinci (1452–1519)—an Italian engineer, artist, inventor, theatrical designer, musician, and sculptor—drew one of the first sketches of a flying machine. His detailed drawing of a helicopter featured a wing and a horizontal propeller. Because da Vinci felt his painting should reflect light, space, and other sciences such as anatomy, he drew hundreds of sketches of nature and of inventions such as his flying machine.

*The man who discovered lift* In the eighteenth century, Daniel Bernoulli (1700–1782)—a Swiss mathematician, botanist, and anatomist—discovered that force arises from differences in pressure as objects move through a gas or liquid. Bernoulli's discovery later was used to explain what gives birds their lift, or ability to glide without falling. His theory would later be used in the design of the airplane.

*Making the "Wright" connection* By the end of the nineteenth century, several people had made significant headway in developing the airplane. But it was Wilbur and Orville Wright who put all the pieces together to create an airplane that could fly.

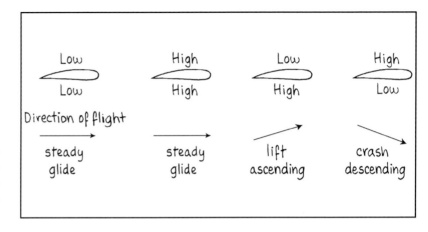

| Low | High | Low | High |
|-----|------|-----|------|
| Low | High | High | Low |

Direction of flight

steady glide     steady glide     lift ascending     crash descending

*Air flows a greater distance over the top of a wing, creating low air pressure there. Higher air pressure under the wing forces the wing upward.* GALE GROUP.

Three men inspired the Wright brothers, setting the stage for this important invention. One was Otto Lilienthal, a German who made 2,000 unpowered flights with his glider. Another was Samuel Pierpont Langley, a prominent scientist and head of the Smithsonian Institution. Langley launched two model airplanes in 1896 that remained airborne long enough to impress the United States Army, which gave him $50,000 for his experiments. The third was Octave Chanute, an American who also conducted gliding experiments. Both Chanute and Lilienthal felt an aircraft's wings should be curved on top and concave underneath. This shape reduced air pressure above the wing and increased it below, providing the aircraft's lift. All three men wrote books about their theories and experiences.

The Wright brothers were successful because they were able to control their aircraft once it flew, an accomplishment that other inventors had been unable to achieve. The key was twisting the wing tips to maintain balance, just as birds alter their wing shape to change flight direction. Beginning in 1899, these persistent, resourceful men pored over any aviation information they could get their hands on and became flying experts. As businessmen, they ran a small, successful bicycle shop in Dayton, Ohio. During off-hours, they tested airfoil sections in a home-made wind tunnel, designed a lightweight internal combustion gas engine, and experimented with kites and gliders. They spent hundreds of

*Otto Lilienthal made over 2,000 gliding experiments.* CORBIS-BETTMANN.

## WORDS TO KNOW

**Aerodynamics:** The study of the motion of gases (particularly air) and the motion and control of objects in the air.

**Centripetal force:** Rotating force that moves towards the center or axis.

**Control experiment:** A set-up that is identical to the main experiment but not affected by the variable being tested in the main experiment. Results from the control experiment are compared to results from the actual experiment to determine the effect of the variable.

**Hypothesis:** An idea in the form of a statement that can be tested by observations and/or experiment.

**Lift:** Upward force on the wings of an aircraft created by differences in air pressure on top of and underneath the wings.

**Propeller:** Radiating blades mounted on a rapidly rotating shaft, which moves aircraft forward.

**Turbulence:** Air disturbance that affects an aircraft's flight.

**Variable:** Something that can change the results of an experiment.

---

hours testing their findings in their shop, on empty fields, and in deserted windy areas like the sand dunes at Kitty Hawk, North Carolina. It was there, on December 17, 1903, their airplane soared for 12 seconds, traveling 120 feet (36 meters) before landing. It became the first flying machine to stay aloft on its own power with a passenger.

Making objects fly was a challenge to the early inventors. Performing basic experiments in aerodynamics will help you understand some of the basic principles of flight.

## EXPERIMENT 1

### Lift-Off: How can a glider be made to fly higher?

**Purpose/Hypothesis** In this experiment you will create an aerodynamic glider capable of moving through the air and modify it so it can soar higher, gaining lift by manipulating the wings. According to Bernoulli's principle, force arises from differences in pressure. Pilots change the degree of lift by manipulating the flaps on the wings' edges. To understand the effects of air

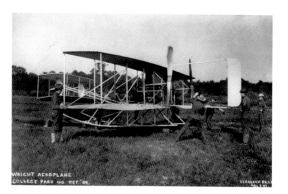

*The Wright brothers' historic first flight took place in 1903.*
PHOTO RESEARCHERS INC.

## What Are the Variables?

Variables are anything that might affect the results of an experiment. Here are the main variables in this experiment:

- the type of balsa wood glider used (both gliders should be identical, simple, and lightweight)
- the type of modifications made to the wing shape of the second glider

In other words, the variables in this experiment are everything that might affect the flight time of the gliders. If you change more than one variable, you will not be able to tell which variable had the most effect on the gliders' flight.

pressure, examine the diagrams illustrated. Before you begin, make an educated guess about the outcome of this experiment based on your knowledge of flight. This educated guess, or prediction, is your hypothesis. A hypothesis should explain these things:

- the topic of the experiment
- the variable you will change
- the variable you will measure
- what you expect to happen

A hypothesis should be brief, specific, and measurable. It must be something you can test through observation. Your experiment will prove or disprove whether your hypothesis is correct. Here is one possible hypothesis for this experiment: "Modifying the wing cross-sectional shape will create more lift under the wing that will allow the glider to fly higher."

In this case the variable you will change is the wing shape of one of the gliders, and the variable you will measure is the distance the gliders fly.

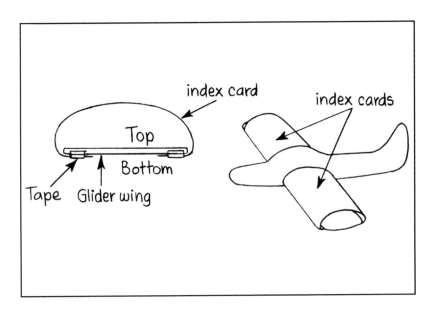

*Steps 3 and 4: Closeup of index card folded over one glider wing and how the glider looks with the index cards on both wings.*

GALE GROUP.

**Level of Difficulty** Easy.

**Materials Needed**

- 2 balsa wood gliders (Styrofoam gliders are acceptable substitutes, but the gliders must have no propellers or landing gear.)
- 1 high power fan, 16 to 24 inches (41 to 61 cm) in diameter
- 2 pieces of string, 18 inches (45 cm) long
- 2 index cards, 4 × 6 inches (10 × 15 cm)
- 1 roll of adhesive tape

**Approximate Budget** $5 for planes. (Borrow the fan from a family member or teacher.)

**Timetable** 30 minutes.

**Step-by-Step Instructions**

1. Prepare the control and test gliders. Assemble as shown on the packing bag.
2. Tie one string to the nose of each glider. If there is a metal or plastic clip on the nose, use it to attach the string.
3. Modify the wing of the test glider to create lift. Fold the top and bottom of the index card as shown in the diagram.
4. Tape the cards over the tops of the wings of the test glider.
5. Modify the index card. Push forward from the back of the wing so that the bubble shape is toward the front of the wing. Once you bend the index card, it molds into the shape as illustrated.
6. Attach the two strings from the planes to the bottom of the fan or the fan grating. (Remember, use caution. Make sure fan is unplugged at this stage.) Aim the fan slightly down toward the surface the planes are resting on.
7. Turn the fan on low, then medium. Record your observations.

> **How to Experiment Safely**
>
> Use caution handling fans. Make sure the fan is unplugged when assembling the experimental apparatus and never touch the blades of the fan when it is operating.

*Step 5: Index card folded and modified to give lift.* GALE GROUP.

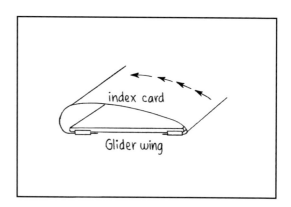

## Troubleshooter's Guide

Sometimes problems may arise during an experiment. Here is an example of a problem, a possible cause, and a way to remedy the problem.

**Problem:** The gliders will not stay in the air.

**Possible cause:** Gliders fly only for short periods because of invisible disturbances in the air, known as turbulence. For this reason, a glider cannot be expected to fly long distances.

**Summary of Results** Record your results by describing how each glider moves in response to the air currents. The modified-wing glider, or test glider, should jump up and glide in the air. The other, the control glider, should constantly dive into the table and flip over. You can measure how high the gliders lift off the table with a ruler.

**Change the Variables** To vary this experiment, use gliders made from different materials, such as Styrofoam or cardboard. Try different fan speeds and change the angle at which the wind hits the glider.

## EXPERIMENT 2

## Helicopters, Propellers, and Centripetal Force: Will it fly high?

*Example of a whirly toy, or propeller on a stick.* GALE GROUP.

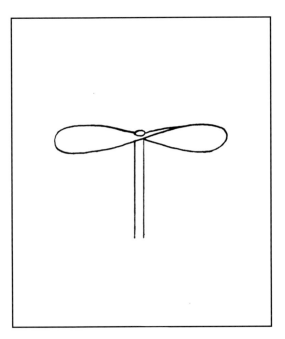

**Purpose/Hypothesis** Centripetal force is force exerted by a spinning object. When objects such as gyroscopes and tops are set in motion, their spinning creates centripetal force. This centripetal force is directed toward the center point of the spinning object. As centripetal force builds momentum, it creates balance. Helicopters rely on this balance and are designed to create centripetal force with their propellers. Before you begin, make an educated guess about the outcome of this experiment based on your knowledge of flight. This educated guess, or prediction, is your hypothesis. A hypothesis should explain these things:

- the topic of the experiment
- the variable you will change
- the variable you will measure
- what you expect to happen

A hypothesis should be brief, specific, and measurable. It must be something you can test through observation. Your experiment will prove or disprove whether your hypothesis is correct. Here is one possible hypothesis for this experiment: "Centripetal force can be disturbed if the balance is disrupted, thus preventing flight."

In this case the variable you will change is the number and position of the dimes on the toy's propeller, and the variable you will measure is the toy's flight.

**Level of Difficulty** Easy.

**Materials Needed**

- Whirly toy—a propeller on a stick
- 4 dimes
- 1 roll of adhesive tape
- meterstick

**Approximate Budget** $3 for whirly toy.

**Timetable** 20 minutes.

**Step-by-Step Instructions**

1. Spin the whirly toy between the palms of your hands and carefully release it.

2. Use the meterstick to record about how high the toy jumps.

3. Tape two dimes onto the propeller of the toy, repeat step 1, and measure the height of its flight. Record the height of the jumps.

4. Remove one of the dimes and test the toy's flight again. Use caution. The flight will be erratic. Record the change in balance and flight.

5. Repeat this test with the dimes in different positions, such as those illustrated.

## What Are the Variables?

Variables are anything that might affect the results of an experiment. Here are the main variables in this experiment:

- the number and position of the dimes (weights) on the propellers

In other words, the variables in this experiment are everything that might affect the flight of the whirly toy. If you change more than one variable, you will not be able to tell which variable had the most effect on the toy's flight.

*Step 3: Toy with dimes attached to each end of the propellers.* GALE GROUP.

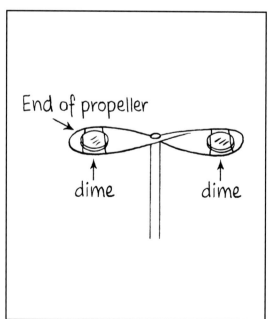

## How to Experiment Safely

Use caution when flying the toys. Avoid contact with eyes.

**Summary of Results** Reflect on your hypothesis. Did you discover centripetal force and the actions that can disrupt its effect or balance? Record your results in a chart. Describe the behavior or draw what happened so others can learn from your experiment.

**Modify the Experiment** Helicopters fly by different principles than other aircraft. In a helicopter, the rotor acts as the wings of an airplane, giving the helicopter lift. The properties of helicopter rotors allows a helicopter to do things a plane cannot, such as hover and move sideways.

For a more challenging experiment, you could make your own whirly toy to discover the shape and size of rotor blades that allow the aircraft to carry the most weight (dimes). First, look at pictures or photograph of helicopter rotor. Note how the rotor blades are not flat. You can use

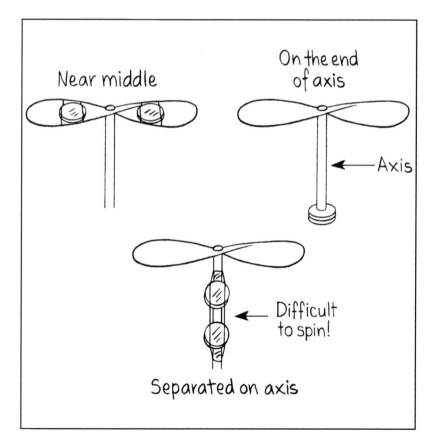

*Step 5: Toy with dimes taped in different positions. Test the flight patterns of each position.*
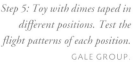

*Experiment Central, 2nd edition*

cardboard, aluminum foil, plastic, or other household materials for your rotors. You can attach the rotors to a dowel, straw, or pencil.

Start out making two blades several inches across. When you have completed the design, rub it in your palms and note how far your makeshift helicopter travels without any weights. Add the weights and repeat. Now continue to improve your helicopter design. You may want to slightly alter the angle of the rotor blades, or add two more. You can also change the length or shape. Remember to change one variable at a time, noting how high it moves on its own before you add the dimes.

---

## Troubleshooter's Guide

Here is a problem that may arise, a possible cause, and a way to remedy the problem.

**Problem:** The toy will not fly when the dimes are attached.

**Possible cause:** The dimes are too heavy. Try lightweight buttons that match each other in size and weight.

---

## Design Your Own Experiment

**How to Select a Topic Relating to this Concept** Investigations and experiments in flight are exciting to explore. A toy box or toy store is a great place to discover objects capable of lift. Keep the ideas simple and work with objects familiar to you. Visit an aerospace museum, or try to arrange a personal tour at a local airport.

Check the Further Readings section and talk with your science teacher or community media specialist to start gathering information on flight questions that interest you.

**Steps in the Scientific Method** To do an original experiment, you need to plan carefully and think things through. Otherwise, you might not be sure what question you are answering, what you are or should be measuring, or what your findings prove or disprove.

Here are the steps in designing an experiment:

- State the purpose of—and the underlying question behind—the experiment you propose to do.
- Recognize the variables involved, and select one that will help you answer the question at hand.
- State a testable hypothesis, an educated guess about the answer to your question.
- Decide how to change the variable you selected.
- Decide how to measure your results.

*Artist and scientist Leonardo da Vinci sketched a flying machine as early as the fifteenth century.* PHOTO RESEARCHERS INC.

**Recording Data and Summarizing the Results** Ask your mom or dad to videotape the takeoff in the glider or pinwheel experiments. Or diagram the flight using photos. Keep the results and data charts simple and easy to use.

**Related Projects** Air pressure is an invisible force that controls many objects and affects our lives. Simple experiments involving balloons or air bags can demonstrate the principles and power of air pressure.

## For More Information

Leuzzi, Linda. *Transportation: Life in America 100 Years Ago.* New York: Chelsea House, 1995. Chronicles aircraft and people who were instrumental in furthering significant inventions.

Nahum, Andrew. *Flying Machine.* London: Dorling Kindersley, 1990. Covers aviation history, its inventors, and principles of flight.

Ohio State University Extension. "Science Fun with Airplanes." http://www.ag.ohio-state.edu/~flight/ (accessed on January 17, 2008). Interactive experiments and information on the science of flight.

Rinard, Judith E. *The Story of Flight.* Buffalo, NY: Firefly Books, 2002. Information on the background and different types of flying crafts.

Weiss, Harvey. *Strange and Wonderful Aircraft.* New York: Houghton Mifflin, 1995. Provides good background on aviation.

## 33

# Flowers

The word flower often brings up images of familiar blooms that enliven homes, such as roses and sunflowers. Yet flowers do far more than beautify the world. A flower is the reproductive structure of flowering plants, which are called angiosperms. Flowering plants include the familiar blooms as well as grasses, shrubs, and trees. The flowers on plants are widely diverse in size, shape, color, and scent. Flower sizes range from the *Wolffia,* which can fit through the eye of a sewing needle, to the Titan Arum, a cone-shaped flower that can tower 9 feet (2.7 meters). Some flowers resemble insects, and others sport brightly colored petals. Yet all flowers share the same key function: to make seeds to give rise to a new generation of the plant.

The evolution of flowers supplied many advantages for plant survival and thus, life on Earth. Flowers provide protection for seeds and a food source for animals. In return for food, the animals supply genetic variation to the flower. Mixing up the genetic material allowed flowers to develop new features that led to plants increasing in types and numbers. First appearing on Earth about 145 million years ago during the era of dinosaurs, today about 90% of plants are flowering plants.

*The inside story* Flowers contain the plant's male and female parts for reproduction. The male part produces powdery grains called pollen. Each pollen grain contains male reproductive cells, called sperm cells. When pollen joins with the female part of the flower it is called pollination. The result is the development of a seed. There are four basic parts to most flowers: the stamen, pistil, petal, and sepal.

The male reproductive organ is called the stamen. The stamens are offshoots that grow in a circle around the blossom. A stamen is made up of the anther located at the top, which holds the pollen, and a filament, which is the thin stalk that supports the anther.

The female reproductive organ is called the pistil. The pistil has three major parts: the stigma, a sticky surface at the top that holds the pollen;

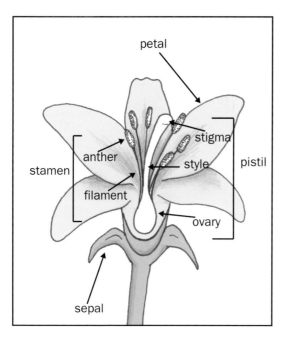

*Parts of a flower.* GALE GROUP.

*Closeup of a Zinnia flower.* FIELD MARK PUBLICATIONS.

the style, the stem that holds the stigma upright; and the ovary, the structure located at the bottom of the stigma that produces ovules, the female reproductive cells or eggs.

The most recognizable part of a flower is its petals. Petals enclose the flower's sex organs. They can bloom in vibrant colors that attract animals to the flower. Sepals are the leaflike structures at the bottom of the petals that protect the flower bud before it opens. When the bud opens, the sepals fold back.

For pollination to occur the pollen must move from the anther of a stamen to the pistil's stigma. The sperm cells in the pollen move down a tube that forms from the style to the ovary. There, the sperm cells can fertilize the eggs in the ovule.

Not all flowers contain all parts. For example, grasses do not contain petals in their flowers. Some flowers produce either the male or female part, and others produce both. The flowers with both pistils and stamens are called perfect flowers. Examples of perfect flowers includes the rose, sweet pea, and lily. Flowers that have only the pistil or the stamen are called imperfect flowers. (The same plant, however, can contain both male and female flowers.)

An imperfect flower prevents a plant from self-pollinating, meaning when the pollen transfers from the male to female parts of a single flower or plant. This can occur simply by gravity causing the pollen to drop. Plants that self-pollinate have the exact same genetic material as the parent, causing them to have a decreased chance of survival if the environment changes. Even if flowers are capable of self-pollinating it is not the desired method of pollination. Flowers have evolved mechanisms to avoid self-pollination such as developing its stamens and pistils at different times, and having its pistil reach far above the stamen.

In cross-pollination pollen is transferred from one flower to another. Cross-pollination combines genetic material and generates greater diversity in the offspring. Plants are usually stronger and healthier over the long run than self-pollinators. While cross-pollination has genetic advantages, it also means that plants are more dependent on a way to have their pollen carried about.

*Pollen on the move* In order for pollen to transfer from one flower to another, it must have a way to move. Some flowering plants depend upon the wind to blow its pollen onto another flower. Examples of wind-pollinated plants include pine trees, corn, and grasses. Plants that pollinate by wind—and sometimes splashes of rain—produce large quantities of light pollen, as a large percntage of the pollen will be wasted by not landing on its target spot. These flowers do not need the vibrant features that tempt pollinators and often have plain, small flowers.

The large majority of flowering plants depend upon animals to ferry the pollen from one flower to another. These pollen-carriers are called pollinators. Insects, birds, butterflies, and even bats are pollinators. Bees are among the most numerous and important pollinators.

Flowers first must attract pollinators by offering food, color, scents, and other temptations. A pollinator that comes into contact with the flower rubs against the anther, causing some pollen to stick to its body. When the pollinator then visits another flower of the same species, its pollen brushes or falls onto that flower's stigma. Animal-pollinated flowers produce less pollen than the wind-pollinators, as the animal carries the pollen directly to a flower.

*Allure of the wild* In the quest to lure pollinators, flowers have evolved several ingenious features. Many flowers offer food in the form of nectar. Nectar is a sweet liquid that provides nourishment for birds, bees, butterflies, and other animals. Nectar is located deep within the flower at the base of their petals. Petals often sport lines or dots that serve as a guide to the hidden nectar. In some flowers nectar accumulates in long pouches that is available to animals with long beaks or tongues. Some flowers time their production of nectar to coincide with

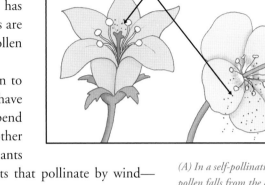

*(A) In a self-pollinating flower, pollen falls from the anther to the stigma; (B) a flower can avoid self-pollination if its pistil reaches above the stamen.* GALE GROUP.

*In cross-pollination, genetic material (pollen) is exchanged from one flower to another.* GALE GROUP.

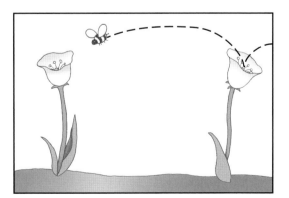

*Bees are among the most numerous and important pollinators.* © GEORGE D. LEPP/CORBIS.

*Flowers have many ways of attracting pollinators. One way is nectar, a sweet liquid located deep within the flower that provides nourishment for birds, bees, butterflies, and other animals.* GALE GROUP.

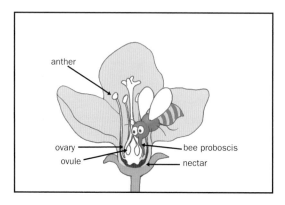

the schedule of their desired pollinator. For example, night-blooming flowers increase their production of nectar at night so the scent attracts bats, moths, and other nocturnal pollinators.

Some plants have many different pollinators, while others are particular to just one type. A plant with many pollinators will have more organisms carrying its pollen, yet there is a greater chance the pollen will not make it to the same type flower. Having a pollinator who only likes one type of flower cuts down the amount of traveling pollen but ensures that the pollen will be delivered to a like flower. For example, the orchid *Angraecum sesquipedale* ensures that only a specific type of insect pollinates it by having its nectar tucked about 10 to 14 inches within the flower. The hawkmoth, which is an insect but is the size of a small bird, with its 12-inch proboscis is the only insect that can reach the nectar.

Animals can get other meals from flowers as well. Some flowers produce a second type of pollen that pollinators can eat. Oils on the flowers are food for some insects.

Flowers also attract pollinators with their petal colors and shapes. Animals all have unique color perception and are attracted to colors that they can spot. Flowers that appeal to birds are often red (some have evolved a landing area for the bird). Bees are attracted to blues, purples, and yellow pigments. Butterflies prefer to eat sitting down so they prefer flat, wide surfaces and bright colors. Bats need large, sturdy and pale-colored flowers to support their weight and show up in the darkness.

Scents—both sweet and foul—are another method of appealing to certain animals. The bee orchid, for example, resembles and smells like a bee. When male bees, tempted by its scent, attempt to mate with the flower they become covered with pollen and spread it to their next flower mate. Another orchid species, the Lady's Slipper, holds a fragrance in its pouch that has a wild attraction for flies. The flies climb around and inside the pouch, getting pollen stuck to them in the process.

Foul odors attract pollinators who feed on decaying matter. The smells are similar to those of the food that these insects and other animals eat. Along with laying claim to the world's largest flower, the Titan's flower is also the world's smelliest. Giving off an odor similar to rotting meat, the stench attracts beetles and flies that feed on or lay eggs in rotting flesh.

Some flowers have mechanisms that force a pollinator to stay for a long visit. With flowers up to one foot across, the giant water lily of the Amazon has to work fast as it only blooms for two days. The flower attracts beetles during the day, then traps them inside when it closes for the night. Covered in pollen, the beetles are released when the flower opens at dusk of the following day. The Dutchman's pipe has a tube-shaped flower with a waxy surface. It emits a putrid smell that appeals to flies. When insects land they slip down the flower and are trapped by its thick hairs. The flies can lap up nectar while they get covered in pollen.

The appearance and smell of a flower provides clues as to its pollinator. In the following two experiments you will explore pollination and how a flower's features shape its pollinators.

*The pouch on a Lady's Slipper orchid, which contains the flower's pollen, has a fragrance that attracts pollinators to it.*
FIELD MARK PUBLICATIONS.

## EXPERIMENT 1

### Self versus Cross: Will there be a difference in reproduction between self-pollinated and cross-pollinated plants of the same type?

Purpose/Hypothesis Flowering plants can be cross-pollinators or self-pollinators. Botanists and flower developers cross-pollinate specific plants intentionally to produce a desired trait in the offspring, such as a specific color. The cross between two parent plants produces a hybrid.

In this experiment, you will both cross-pollinate and self-pollinate the same type of plant. Because of possible variations, you will use two plants for each trial. You will then wait for the plants to develop and observe any differences in the flowers and outcome.

## WORDS TO KNOW

**Angiosperm:** A flowering plant that has its seeds produced within an ovary.

**Anther:** The male reproductive organs of the plant, located on the tip of a flower's stamen.

**Control experiment:** A setup that is identical to the experiment, but is not affected by the variable that acts on the experimental group.

**Cross-pollination:** The process by which pollen from one plant pollinates another plant of the same species.

**Filament:** In a flower, stalk of the stamen that bears the anther.

**Flower:** The reproductive part of a flowering plant.

**Hypothesis:** An idea in the form of a statement that can be tested by observation and/or experiment.

**Imperfect flower:** Flowers that have only the male reproductive organ (stamen) or the female reproductive organs (pistil).

**Nectar:** A sweet liquid, found inside a flower, that attracts pollinators.

**Ovary:** In a plant, the base part of the pistil that bears ovules and develops into a fruit.

**Ovule:** Structure within the ovary that develops into a seed after fertilization.

**Perfect flower:** Flowers that have both male and female reproductive organs.

**Petal:** Leafy structure of a flower just inside the sepals; they are often brightly colored and have many different shapes.

**Pistil:** Female reproductive organ of flowers that is composed of the stigma, style, and ovary.

**Pollen:** Dust-like grains or particles produced by a plant that contain male sex cells.

**Pollination:** Transfer of pollen from the male reproductive organs to the female reproductive organs of plants.

**Pollinator:** Any animal, such as an insect or bird, that transfers the pollen from one flower to another.

**Self-pollination:** The process in which pollen from one part of a plant fertilizes ovules on another part of the same plant.

**Sepal:** The outermost part of a flower; typically leaflike and green.

**Stamen:** Male reproductive organ of flowers that is composed of the anther and filament.

**Stigma:** Top part of the pistil upon which pollen lands and receives the male pollen grains during fertilization.

**Style:** Stalk of the pistil that connects the stigma to the ovary.

**Variable:** Something that can affect the results of an experiment.

Before you begin, make an educated guess about the outcome of this experiment based on your knowledge of flowers and pollination. This educated guess, or prediction, is your hypothesis. A hypothesis should explain these things:

- the topic of the experiment
- the variable you will change

- the variable you will measure

- what you expect to happen

A hypothesis should be brief, specific, and measurable. It must be something you can test through further investigation. Your experiment will prove or disprove whether your hypothesis is correct. Here is one possible hypothesis for this experiment: "The flowers that are cross-pollinated will produce seeds and the self-pollinated plant will not."

In this case, the variable you will change is the source of the pollen. The variable you will measure is the development of the flowers and seeds.

Conducting a control experiment will help you isolate each variable and measure the changes in the dependent variable. Only one variable will change between the control and the experimental setup, and that is the pollen a plant receives. For the control, you will place a plant in an isolated, indoor area to ensure it receives no pollen from another plant. At the end of the experiment you can compare the results of the control to the experimental plants.

## What Are the Variables?

Variables are anything that might affect the results of an experiment. Here are the main variables in this experiment:

- the type of plant
- the source of pollen
- the environment (for example, sunlight, wind, air temperature)
- the amount of water applied to the plant after pollination

In other words, the variables in this experiment are everything that might affect pollination. If you change more than one variable at the same time, you will not be able to tell which variable had the most effect on plant reproduction.

Level of Difficulty Moderate.

Materials Needed

- eight young flowering, cross-pollinating plants of one type, purchased before any flowers have grown (if not available as young plants, you can grow with seeds, potting soil, and pots. For a faster option, you can order Wisconsin Fast Plant seeds from Carolina Biological; see Further Readings). Talk with an expert at a gardening store or conduct research to make sure that you have selected a plant that cross-pollinates. (In general, geraniums, corn, and cucumbers work well; avoid tomatoes, beans, and peas.)

- several cotton swabs
- several toothpicks
- tweezers
- marking pen
- magnifying glass (optional)

## How to Experiment Safely

There are no safety hazards in this experiment. If you have strong allergies to pollen you may want to check with an adult before conducting this experiment.

**Approximate Budget** $20.

**Timetable** Varies widely depending on plant; 30 minutes for pollination; about 10 minutes of regular observations for six to 14 weeks.

**Step-by-Step Instructions**

1. Conduct the experiment inside and away from other plants of the same species. There should be two plants in each trial: Label two plants "A," two plants "B," two plants "C," and two plants "D." The plants labeled "D" will be the Control. Set plants in distant locations from one another, such as in separate parts of a room, or even in separate rooms. Make sure each plant has equal light.

2. After the plants have formed blossoms and before the petals open, gently push aside the petals with a toothpick. On Plants A use the tweezers to remove all the stamens on each flower, leaving the stigma. Label the pot: "Female/Cross."

3. When all the plants have open flowers, (this should occur at roughly the same time) note whether the stigma stands below, equal, or higher to the anthers. You will need to pollinate, self-pollinate, and not pollinate the same number of flowers on each plant. Count the least number of flowers on one of the plants and use that as the guide. Gently snip off the remaining flower shoots that you will not need. For example, if one of the plants only has three flowers and the rest have over six, snip off the extras on the other plants so all plants have three flowers.

4. Rub a cotton swab against the stamens of Plants B. You should see pollen grains on the swab. You may want to use a magnifying glass. Gently rub those pollen grains against the tip of the stigmas on Plants A. Make sure you see the pollen grains on the stigma.

5. Repeat with a fresh swab for each transfer of pollen flowers.

*Step 4: Gently rub the pollen grains from the stamen against the tip of the stigma.* GALE GROUP.

6. Self-pollinate Plants C by taking a fresh swab and moving the pollen from the stamen to the stigma in each flower. Label plants: "Self-Pollinated."

7. At regular intervals, (depending on plant, could be every three days) note any changes in the pistil in Plants A, C, and D. Note what day the petals fall off and any changes in the sepals.

**Summary of Results** As the flowers continue to develop, construct a chart with the similarities and differences among the plants. Note the pistil development and count the number of seeds in each pistil. Average the seeds for each of the two plants in each group. Compare the control to the self-pollinated plant. How did the groups of plants differ? How were they the same?

**Change the Variables** To change the variable in this experiment you can change the type of plant. You can also conduct the same type of pollination on each plant, and alter the environmental conditions. You can also alter the nutrition of the plants by changing the soil content. Use a soil with few nutrients, and then add specific nutrients one by one to determine which nutrients affect seed production.

---

## Troubleshooter's Guide

Below is a problem that may arise during this experiment, some possible causes, and some ways to remedy the problem.

**Problem:** The plants did not produce seeds.

**Possible cause:** There can be several possible causes: The plant may have been exposed to too much heat, or it may not have had enough water or nutrients. Make sure you use a rich soil that contains nutrients, and follow the directions for the seed carefully. You may want to talk with a professional at a plant store.

**Possible cause:** You may not be able to see the seeds. The pistil should be enlarged, change shape, and become dry. When this happens, carefully look inside the pistil to see if there are seeds, then remove each seed carefully.

---

## EXPERIMENT 2

### Sweet Sight: Can changing a flower's nectar and color affect the pollinators lured to the flower?

Purpose/Hypothesis Among the many characteristics a flower uses to attract pollinators are its color and nectar. There are some pollinators that respond to certain colors. For example, in general butterflies are attracted to bright reds and oranges; bees to blues and yellows; and beetles to many different colors. Nectar also varies among flowers in the amount of sugar it contains. Some pollinators are attracted to nectar that has about 20 to 25% sugar; other pollinators, such as bees, prefer a richer sugar content of about 50%.

In this experiment, you will determine if you can attract a certain type of pollinator based on the color and sugar-concentration of nectar. You can

## What Are the Variables?

Variables are anything that might affect the results of an experiment. Here are the main variables in this experiment:

- the shape of the bowl/cup
- the environment the cup is placed
- the weather conditions
- the time of observations
- the concentration of nectar
- the color of the flower

In other words, the variables in this experiment are everything that might affect the pollinators who approach the cups. If you change more than one variable at the same time, you will not be able to tell which variable had the most effect on attracting pollinators.

measure the results by noting the numbers and types of pollinators. Among the animals to look out for are ants, butterflies, bees, birds, and spiders. You will first apply a constant nectar content to three colors: yellow, blue, and white. After finding one color that attracts the most pollinators, you will then vary the nectar by placing an artificial nectar on the color.

Nectar is a syrupy-solution made up of several types of sugar, primarily sucrose, which is common table sugar. You will make varying concentrations of artificial nectar: a 20% sugar syrup and a 50% sugar syrup.

Before you begin, make an educated guess about the outcome of this experiment based on your knowledge of flowers and pollinators. This educated guess, or prediction, is your hypothesis. A hypothesis should explain these things:

- the topic of the experiment
- the variable you will change
- the variable you will measure
- what you expect to happen

A hypothesis should be brief, specific, and measurable. It must be something you can test through further investigation. Your experiment will prove or disprove whether your hypothesis is correct. Here is one possible hypothesis for this experiment: "There will be one combination of color and nectar that will attract the most of one type of pollinator: The yellow, high nectar concentration will lure the most bees."

In this case, the variables you will change, one at a time, are the color and then the concentration of the artificial nectar. The variable you will measure is the number and type of pollinators.

Conducting a control experiment will help you isolate each variable and measure the changes in the dependent variable. Only one variable will change between the control and your experiment. After determining the color that attracts the most of a certain type of pollinator, your control will change the concentration of nectar. For the control in this part of the experiment, you will use plain water instead of nectar. At the end of the experiment you can compare the experimental data to the control data.

**Level of Difficulty** Moderate to Difficult, because of the attention to detail and time involved.

**Materials Needed**

- 3 cups sugar
- outside area with a high ledge area
- 2 nice days
- 6 cups water
- six clear plastic cups
- swatches of blue, yellow, and white felt: enough to fit in the plastic cups
- colored felt
- small rocks
- stirring spoon
- measuring cup
- marking pen

**Approximate Budget** $5.

**Timetable** 1 hour for experiment setup; 1 hour each day for 2 days.

*Steps 3 and 4: After selecting one color, alter the concentration of the sugar in the artificial nectar.* GALE GROUP.

## Troubleshooter's Guide

Below is a problem that may arise during this experiment, some possible causes, and some ways to remedy the problem.

**Problem:** There were too few pollinators to draw any conclusions.

**Possible cause:** Vary the time of day you are making your observations. You may also want to change the location to one with more plant growth and surrounding flowers.

### Step-by-Step Instructions

1. Day 1: Cut a swatch of the colored felts and scrunch each one into a clear cup. Place a small stone in the felt to weigh it down.

2. Set each of the cups in the same general area outside on a high ledge, at roughly 2 feet apart from one another. Choose two times of day to observe the colored cups for a 30-minute period each time: one time in the morning and one in the afternoon or early evening. You will need to observe at the same two times the following day. For each color, note the number and type of pollinators that visit the cup.

3. Day 2: Vary the nectar concentration. Use your data from the previous day to select one of the colors that attracted the most pollinators. Place a swatch of the selected color into each of three clear plastic cups.

4. Label the cups according to the ratio of sugar to water: "1:1," "1:4," and "Control." The Control will be plain water.

5. Boil the 6 cups of water. Pour 2 cups of sugar into a glass bowl labeled 1:1. Add 2 cups of boiled water and stir until all sugar has dissolved. Allow the artificial nectar to cool.

6. Pour $\frac{1}{2}$ cup sugar into a glass bowl labeled 1:4. Add 2 cups of boiled water and stir until all sugar has dissolved. Allow to cool.

7. Fill the 1:1 cup and the 1:4 cup with their designated artificial nectar. Fill the Control cup with 2 cups of cooled boiled water without any sugar. Place the cups outside on a ledge.

8. At the same two times of day as the previous day, observe the flowers for 30-minute periods and note the type and number of visitors to each cup.

Summary of Results Examine your results for both the color and concentration. Graph the major pollinators number of visits by the color. Create another graph of the major pollinators number of visits by the nectar concentration. Could you attract one specific pollinator by altering the nectar and color? Conduct some research and determine what types of flowers this pollinator(s) visits the most frequently. How do the characteristics of these flowers compare to your experimental results?

Change the Variables As it is the combination of many different factors that influence a flower's pollinators, you can vary this experiment in many ways to determine the relative effect of each characteristic.

- Change the shape of the setup by creating petals of different shapes, then using one concentration of nectar.
- Change the colors of the setup, using single colors and multiple colors
- Vary the scent of the setup, either by purchasing flower scents or by extracting scents from real flowers
- Change the environment to compare pollinators, such as in a wooded area, park, and backyard.

Modify the Experiment This experiment involves examining how flower nectar and color both attract pollinators. You can simplify the setup and focus of this experiment by working with artificial flowers. By comparing artificial flowers to real flowers, which contain nectar, you can determine how flower characteristics affect pollinators.

You will need two types of artificial flowers and their matching natural flowers. The flowers should be different colors. Try to chose flowers that have large petals and bright colors, such as roses, sunflowers, or hydrangeas. You will only need one of each. If possible, try to match the artificial flowers to a flower naturally growing outside. If you purchase real flowers, make sure they are freshly cut. To begin the experiment, you should have four flowers: two of one type, one real and one artificial; two of another type, one real and one artificial.

On a nice morning, place the artificial flowers several feet away from the natural flowers. Now stand back several feet and observe the insects or other pollinators that visit each flower. It helps to have a friend or adult observe and make notes also. Observe the flowers for at least 15 minutes at least two different times. Does one color flower attract more pollinators than the other? Do the natural flowers attract more pollinators? Do the pollinators stay for a longer period of time at the natural flowers? You can repeat this experiment with several different color and types of flowers? When you have finished, look at all your data and see if you notice a pattern with color or nectar. Chart your results or write a summary of your findings.

## Design Your Own Experiment

How to Select a Topic Relating to this Concept While flowers all have the same function, they are widely diverse in appearance. Many flowers, especially the self-pollinators, are so small and nondescript that you may not notice them. To gather ideas for a topic you can look at the many different types of flowers that grow in your area. Visit a greenhouse or a florist to observe species' shapes, colors, and scents. As flowers are unique to a geographic region, you may want to look up photographs and descriptions of flowers in different locations around the United States and the world. Examine how the flower's appearance shapes its role, if any, with possible pollinators.

Check the Further Readings section and talk with your science teacher to learn more about flowers and pollination. You could also speak with a professional at a local greenhouse or nursery.

**Steps in the Scientific Method** To conduct an original experiment, you need to plan carefully and think things through. Otherwise, you might not be sure what question you are answering, what you are or should be measuring, or what your findings prove or disprove.

Here are the steps in designing an experiment:

- State the purpose of—and the underlying question behind—the experiment you propose to do.
- Recognize the variables involved and select one that will help you answer the question at hand.
- State your hypothesis, an educated guess about the answer to your question.
- Decide how to change the variable you selected.
- Decide how to measure your results.

**Recording Data and Summarizing the Results** Your data should include charts and graphs such as the one you did for these experiments. They should be clearly labeled and easy to read. You may also want to include photographs and drawings of your experimental setup and results, which will help other people visualize the steps in the experiment.

If you are preparing an exhibit, you may want to display your results, such as any experimental setup you designed. You may also want to display any flowers that you studied. If you have completed a nonexperimental project, explain clearly what your research question was and illustrate your findings.

**Related Projects** With the wide variety of flowers and their pollinators, there are numerous flower-related projects. You can use a magnifying glass to carefully dissect a flower, separating and labeling each of its parts.

By doing this with several different types of flowers you can compare the flower parts. Flowers have several main attractants to pollinators: color, nectar, shape, and scent. You can examine the relationship between one or all of these with the pollinator. For example, you can examine the effect of flower scents on pollinators. You can look up techniques to capture the scent of a flower and then place the scents outside on the same substance.

Different species of flowers release pollen of varying appearance. You can collect and compare the pollen grains from several types of flowers. Look at how the grains from self-pollinators compares to cross-pollinators. You can also examine what types of pollinators are attracted to each of the pollen types. For a research paper, you can examine what the pollen grains offer the pollinator, such as protein, sugar, and shelter. Some flower species have evolved deceptive appearances and smells to entice pollinators that you could also observe and research. You could also look at the biology of pollination and map out the genetics of plant reproduction.

## For More Information

Attenborough, David. *The Private Life of Plants: A Natural History of Plant Behaviour.* Princeton, NJ: Princeton University Press, 1995. These stories of plant life and survival feature plants from all over the world with full-color photographs.

Bailey, Jill. *Plants and Plant Life: Flowers & Fruits.* Danbury, CT: Grolier Educational, 2001. This volume of the series on plants covers reproduction.

Black, David, and Anthony Huxley. *Plants: The World of Science.* New York: Orbis Publishing, 1985. Contains comprehensive information on plants, with photographs.

Ganeri, Anita. *Plant Science.* New York: Dillon Press, 1993. Answers questions on basic plant characteristics and behavior.

Missouri Botanical Garden. "Pollination." *Biology of Plants.* http://www.mbgnet.net/bioplants/pollination.html (accessed on February 6, 2008). Information and video about pollination.

"Plants and Animals: Partners in Pollination." *Smithsonian Center for Education and Museum Studies.* http://www.smithsonianeducation.org/educators/lesson_plans/partners_in_pollination/index.html (accessed on February 16, 2008) Covers various aspects of how animals help pollinate plants.

"Rice Anatomy." *Plant Biology Division of Biological Sciences, University of California, Davis.* http://www-plb.ucdavis.edu/labs/rost/Rice/reproduction/flower/flower.html (accessed on February 18, 2008) Shows the various reproductive components of rice flowers and how they interact.

Souza, D.M. *Freaky Flowers.* New York: Franklin Watts, 2002. Filled with photographs that show intriguing flowers from around the world.

U.S. Department of Agriculture Forest Service. "Pollinators." *Celebrating Wildflowers.* http://www.fs.fed.us/wildflowers/pollinators/index.shtml (accessed on February 16, 2008). A lot of information on pollination, with pictures and examples.

# 34

# Fluids

When people talk about fluids, we are often referring to liquids. In scientific terms, a fluid is both a liquid and a gas. In solids, the particles are packed tightly together and in a regular pattern. Particles in fluids move about freely are in constant motion—they are fluid.

*What makes a fluid a fluid* There are many properties that set fluids and solids apart. A few key properties include:

- Pressure Direction: Right now, there is pressure all around you from air, a fluid. You cannot feel this pressure because you are supported by equal air pressure on all sides and your body is filled with fluids (gases and liquid) that push back. For solids, the pressure pushes downward. When you stand up the weight of your body is pushing down on the floor. For a fluid, the pressure at any one point is the same in all directions.

- Density: One property of all matter is density. Density is a measure of a solid or fluid's mass in a set amount of space (volume). Any fluid (or solid) at a given temperature and pressure will have a fixed volume. The fluid will also have a certain mass, which is usually measured in pounds or kilograms. Density is a ratio of the mass to its volume. For example, one cup of motor oil weighs far more than one cup of air, making the density of oil higher than the density of air.

- Viscosity: Viscosity is a measure of a fluid's resistance to flow. It is sometimes referred to as the "flowability" of the liquid. This is a common property to measure in science, as it gives information as to how the material will behave. In general, thicker fluids have a greater

*For a fluid, the pressure at any one point is the same in all directions.* ILLUSTRATION BY TEMAH NELSON.

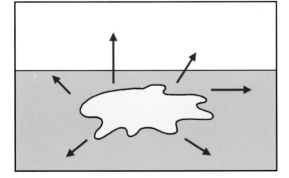

**439**

## WORDS TO KNOW

**Density:** The mass of a substance divided by its volume.

**Fluid:** A substance that flows; a liquid or gas.

**Hypothesis:** An idea phrased in the form of a statement that can be tested by observation and/or experiment.

**Mass:** Measure of the total amount of matter in an object. Also, an object's quantity of matter as shown by its gravitational pull on another object.

**Matter:** Anything that has mass and takes up space.

**Newtonian fluid:** A fluid that follows certain properties, such as the viscosity remains constant at a given temperature.

**Non-Newtonian fluid:** A fluid whose property do not follow Newtonian properties, such as viscosity can vary based on the stress.

**Shear stress:** An applied force to a give area.

**Surface tension:** The attractive force of molecules to each other on the surface of a liquid.

**Variable:** Something that can affect the results of an experiment.

**Viscosity:** The measure of a fluid's resistance to flow; its flowability.

**Volume:** The amount of space occupied by a three-dimensional object.

resistance to flow, which means a higher viscosity. Motor oil, for example, has a high viscosity when compared to water. In some fluids, viscosity can change. Motor oil thins as it heats and thickens as it cools.

*Fluid categories* Because fluids is such a large category there are many ways to identify and categorize them. One category of fluids is whether it acts as a Newtonian or non-Newtonian fluid. This is named after the English scientist Isaac Newton (1642–1727).

Newtonian fluids in general have a constant viscosity given the same temperature and pressure. Water is a Newtonian fluid. When you pour out a large bottle of water the first cup flows at the same rate as the last. If you shake the bottle and pour it again, the water will flow at the same rate. But many fluids fall under the category of non-Newtonian fluids.

In non-Newtonian fluids, the viscosity changes depending on the forces acting on the

*A water strider utilizes surface tension of water to float.* © VISUALS UNLIMITED/CORBIS.

fluid. The force is known as the shear stress, meaning the fluids are sheared or deformed. Applying shear stress to non-Newtonian fluids will change the viscosity. Turn a bottle of ketchup upside down and you'll usually wait for the ketchup to flow. But if you shake the ketchup bottle and pour again, the ketchup will flow at a much faster rate. Its viscosity has lowered.

Some non-Newtonian fluids will become more viscous (thicker) when shear force is applied. A non-Newtonian fluid also may change viscosity with temperature and pressure changes. Yogurt, quicksand, and paints are other examples of non-Newtonian fluids.

*Fun with fluids* Another important property of fluids is the surface tension, which is a measurement of how much the liquid molecules tend to stick together. Compared to many fluids, water has a relatively high surface tension. This is why water bugs can "walk" along the water's surface.

Fluids also move at different speeds or velocities. Then there are fluids that form a coil, like a rope, when it streams downwards and others that drop in a straight line. Some fluids spatter more than others.

In the experiments that follow, you will examine different properties of fluids. As you conduct the experiments, consider questions about the fluids that you would like to explore further.

> ## What Are the Variables?
>
> Variables are anything that might affect the results of an experiment. Here are the main variables in this experiment:
>
> - the type of fluid
> - the temperature of the fluid
> - the container holding the fluid
> - the object moving through the fluid
> - the amount of fluid
>
> In other words, the variables in this experiment are everything that might affect the time it takes for the object to sink. If you change more than one variable at a time, you will not be able to determine which variable had the most effect on the viscosity.

## EXPERIMENT 1

## Viscosity: How can temperature affect the viscosity of liquids?

Purpose/Hypothesis Viscosity is an important property of fluids. In general, liquids that are thick have a relatively high viscosity and thin liquids have a low viscosity. Most fluids have a constant viscosity at a fixed temperature. In this experiment, you will explore how changing the temperature of fluids may affect the viscosity.

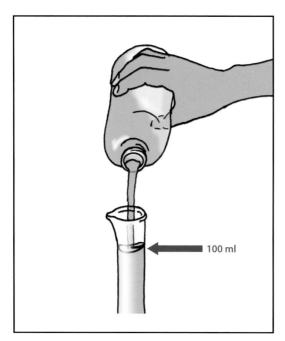

100 ml

*Step 1: Pour honey into the graduated cylinder to the 100 ml mark.* ILLUSTRATION BY TEMAH NELSON.

You will first test the viscosity of the fluid at room temperature by timing how long it takes for an object to move through the fluid. The thicker the fluid, the longer it takes for the object to fall. The fluids in this experiment are honey and cooking oil. By lowering and increasing the temperature of the honey and oil, you can measure how temperature affects the viscosity of the two fluids.

To begin the experiment, use what you have learned about fluids and make an educated guess about how temperature will affect the viscosity of a fluid. This educated guess, or prediction, is your hypothesis. A hypothesis should explain these things:

- the topic of the experiment
- the variable you will change
- the variable you will measure
- what you expect to happen

A hypothesis should be brief, specific, and measurable. It must be something you can test through observation. Your experiment will prove or disprove whether your hypothesis is correct. Here is one possible hypothesis for this experiment: "The colder the liquid; the higher its viscosity and the warmer the liquid, the lower its viscosity."

In this case, the variable you will change for each material is the temperature. The variable you will measure is the time it takes an object to move through the fluid.

**Level of Difficulty** Moderate.

**Materials Needed**

- stopwatch
- graduated cylinder, 100 ml (or a narrow see-through container about a foot tall, such as a shampoo bottle)
- honey
- cooking oil
- small paperclips, at least 6

- 2 pots, which the graduated cylinder fits into (stew pots work well); 1 pot will also work
- potholders
- chopsticks or other long, slender item

**Approximate Budget** $5 (assuming you can find or borrow a stopwatch).

**Timetable** One hour and 30 minutes.

**Step-by-Step Instructions**

1. Pour honey into the graduated cylinder to the 100 ml mark. If you are using another container, mark a line where you fill the honey.

2. Drop the paperclip into the honey. Use the stopwatch to time how long it takes for the paperclip to hit the bottom. Repeat for two more trials and make a note in a chart.

3. Remove the paperclips (chopsticks work well) and fill the honey again to the 100 ml or to the line.

4. To heat the honey: Fill the pot with water until is slightly below the top of the graduated cylinder. (Be careful not to get any water into the honey) Remove the graduated cylinder and heat the pot of water until it simmers. Turn off the heat. Carefully, place the graduated cylinder in the middle of the pot. Allow it to sit in the hot water for 15 to 20 minutes.

5. Use the potholders to remove the graduated cylinder. Again, drop a paperclip into the honey and time how long it takes for it to hit the bottom. Repeat two more times.

6. Remove the paperclips and fill the honey to the same height.

7. To cool the honey: Fill the second pot with ice. (If you only have one pot, pour

*Step 2: Drop the paperclip into the honey.* ILLUSTRATION BY TEMAH NELSON.

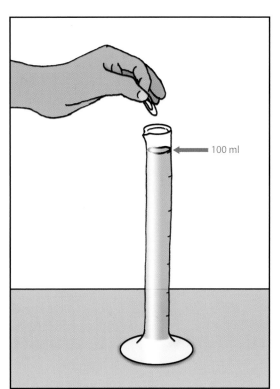

100 ml

## Troubleshooter's Guide

It is common for experiments to not work exactly as planned. Learning from what went wrong can also be a learning experience. Below are some problems that may arise during this experiment, some possible causes, and ways to remedy the problems.

**Problem:** There was no change in viscosity when the liquids changed temperature.

**Possible causes:** If you were using a container that was insulated, the honey and oil may have been too insulated from the surrounding water temperatures. Make sure the hot water is hot and the cold water is ice-cold, and that the container is not insulated. You can use a thermometer to make sure that the honey and oil are changing temperatures. Repeat the trials.

**Problem:** The paperclip is dropping too quickly to measure.

**Possible causes:** Use a taller container, such as a 100 ml graduated cylinder, and make sure you are using a small paperclip. You may also need to find a more accurate timer or stopwatch. Repeat the experiment.

out the hot water.) The ice should not be higher than the honey in the graduated cylinder. Add cold water and set the graduated cylinder in the middle of the pot. Allow it to set for 20 minutes.

8. Remove the honey and conduct three trials on how long the paperclip takes to fall to the bottom.

9. Clean the graduated cylinder, and repeat the entire process, replacing the honey with cooking oil.

**Summary of Results** Average the three trials for each of the liquids. How does the viscosity of the liquids compare to one another? How did temperature affect both fluids? You may want to make a bar chart of your results. Write a paragraph summarizing and explaining your findings.

**Change the Variables** If you want to change the variables in this experiment, you can try changing the fluids. Compare the viscosity of several different liquids. You can focus on different types of oils, for example, or test a variety of liquids. You can also examine how gradations of heat or cold affect viscosity. You can use a thermometer and measure viscosity at specific temperature increments.

## EXPERIMENT 2

### Spinning Fluids: How do different fluids behave when immersed in a spinning rod?

**Purpose/Hypothesis** One property of some non-Newtonians fluids is the tendency for the liquid to climb up a spinning rod. This characteristic is known as the Weissenberg effect—named after the scientist Karl Weissenberg, whose experiments demonstrated many properties of non-Newtonian fluids.

In this experiment you will compare the properties of three fluids when the fluids are submerged in a spinning rod. You can compare water, a Newtonian fluid, to two different fluids: egg whites and a viscous fluid made up of glue and borax. Before you begin, make an educated guess about the outcome of this experiment based on your knowledge of fluids. This educated guess, or prediction, is your hypothesis. A hypothesis should explain these things:

- the topic of the experiment
- the variable you will change
- the variable you will measure
- what you expect to happen

A hypothesis should be brief, specific, and measurable. It must be something you can test through observation. Your experiment will prove or disprove whether your hypothesis is correct. Here is one possible hypothesis for this experiment: "Only the fluid made from glue will climb up a spinning rod."

In this case, the variable you will change is the liquid, and the variable you will measure is whether the object moves up the rod or not.

**Level of Difficulty** Easy/moderate (due to the use of a power tool and cutting).

**Materials Needed**

- drill
- white school glue, washable
- borax
- thick plastic glass
- plastic cup
- plastic spoons
- drill
- 3 eggs
- ruler
- clock with a minute hand

## What Are the Variables?

Variables are anything that might affect the results of an experiment. Here are the main variables in this experiment:

- the composition of the liquids
- the speed of the spinning rod
- the amount of time the rod spins
- the temperature of the liquids

In other words, the variables in this experiment are everything that might affect the properties of the fluid. If you change more than one variable, you will not be able to tell which variable had the most effect on whether the fluid climbed up the rod or not.

## How to Experiment Safely

Have an adult cut the aluminum rod. Be careful when working with the drill and have an adult present.

- waterproof marker
- 1/4-inch diameter aluminum rod (available from hardware stores)
- paper towels
- hack saw or other tool to cut metal

**Approximate Budget** $8. (If your household does not have a drill try to borrow one.)

**Timetable** 20 minutes.

**Step-by-Step Instructions**

1. Have an adult cut the aluminum rod at about the 9-inch (23-centimeter) mark. The exact length does not matter; the rod should be about 2 to 3 inches (5–7 centimeters) longer than the top of the glass.

2. Use the marker and ruler to mark one-quarter inch (0.64 centimeters) notches on the rod. Start at the 1-inch (2.54-centimeter) mark and continue until you reach about half-way up the rod.

3. Set the rod in the drill and have an adult help you tighten the rod in the drill.

4. Pour approximately three-quarters of a cup of water into the glass.

5. Set the glass on a counter so it is about eye level, or you may need a helper to hold the drill. You should be able to see the marks on the rod.

6. With an adult helping, place the drill in the glass and turn it on for one minute. Observe how the water is behaving as the rod is spinning.

7. Note if the water climbed up the rod at all by looking at the marks.

8. Empty out the glass and wipe off the rod.

9. Carefully, separate the eggs and drop the egg whites into the glass.

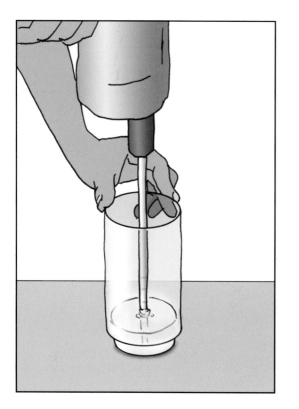

*Step 6: Place the drill in the glass and turn it on for 1 minute.*
ILLUSTRATION BY TEMAH NELSON.

10. Repeat Steps 5–8, noting how far the egg whites climbs up the rod.

11. Use the plastic spoons to measure out 8 teaspoons (2 tablespoons) of white glue and 8 teaspoons of water into the cleaned glass.

12. In a plastic cup and using a clean spoon, place one-half of a teaspoon of borax and 8 teaspoons of water (one-half cup). Mix well.

13. Pour the borax solution into the glass and briefly stir.

14. Repeat Steps 5–8, noting how far the glue fluid climbs up the rod.

*Step 11: Use the plastic spoons to measure out 8 teaspoons (2 tablespoons) of white glue.* ILLUSTRATION BY TEMAH NELSON.

**Summary of Results** Examine how far each fluid climbed up the rod. Was there a large difference among the fluids? Was your hypothesis correct? Consider the similarities and differences in how the three fluids behaved. You might want to graph your results and write a paragraph on your conclusions.

**Change the Variables** To change the variables, you can use one of the fluids and experiment with changing the temperature. What would happen in a cooler or warmer environment? You could also use many different fluids.

## Design Your Own Experiment

**How to Select a Topic Relating to this Concept** The experiments presented here touch upon only a few aspects of the properties of fluids. With so many fluids, there are many categories and characteristics fluids demonstrate. Consider fluids you use and come across in daily life. Are there questions you have about why they behave in certain ways?

Check the Further Readings section and talk with your science teacher for experiment idea that interest you related to fluids. You might also want to read about and investigate polymers.

**Steps in the Scientific Method** To do an original experiment, you need to plan carefully and think things through. Otherwise, you might not be

## Troubleshooter's Guide

When doing experiments, you may not get the results you intended but your findings can still be a learning experience. Here are some problems that may arise during this experiment, some possible causes, and ways to remedy the problem.

**Problem:** None of the solutions climbed up the rod.

**Possible cause:** Your drill may not have had enough power. If your drill has settings, turn the drill to the most powerful setting and allow the rod to spin for longer. Repeat the experiment.

**Problem:** The glue solution became too putty-like for it to move.

You may have used too much borax. If you are using plastic spoons, make sure you are not heaping borax into the teaspoon. You can also try adding a couple teaspoons more water and repeat the experiment.

**Problem:** The rod keeps moving around.

**Possible cause:** The rod may not be centered in the drill. Have an adult help loosen and center the rod, then retighten. Repeat the experiment.

sure what question you are answering, what you are or should be measuring, or what your findings prove or disprove.

Here are the steps in designing an experiment:

- State the purpose of—and the underlying question behind—the experiment you propose to do.
- Recognize the variables involved, and select one that will help you answer the question at hand.
- State a testable hypothesis, an educated guess about the answer to your question.
- Decide how to change the variable you selected.
- Decide how to measure your results.

Recording Data and Summarizing the Results In the experiments included here and in any experiments you develop, you can look for ways to display your data in more accurate and interesting ways.

Remember that those who view your results may not have seen the experiment performed, so you must present the information you have gathered in as clear a way as possible. Including photographs or illustrations of the steps in the experiment is a good way to show a viewer how you got from your hypothesis to your conclusion.

Related Projects To develop other experiments related to fluids, think about liquids you have used or are familiar with. Why does paint stick to the brush? Investigate the surface tension of water compared to other fluids. Investigate the fluid properties of oobleck, a cornstarch and water mixture. You can also investigate how knowing the properties of fluids can help in food science, crime solving, or materials science.

## For More Information

Polymer Science Learning Center, University of Southern Mississippi. *The MacroGalleria.* http://pslc.ws/macrogcss/maindir.html (accessed on

February 26, 2008). Detailed site on all aspects of polymers, from studying them to everyday applications.

Ray, C. Claibourne. *The New York Times Book of Science Questions and Answers.* New York: Doubleday, 1997. Addresses both everyday observations and advanced scientific concepts on a wide variety of subjects.

"The States of Matter." *Faces in the Molecular Sciences: Faces in Polymers.* http://www.chemheritage.org/educationalservices/faces/poly/tutorial/states.htm (accessed on April 22, 2008). Information on the states of matter.

Van Cleave, Janice. *Chemistry For Every Kid.* New York: John Wiley and Sons, Inc., 1989. Contains a number of simple and informative demonstrations and investigations, including the properties of water.

# 35

# Food Preservation

Food preservation is easy to take for granted. It's become common to open a can of fruit in the winter or keep a bag of frozen vegetables for weeks. We store produce and meats in the refrigerator where we might not grab it for days. If the foods are dried, they can sit on a shelf for months before making their way into a meal. Food preservation certainly makes life more convenient but because we need food to live, it also improves people's lives.

*The back story* Food preservation is the process of treating foods in order to stop or slow spoilage. The moment after a plant is harvested or an animal is slaughtered, the spoilage process begins. Spoiled food can cause vomiting, nausea, or more severe symptoms. Bugs, microorganisms, and the natural environment can all cause food to spoil. In many cases, spoiled food is noticeable by its odor, sight, or texture.

Life before food preservation was challenging. The goal was to eat food before it spoiled. People needed to live near where food was produced or grown so they could eat it soon after it was collected. During seasons when food was scarce, people were hungry. In seasons when there was plenty of food, with no way to preserve it the extra food would spoil.

When cultures discovered preservation methods, they could stay in one place instead of constantly traveling to find fresh food. For people who wanted to travel, they now could bring food with them.

*Oldies but goodies* Ancient cultures used some of the same preservation methods we still use today. Many preservation techniques center around removing water and oxygen. Microorganisms need water and oxygen to live, and many chemical reactions that can cause spoilage use these substances.

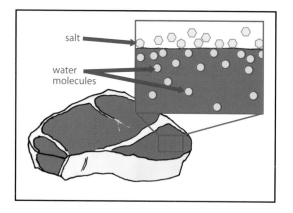

*Salt pulls water out of the food through the process of osmosis.*
ILLUSTRATION BY TEMAH NELSON.

*Pickling is one way used to help preserve food.* © OWEN FRANKEN/CORBIS.

- Salting: Covering a food in salt is one of the oldest forms of food preservation. Salt pulls water out of the food through the process of osmosis. In osmosis, a substance moves across a semipermeable membrane from an area of high concentration to an area of low concentration. A semipermeable membrane lets some substances through but not others. The salt concentration on the outside of the food is higher than the salt concentration inside the cells in the food, and the water moves out of the cells to balance out the concentration. Along with removing water from the food, a high-salt content is not an environment where many microorganisms can grow.

- Sugar: Sugar can also cause osmosis, pulling water out of the food. Sugar that is combined with salt and/or other substances is curing. Meats are commonly preserved by curing.

- Pickling: Combining the preservation properties of salt with those of an acid is pickling. An acid environment, such as vinegar, is not a desirable living environment for microorganisms. Pickled foods are first soaked in a salt solution and then stored in vinegar, often with spices.

- Canning: In the late 1700s, French Emperor Napoleon Bonaparte realized that a lot of the men fighting in his army were starving and sick from poor nutrition. He offered a large amount of money to anyone who could come up with a way of preserving food. Nicholas Appert, a French candy maker, won the prize 14 years later with the first canning method. He placed the food in sealed glass bottles and then heated it. Decades later the French chemist Louis Pasteur (1822–1895), found out why this method worked. (He saw that it was microorganisms causing disease, and that heating the food killed the microorganisms.) Canning kills the microorganisms and then seals up the food from air and microorganisms. Once the can is opened, the food is at risk of becoming spoiled. Fruits, soups, and vegetables are foods commonly canned.

• Drying: Also called dehydration, drying is one of the oldest preservation methods that is still widely used today. In drying, heated air evaporates the water in the food. Without water, the microorganisms cannot grow and spoilage chemical reactions cannot take place. Ancient cultures dried food in the sun. The French developed the first artificial dehydrator where it was used in 1795 to dry vegetables. Eggs, milk, pasta, fruits, and vegetables are a few of the foods typically dried.

• Freeze drying: A form of drying, freeze drying was first used to preserve blood back in the 1890s. Food that is freeze dried removes water from the food while the food is frozen. The frozen food is placed in a strong vacuum chamber and is heated. Water in the food evaporates, moving from ice straight to gas without ever turning into a liquid. Freeze dried food is light and lasts a relatively long time. Coffee is a food that is typically freeze-dried, along with apples and other fruit. Food for astronauts is freeze-dried. When water is added back to the food, the natural flavor of the food returns.

*Basic preservations* There are several other basic methods of food preservation. Keeping food cold in the refrigerator or freezer slows the growth of microorganisms. When food is vacuum-sealed, the oxygen is removed and microorganisms cannot survive. Chemical additives are also used to preserve food. Some chemicals are natural, such as vitamin C, and others are synthesized (manmade).

All food preservation techniques can affect the flavor. The type of preservation used depends upon the food and its intended storage time. In the following two experiments, you can experiment with different methods of food preservation. As you conduct these experiments, consider questions you want to find out about food preservation.

*Keeping food cold in the refrigerator slows the growth of microorganisms* AP PHOTO/ JIM MCNIGHT.

## WORDS TO KNOW

**Canning:** A method of preserving food using air-tight, vacuum-sealed containers and heat processing.

**Concentration:** The amount of a substance present in a given volume, such as the number of molecules in a liter.

**Control experiment:** A set-up that is identical to the experiment but is not affected by the variable that will be changed during the experiment.

**Dehydration:** The removal of water from a material.

**Hypothesis:** An idea in the form of a statement that can be tested by observation and/or experiment.

**Osmosis:** The movement of fluids and substances dissolved in liquids across a semipermeable membrane from an area of its greater concentration to an area of its lesser concentration until all substances involved reach a balance.

**Semipermeable membrane:** A thin barrier between two solutions that permits only certain components of the solutions, usually the solvent, to pass through.

**Synthesize:** Something that is made artificially, in a laboratory or chemical plant, but is generally not found in nature.

**Variable:** Something that can affect the results of an experiment.

## EXPERIMENT 1

## Sweet Preservatives: How does sugar affect the preservation of fruit?

Purpose/Hypothesis The purpose of this experiment is to measure how sugar is used in keeping fruit from spoiling. The fruit you will use is strawberries. When strawberries spoil they can become soft and form black or white rot on them, caused by fungus. The experiment will have four strawberry setups. You will use table sugar and water to make two different concentrations of syrup. You can then compare the preservation of strawberries soaked in syrups against a strawberry coated in sugar, and a plain strawberry. The strawberry with nothing added to it will be the control.

Before you begin, make an educated guess about the outcome of this experiment based on your knowledge of food preservation and fruit. This educated guess, or prediction, is your hypothesis. A hypothesis should explain these things:

- the topic of the experiment
- the variable you will change

- the variable you will measure
- what you expect to happen

A hypothesis should be brief, specific, and measurable. It must be something you can test through observation. Your experiment will prove or disprove whether your hypothesis is correct. Here is one possible hypothesis for this experiment: "The strawberry with the heaviest syrup—the most sugar—will be preserved the longest."

In this case, the variable you will change is the sugar environment surrounding the strawberry. If the strawberry in the heaviest syrup remains unblemished longer than the other test strawberries, you will know your hypothesis is correct.

**Level of Difficulty** Moderate.

**Materials Needed**

- sugar
- pot
- measuring cups and tablespoons
- stirring spoon
- 2 bowls
- toothpicks
- paper and markers, for labeling
- 4 narrow glasses or small, shallow dishes
- 4 strawberries, all the same type and purchased at the same time

**Approximate Budget** $5.

**Timetable** 1 hour working time; 10 minutes daily over four to seven days.

**Step-by-Step Instructions**

1. Label each of the glasses: 1) heavy syrup; 2) light syrup; 3) sugar; 4) control.
2. To prepare the heavy syrup: In a pot, add 1 cup water and 10 tablespoons sugar (½-cup plus 2 tablespoons).

## What Are the Variables?

Variables are anything that might affect the results of an experiment. This experiment involves both environmental variables and biological variables. Here are the main variables in this experiment:

- the presence of air
- the type of strawberry
- the ripeness of the strawberry
- the type of sugar
- the temperature of the environment

In other words, the variables in this experiment are everything that might affect the spoilage of the strawberry. If you change more than one variable, you will not be able to tell which variable had the most effect on the preservation.

*Step 2: Add 1 cup water and 10 tablespoons sugar (½-cup plus 2 tablespoons).*
ILLUSTRATION BY TEMAH NELSON.

## How to Experiment Safely

Ask an adult to help you when working over the hot stove. This experiment will need an environment outside of the refrigerator where food will remain undisturbed for up to a week. Ask an adult for the best place to setup the experiment. After the experiment is complete, throw away all the foods and clean the dishes well.

When experimenting with food preservation, do not taste or ingest any of the food items, and make sure to mark the item clearly to keep others away.

3. Heat slowly while stirring until the sugar is dissolved and the water comes to a boil. Pour into a bowl and place in the refrigerator. (If a refrigerator is not available, you can set the bowl in a larger bowl with ice.) Rinse the pot.

4. To prepare the light syrup: In a pot, add 1 cup water and 4 tablespoons sugar. Bring to a boil, stirring occasionally until the sugar is dissolved. Pour into another bowl and place in the refrigerator.

5. Wait approximately 30 minutes. The syrups should be cool to the touch.

6. When the syrups are room temperature or slightly below, place one strawberry in each of the four glasses. Try to find strawberries that are approximately the same size, and make sure each strawberry does not have any blemishes.

*After setting up the experiment, inspect all your strawberries without touching them.*
ILLUSTRATION BY TEMAH NELSON.

7. Coat the strawberry in the "sugar" glass with sugar and set back in the glass.

8. Pour the heavy syrup over the strawberry in the designated glass and the light syrup in the "light syrup" glass. The syrup should just cover the top of the strawberry.

9. Set the glasses aside in a place where they will be undisturbed (and no one will eat them!).

10. The next day, inspect all your strawberries without touching them. Make a chart and note if there are marks, colors, or any signs of spoilage on each strawberry. Use a toothpick to poke each strawberry and test if it is soft or hard, compared to the control. You may want to sketch a picture of each strawberry.

11. Repeat Step 10 every day, for up to a week or until some of the strawberries are noticeably spoiled.

## Troubleshooter's Guide

Here is a problem that may arise during this project, a possible cause, and a way to remedy the problem.

**Problem:** One of the strawberries that was preserved spoiled faster than the control.

**Possible cause:** You may have selected a strawberry that was already bruised and in the process of spoiling. Repeat the experiment, making sure that all the strawberries are fresh and firm. If you see any blemishes or black indentations in the berry, choose another strawberry.

**Summary of Results** Analyze your results and if you have pictures or sketches compare them to one another. Look at what day each of the strawberries began to show signs of spoilage. How does the strawberry covered with water compared to those in sugar-water? What does the strawberry coated in sugar illustrate about osmosis? Consider how you would want to preserve strawberries, based on your results. Write up a summary of your experiment.

**Change the Variables** To further explore how sugar affects fruit preservation, you can vary the experiment in the following ways:

- Use different types of strawberries, organic versus non-organic, for example, and keep the sugar syrup the same.

- Try experimenting with different types of sugar, such as brown sugar or natural cane sugar.

- Alter the environment of the strawberries, using a warmer or cooler environment

## What Are the Variables?

Variables are anything that might affect the results of an experiment. Here are the main variables in this experiment:

- the time of day
- the condition of the fruit
- the environment the fruits are kept in
- the length of time the fruits sit out
- the size of the fruit
- the type of fruit

In this case, the variable you will change is the moisture content of the fruit. The variable you will measure is mold, blemishes, or an other appearance of spoilage. At the end of the experiment you will compare the dry fruit and moist fruit.

*Step 4: Weigh the peach slices on the gram scale.*
ILLUSTRATION BY TEMAH NELSON.

# EXPERIMENT 2

## Drying Foods: Does drying fruits help prevent or delay spoilage?

Drying foods in the sun is one of the oldest preservation techniques people have used. Bacteria and other organisms need water to live, and drying removes the moisture from the food. In this experiment you will dry fruits in the sun and calculate how much moisture the fruit contained. You can then compare spoilage of the dried fruits to the non-dried fruit.

Before you begin, make an educated guess about the outcome of this experiment based on your knowledge of food preservation and drying. This educated guess, or prediction, is your hypothesis. A hypothesis should explain these things:

- the topic of the experiment
- the variable you will change
- the variable you will measure
- what you expect to happen

A hypothesis should be brief, specific, and measurable. It must be something you can test through further investigation. Your experiment will prove or disprove whether your hypothesis is correct. Here is one possible hypothesis for this experiment: "The dried fruits will delay the appearance of spoilage when compared to the same fruit that is not dried."

**Level of Difficulty** Moderate.

**Materials Needed**

- 2 peaches of about the same size and ripeness
- gram scale
- wax paper

- netting, about 14 inches (36 centimeters) square (available from fabric stores)
- 4 strips of wood or other material, each about 12 inches (30 centimeters) long and an inch (2.5 centimeters) thick, that you can apply tape to
- Duct or masking tape
- knife
- helper
- props, such as chairs or books to lift the drying rack off the ground
- warm, sunny day

**How to Experiment Safely**

Be careful when handling the knife. Never eat the foods when experiment with food preservation and spoilage. When you have finished the experiment, throw all the foods away and wash your hands. When experimenting with food preservation, do not taste or eat any of the food items, and make sure to mark the item clearly to keep others away. Make sure you tell an adult you are conducting this experiment.

**Approximate Budget** $10 (assuming you can find or borrow a gram scale).

**Timetable** Approximately one week. (About one hour working time in total; with one day needing to check on the experiment every two hours over a minimum of eight-hours waiting time.) You will need to start this experiment in the early morning.

**Step-by-Step Instructions**

1. In the early morning just as the sun is coming out, begin to make a drying rack. Lay out four pieces of wood blocks or other material into a rectangle. Lay the netting half-way over the pieces. Tape the netting to each of the blocks. The netting should be taut (tight); you will probably need a helper to pull the wood while you tape the netting.
2. Cut one peach into thin slices. Cut as much of the peach as you can and place the slices on a piece of wax paper.
3. Leave the second peach on the counter, at room temperature.
4. Weigh the peach slices on the gram scale and note the weight.
5. Transfer all the peach slices onto the netting.
6. Bring the drying rack to a clear spot in the sun. Use two chairs, books, pots, or other props to set down the drying rack and keep it away from bugs. If you are in an

*Step 6: Bring the drying rack to a clear spot in the sun.*
ILLUSTRATION BY TEMAH NELSON.

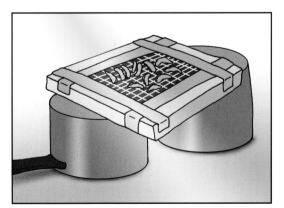

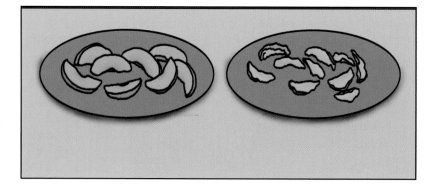

area where there are a lot of flying bugs, set a piece of netting over the fruit. Set it on the books or other material so that it does not touch the peaches.

7. Check in on the peaches about every two hours. Turn the peaches over and make sure the drying rack remains in the sun. You may need to move it throughout the day.

8. At the end of the day, bring the dried peaches inside and weigh them. Note the weight.

9. Cut up the second peach and place the slices on the piece of wax paper.

10. Weigh the peach slices. It should be similar to the weight of the first peach before it was dried. If it is not, take away or cut up more peach until the weights are similar.

11. Place both peaches on a clean sheet of wax paper and set aside. They should be at room temperature.

12. Check on both peaches every day for the next six days. Note any appearances of spoilage every day.

**Summary of Results** Compare the spoilage appearance and rates of the two peaches. Subtract the starting and ending weight of the peach slices to determine how much water the dry peach lost. Was your hypothesis correct? Did the dried fruit show fewer signs of spoilage than the fruit that contained more water. Today, people dry food in a food dehydrator or an oven. Consider how the taste of the food would change with different food drying techniques. Write up a summary of your findings. You may want to include pictures.

**Modify the Experiment** You can modify this experiment in several ways:

- Change the type of fruit, you can apples or bunches of smaller fruits, such as strawberries or grapes.

- Change the amount of time you allow the fruit to dry: what happens if the fruit dries for only four hours compared to eight hours.
- Change the environmental conditions the fruit is left out in.

## Design Your Own Experiment

How to Select a Topic Relating to this Concept Because food spoilage is a serious and common problem, people have developed many methods of preserving foods. You can start thinking of ideas by identifying some common preservatives and techniques used in the foods you eat. Look at food labels to identify the preservative. You can separate the natural and synthetic preservatives. Consider how leftovers are preserved in your home.

Check the Further Readings section and talk with your science teacher to learn more about food preservation. You could also talk with a microbiologist for details on the microorganisms involved in spoilage.

When experimenting with food, do not taste or eat any of the food items, and make sure to mark the item clearly to keep others away. When you conduct an experiment with food in the home, make sure you tell an adult.

Steps in the Scientific Method To conduct an original experiment, you need to plan carefully and think things through. Otherwise, you might not be sure what question you are answering, what you are or should be measuring, or what your findings prove or disprove.

Here are the steps in designing an experiment:

- State the purpose of—and the underlying question behind—the experiment you propose to do.
- Recognize the variables involved and select one that will help you answer the question at hand.
- State your hypothesis, an educated guess about the answer to your question.

## Troubleshooter's Guide

Below is a problem that may happen during this experiment, a possible cause, and a way to remedy the problem.

**Problem:** The peach did not really lose that much water in the sun.

**Possible cause:** The sun may not be strong enough, or it may not have been in the sun the entire day. Try to plan this experiment for a day that will be warm and sunny for the whole day. Also, make sure to move the drying rack so it is facing the sun throughout the day. When you think you will have a sunny day, repeat the experiment.

**Problem:** Neither peach showed more appearance of spoilage.

**Possible cause:** Depending upon the peaches and environment, you may need to leave the peaches out for a longer period of time. Look for any brown spots, and continue monitoring the peaches.

- Decide how to change the variable you selected.
- Decide how to measure your results.

**Recording Data and Summarizing the Results** Your data should include charts and graphs such as the one you did for these experiments. They should be clearly labeled and easy to read. You may also want to include photographs and drawings of your experimental setup and results, which will help other people visualize the steps in the experiment.

If you are preparing an exhibit, you may want to display your results, such as any experimental setup you designed. If you have completed a nonexperimental project, explain clearly what your research question was and illustrate your findings.

**Related Projects** There are projects related to food preservation that are inexpensive and waiting in the kitchen. You could conduct a project examining the uses of synthesized versus natural preservatives. You could explore how preservative delay spoilage for different types of foods. You could examine packaging that preserves food. How are the properties of different packaging materials designed to preserve specific foods. You could also use expiration dates to compare different food preservatives.

## For More Information

Dalton, Louisa. "What's that Stuff?: Food Preservatives." *Chemical & Engineering News,* November 11, 2002. http://pubs.acs.org/cen/science/8045/8045sci2.html (accessed on May 16, 2008). Information on various food preservatives.

D'Amico, Joan and Karen Eich Drummond. *The Science Chef Travels Around the World: Fun Food Experiments and Recipes for Kids.* New York: John Wiley, 1996. Food experiments and recipes from around the world.

*Eating for Health.* Vol. 3. Chicago: World Book Inc., 1993. Part of the "Growing Up" series, this volume provides thorough, interesting information about carbohydrates, vitamins, and minerals as well as metabolism, eating disorders, and processing.

"Food: Nutrition, Safety and Cooking." *University of Nebraska Lincoln.* http://lancaster.unl.edu/food/myths-ss/index.htm (accessed on May 18, 2008). Quiz and common myths on food safety.

"From Farm to Table." *www.foodsafety.gov.* http://www.foodsafety.gov/~fsg/fsgkids.html (accessed on May 18, 2008). Links to government sites on food safety and spoilage.

"Kids World: Food safety." *N.C. Department of Agriculture and Consumer Services.* http://www.ncagr.com/cyber/kidswrld/foodsafe/index.htm (accessed on May 18, 2008). Food safety facts and interactive question on spoilage.

# 36

# Food Science

Have you ever wondered why bread rises? Or why some chocolates melt in your hand and others remain hard? Why does cooking change the color of some vegetables and cause meat to become more tender? The area of food science covers all of these questions and many more.

Food science is a broad topic that applies scientific principles to foods in order to better understand them. We use the applications of food science every day in how we prepare and preserve foods. Food science helps us understand the nutrients in foods and how heat, cold, light, and air can affect them. It explores what foods are made of and looks at chemical reactions that occur when foods are combined. Food scientists also work to develop or improve a food's flavor, texture, and nutrition. Chemistry, microbiology, and botany are some of the key areas food science covers.

*Cooking and flavors* Meat is one of the more apparent examples of a reaction that produces a lot of flavor: the Maillard reaction. The Maillard reaction is named after French chemist Louis Camille Maillard who began studying the reaction in 1912. Meats contain a lot of protein molecules, which are held together by bonds. Heat breaks the bonds and the protein unravels. This is called a denatured protein. The reaction between denatured proteins combines with natural sugars (a form of carbohydrates) in the meat. The reaction leads to changes in color and hundreds of flavors.

The Maillard reaction is often referred to as the browning reaction, because meat does turn brown. The Maillard reaction also produces the toasty flavor on bread crust and the sweetness of browned onions. Researchers use the Maillard reaction to create many artificial flavors.

If you have ever heated sugar and watched it brown you have witnessed another chemical process called caramelization. In caramelization, which is not related to the caramel candy, sugars move through a series of reactions at high temperature. Heating causes the sugar molecules to lose water and break down. The sugars turn brown and form new flavors.

The Maillard reaction and caramelization reactions are so complex that researchers are still trying to understand exactly how they work.

*The rising of chemical leaveners* Place a cake or bread dough in the oven and when it's cooked, it is a lot higher. A leavening agent is any substance that causes dough or batter to rise, or increase in volume. In general the leavening agent makes food rise by producing air or gas that pushes the food ingredients apart, causing it to expand and increase in volume. In cooking, leavening agents work by chemical reactions and physical changes.

Baking powder and baking soda are called chemical leavening agents because they work by chemical reactions. Baking soda is sodium bicarbonate. When moisture and an acid are added to sodium bicarbonate, it causes a reaction that releases the gas carbon dioxide. The bubbles of carbon dioxide push the food apart, causing its volume to increase. Like air, carbon dioxide also expands when heated. The reaction of baking soda starts to work immediately so cooks need to bake the food immediately.

Baking powder is a mixture of sodium bicarbonate and an acid ingredient, such as tartaric acid (cream of tartar), along with other dry ingredients. Baking powder does not need an acid added because it is already in there.

There are two types of baking powder. Single-acting baking powders start to react immediately with moisture, whether it is warm or cool. Double-acting baking powder reacts "double" because it releases gas in two reactions. Some gas is released immediately when moisture is added. Even more gas is released with heat. That means double-acting baking powder can still cause the recipe to rise even if it sits at room temperature for a period of time.

*The physical agents that lead to rising* When making bread, the typical leavening agent is yeast. Yeast is a natural leavening agent that people have used for thousands of years. It is a live single-celled fungus. Yeast eat sugar in the form of starch, such as in flour, and release carbon dioxide gas and alcohol. Along with making dough rise, people use yeast to produce the alcohol in beer and wine.

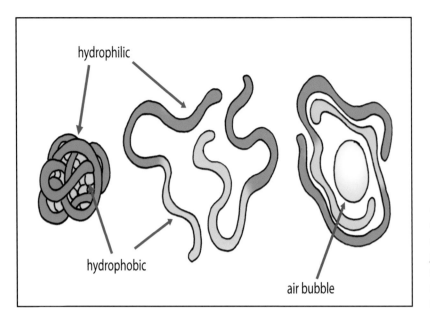

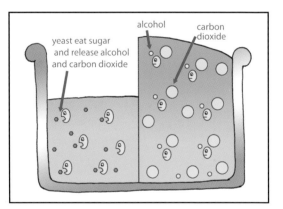

*Parts of the protein are attracted to water (hydrophilic or water-loving) and other parts avoid the water (hydrophobic or water-fearing).* ILLUSTRATION BY TEMAH NELSON.

Another method of leavening is whipped egg whites. Egg whites are about 90% water and 10% protein. Parts of the protein are attracted to water (hydrophilic or water-loving) and other parts avoid the water (hydrophobic or water-fearing). In its natural state, the hydrophobic parts of the proteins are curled up in the center and the hydrophilic parts are surrounded by water.

Beating raw egg whites causes air bubbles to form and the protein molecules to uncurl. The uncurled protein molecules twist about so that the parts that don't like water touch air. The result is a network of protein molecules that trap the air bubbles in place, causing the egg whites to froth and increase in volume and froth. Baking the frothy egg whites makes the bubbles become firm.

*Heating and change* The best method of heating foods is another area of food science. Heating not only can kill harmful microorganisms, but it also affects the flavor, texture, and color of many foods.

Plants contain chlorophyll, the substance that gives plants its green color. The greener the vegetable, the more chlorophyll it contains.

*Yeast eat sugar in the form of starch, such as in flour, and release carbon dioxide gas and alcohol.* ILLUSTRATION BY TEMAH NELSON.

## WORDS TO KNOW

**Blanching:** A cooking technique in which the food, usually vegetables and fruits, are briefly cooked in boiling water and then plunged into cold water.

**Caramelization:** The process of heating sugars to the point at which they break down and lead to the formation of new compounds.

**Cell wall:** A tough outer covering over the cell membrane of bacteria and plant cells.

**Chlorophyll:** A green pigment found in plants that absorbs sunlight, providing the energy used in photosynthesis.

**Control experiment:** A setup that is identical to the experiment, but is not affected by the variable that acts on the experimental group.

**Fermentation:** A chemical reaction in which enzymes break down complex organic compounds (for example, carbohydrates and sugars) into simpler ones (for example, ethyl alcohol).

**Fungi:** Kingdom of various single-celled or multi-cellular organisms, including mushrooms, molds, yeasts, and mildews, that do not manufacture their own food.

**Hydrophilic:** Having an attraction for water.

**Hydrophobic:** Having an aversion to water.

**Hypothesis:** An idea in the form of a statement that can be tested by observation and/or experiment.

**Leavening agent:** A substance used to make foods like dough and batter to rise.

**Maillard reaction:** A reaction caused by heat and sugars and resulting in foods browning and flavors.

**Pectin:** A natural carbohydrate found in fruits and vegetables.

**Yeast:** A single-celled fungi that can be used as a leavening agent.

**Variable:** Something that can affect the results of an experiment.

Chlorophyll lies in the plants' cell and heat causes the cell walls to break down. This leads to changes in the chlorophyll, which leads to the vegetable turning browner.

One method used to retain the color and texture of vegetables is blanching. In blanching, the food is briefly placed into boiling water and then plunged into cold water. The heat causes the air in the vegetables to expand and boil away, which leads to a more vibrant color. Carrots become more orange and green beans a richer green. The cold water immediately stops the cooking process.

In the following two experiments, you will explore two aspects of food science. You will investigate how jelly becomes firm and how different leavening agents make foods rise.

# EXPERIMENT 1

## Jelly and Pectin: How does acidity affect how fruit gels?

Purpose/Hypothesis Pectin is what helps make the gel in fruit gels, such as jellies and marmalades. Pectin is a type of carbohydrate found in plant cell walls. It is found in apples and citrus fruits, such as limes and lemons, and is most plentiful in the skin and core. Pectin forms naturally as the fruit ripen.

When fruit is cooked, the heat causes the cell walls to break down and release the pectin. If the fruit is cooked in water the pectin moves into the water. The pectin molecules all have the same charge and so they repel one another. In order to make the pectin molecules bond, you need sugar and the right acidity. Sugar pulls the water molecules together and leaves the pectin on its own. Adding an acidic substance gets rid of the pectin's negative charges. The pectin can then bond to one another and form a gel.

### What Are the Variables?

Variables are anything that might affect the results of an experiment. Here are the main variables in this experiment:

- the temperature of the mixture
- the amount of time the fruit is cooked
- the type of fruit
- the amount of lemon juice
- the amount of time the gel is allowed to cool
- the amount of fruit
- the amount of sugar

In other words, the variables in this experiment are everything that might affect the formation of an apple jelly. If you change more than one variable, you will not be able to tell which variable had the most effect on the gelling of the apples.

In this experiment you will make apple jam and test how the pH of the mixture affects the gelling of the jam. The pH is a measure of the acidity of a substance. A pH of 7 means the substance is neutral. Water is a neutral substance. The lower the pH, the higher its acidity. For the apple jam, the apples will supply the pectin and lemon juice will provide the acid. Lemons contain citric acid, which gives lemon a pH of approximately 2 to 3. You will make three jams: in one jam you will add lemon juice; the second jam you will add half the amount of lemon juice; and the third jam will not include any lemon juice.

Before you begin, make an educated guess about the outcome of this experiment based on your knowledge of food science and gels. This educated guess, or prediction, is your hypothesis. A hypothesis should explain these things:

- the topic of the experiment
- the variable you will change

## How to Experiment Safely

Be careful when handling the knife and working on the stove. Ask an adult for help when pouring the hot apple liquid into the strainer.

- the variable you will measure
- what you expect to happen

A hypothesis should be brief, specific, and measurable. It must be something you can test through observation. Your experiment will prove or disprove your hypothesis. Here is one possible hypothesis for this experiment: "The apple jam with the most lemon juice will form the firmest gel."

In this case, the variable you will change will be the amount of lemon juice. The variable you will measure will be the firmness of the gel.

**Level of Difficulty** Moderate.

**Materials Needed**

- 3 tart apples, about the same size (Macintosh or Jonathan work well)
- pot
- measuring cup
- strainer or colander
- bowl that fits under strainer or colander
- lemon juice
- teaspoons
- toothpicks
- plastic wrap
- stirring spoon
- cutting knife
- spatula or stirring spoon
- 3 small thick glass jelly jars, the same size (you could also use small bowls)

**Approximate Budget** $5.

**Timetable** Approximately two hours (one hour working time and one hour waiting).

**Step-by-Step Instructions**

1. Label one glass (or bowl) "1 tsp. lemon;" the second glass "½ tsp;" and the third glass "0."

*Step 1: Gather the sugar, lemon juice, and apples.*
ILLUSTRATION BY TEMAH NELSON.

2. Cut the three apples into quarters and cut those quarters again. You should include the skins and cores.

3. Pour ³/₄-cup water into a pot. Add the apple chunks and heat until the apple mixture is mushy. This should take about 20 minutes.

4. When the apples are soft, place the bowl under the colander and pour the apple-water mixture into the colander. The colander should strain out the seeds and skin. You will need to press the apple mixture through the colander with a spoon or spatula.

5. Allow the mixture to cool for about 15 minutes and then divide the apple mixture evenly into thirds.

6. Place one-third of the mixture back in the pot.

7. Add 3 and ½-tablespoons of sugar.

8. Add 1 teaspoon of lemon juice.

9. Boil for approximately five to six minutes, stirring occasionally, until large bubbles appear. The droplets should be large and come together to form a "sheet." (See illustration)

10. Pour the mixture into the 1 tsp jelly glass until the glass is about ³/₄ full. Rinse out the pot

11. Repeat Steps 6 through 9 for each of the two remaining test jellies. Replace the 1 teaspoon of lemon juice with ½-teaspoon for the second jelly and no lemon juice for the third jelly.

12. Allow all the jellies to cool for at least an hour, until they have reached room temperature.

13. If a "skin" has formed on any of the jellies, carefully remove it.

14. Poke each jelly with a toothpick and note the results.

15. Cover the glass jars with plastic wrap and flip each jar upside. Note your observations.

**Summary of Results** Look over your observations of each of the jellies. Was your hypothesis correct? Note any other differences between the

*Step 4: You will need to press the apple mixture through the colander with a spoon or spatula.* ILLUSTRATION BY TEMAH NELSON.

*Step 9: The droplets should be large and come together to form a "sheet."* ILLUSTRATION BY TEMAH NELSON.

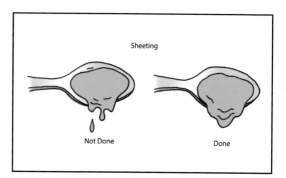

## Troubleshooter's Guide

Here is a problem that may arise during this experiment, possible causes, and a way to remedy the problem.

**Problem:** None of the jellies formed a gel.

**Possible cause:** The fruit may have been too overripe, in which case the fruit does not contain enough pectin. Try the experiment again, using apples that are just slightly under-ripe.

**Possible cause:** You may not have heated the apple mixture for enough time. When a cold metal spoon is placed in the mixture, the droplets should come together before falling off the spoon. Repeat the experiment, heating the mixture for 1 or 2 minutes longer.

jellies, such as the color or texture. Write a paragraph summarizing your results.

**Change the Variables** You can conduct several similar experiments by changing the variables. You can change the type of acid. You can also try peeling and coring the apple, to determine what parts of the apple contains the most pectin. You could also try altering the environment the jelly sets in.

## EXPERIMENT 2

### Rising Foods: How much carbon dioxide do different leavening agents produce?

**Purpose/Hypothesis** Chemical leavening agents need an acid and moisture to produce carbon dioxide. Double-acting baking powder releases carbon dioxide in two chemical reactions: with the addition of an acid and heat.

In this experiment you will measure the amount of carbon dioxide produced by baking soda, baking powder, and double acting baking powder. After adding water, you will trap the carbon dioxide in a balloon. By measuring the balloon's circumference (the distance around the balloon), you can determine the rate at which carbon dioxide is produced. For each of the leavening agents you will measure the amount of gas in the balloon with the leavening agent at room temperature and heated. Which leavening agent do you think will produce the greatest amount of carbon dioxide with heat?

Before you begin, make an educated guess about the outcome of this experiment based on your knowledge of food science and leavening. This educated guess, or prediction, is your hypothesis. A hypothesis should explain these things:

- the topic of the experiment
- the variable you will change
- the variable you will measure
- what you expect to happen

A hypothesis should be brief, specific, and measurable. It must be something you can test through further investigation. Your experiment will prove or disprove whether your hypothesis is correct. Here is one possible hypothesis for this experiment: "The double acting baking powder will produce the greatest amount of carbon dioxide when heat is applied."

In this case, the variable you will change is the leavening agent. The variable you will measure is the circumference of the balloon as it fills with carbon dioxide.

**Level of Difficulty** Moderate.

**Materials Needed**

- 3 balloons, the same size and type
- string
- marker
- ruler or tape measure
- baking powder
- double acting baking powder
- baking soda
- vinegar or lemon juice
- measuring spoons
- bowl
- cup
- 3 small plastic or glass bottles, approximately 3 inches (7.6 centimeters) high and with a top small enough to pull a balloon over (small spray or lotion bottles work well); you can also use one bottle and rinse it out
- timer or clock with minute hand
- funnel
- wax paper (optional)
- small pan
- helper

**Approximate Budget** $10.

**Timetable** 45 minutes.

## What Are the Variables?

Variables are anything that might affect the results of an experiment. Here are the main variables in this experiment:

- the time allowed for the leavening agent to produce gas
- the type of leavening agent
- the temperature of the water added to the leavener
- the volume of the bottle
- the type and shape of the balloon

In other words, the variables in this experiment are everything that might affect the amount of carbon dioxide the leavening agent produces. If you change more than one variable at the same time, you will not be able to tell which variable affected the circumference of the balloon.

## How to Experiment Safely

In this experiment you will be working with boiling water. Be careful when pouring and working around the water.

### Step-by-Step Instructions

1. Fill up the bowl with room temperature water. You will need about a cup.

2. Set several cups of water in the pot or kettle to boil.

3. Stretch out all the balloons several times. Line up the balloons next to one another so that they are even. Mark a line on the balloons at the widest part, so that all the marks are even. This is the point where that should be the widest part; where you will measure the balloons circumference.

4. Place a teaspoon of baking soda in the bottle. Depending upon how large the bottle opening is, you may need to pour the baking soda onto wax paper and then fold the wax paper to direct the soda in.

5. With a helper, place the funnel in the balloon opening and pour in 3 tablespoons of the water from the bowl. If the balloon fills up, stretch it out and keep adding the water. When you are done the top of the balloon should not have water in it.

6. With someone holding the bottle, slip the balloon opening over the bottle top. Empty the water into the bottle and begin timing.

7. After one minute, wrap the string around the balloon at the marked spot (the widest part) and draw a line on the string where it has wrapped.

8. After two minutes wrap the string around the balloon at the same line and mark its circumference. Repeat after three minutes.

9. Pour boiling water into the cup until it is about half way full and set the bottle in the cup. Hold the bottle down so that the hot water surrounds the water inside the bottle.

10. Every minute for the next three minutes, place the string around the balloon and mark its circumference. Remember to

*Step 6: With someone holding the bottle, slip the balloon opening over the bottle top.*
ILLUSTRATION BY TEMAH NELSON.

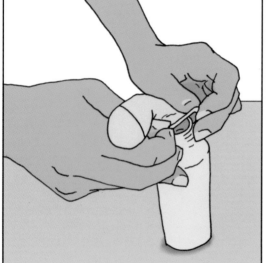

line the string up with the mark on the balloon.

11. Repeat Steps 4–10 for the baking powder and then the double acting baking powder. For each leavening agent, use a new piece of string and line it up with the mark on the balloon. If you use the same bottle, make sure to rinse it well after each use.

12. Measure each of the marks on the three strings and record your data.

Summary of Results Create a data table to record your observations. You may want to graph your results, with the rate of expansion on one axis and the number of minutes on the other axis. Make a separate line or color for each of the leavening agents. Was your hypothesis correct? You may want to look through recipes to see which leavening agents are used for which types of foods. What are the other ingredients in the recipe that would activate the leavening agent?

Change the Variables There are several ways that you can change this experiment. You can focus on the leavening properties of baking soda and change the type of acid. Buttermilk and orange juice are two other acid solutions. You can also change the proportions of acid you mix with the baking soda. Using the same recipe, you can test how different leavening agents cause the food to rise. If you were making cookies, what results would each leavening agent produce?

# Design Your Own Experiment

How to Select a Topic Relating to this Concept Food is such an important part of people's lives that ideas to explore the science behind foods and how they work together are all around. You might want to look at the ingredients in your favorite food items or dishes. Think about what

*Step 9: Hold the bottle down so that the hot water surrounds the water inside the bottle.* ILLUSTRATION BY TEMAH NELSON.

*Step 10: Every minute for the next three minutes, place the string around the balloon and mark its circumference.* ILLUSTRATION BY TEMAH NELSON.

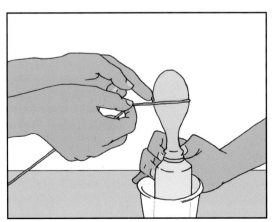

## Troubleshooter's Guide

Below are some problems that may arise during this experiment, some possible causes, and some ways to fix the problem.

**Problem:** The balloon did not expand much for any of the leavening agents.

**Possible cause:** The leavening agent(s) may be too old to produce a reaction. To test whether the baking powder has expired, and a few pinches of baking powder to a couple tablespoons of room temperature water. The mixture should bubble and fizz. Replace the water with vinegar to test the baking soda. If the leavening agents are too old, buy a new baking powder or soda and repeat the experiment.

**Problem:** The balloon kept tearing when placing it over the bottle.

**Possible cause:** The balloon is probably too small and stretching may not help. Try finding a bottle with a smaller cap or a larger balloon. Make sure to stretch the balloon several times, and repeat the experiment.

the properties of all the ingredients add to the food. Consider your favorite meals, snacks, and drinks and you may want to explore how these foods are prepared and why.

Check the Further Readings section and talk with your science teacher to gather information on food science questions that interest you. You may want to talk with someone you know who enjoys cooking. As you consider possible experiments, be sure to discuss them with a knowledgeable adult before trying them.

**Steps in the Scientific Method** To do an original experiment, you need to plan carefully and think things through. Otherwise, you might not be sure what question you are answering, what your are or should be measuring, or what your findings prove or disprove.

Here are the steps in designing an experiment:

- State the purpose of—and the underlying question behind—the experiment you propose to do.
- Recognize the variables involved, and select one that will help you answer the question at hand.
- State a testable hypothesis, an educated guess about the answer to your question.
- Decide how to change the variable you selected.
- Decide how to measure your results.

**Recording Data and Summarizing the Results** It's always important to write down data and ideas you gather during an experiment. Keep a journal or record book for this purpose. If you keep notes and draw conclusions from your experiments and projects, other scientists could use your findings in their own research.

**Related Projects** Food science experiments can go in many different directions. For example, you might focus on the properties of one food type, such as milk or chocolate. How does this one food react to heat, cold, or with other commonly added substances? Does the order of ingredients make a difference in the finished texture or flavor? What chemical properties of the food cause it to react this way? You might also look at blending certain foods together. For example, why does salt alter the taste of certain dishes?

Another possibility is to experiment with how cooking methods affect foods. Blanching, boiling, and baking all can affect the same food in different ways. You can look at techniques chefs use to preserve certain flavors while they are cooking foods.

## For More Information

Arnold Nick. *Freaky Food Experiments.* United Kingdom: Scholastic, 2007. Experiments with and about food.

BBC. "Science of Cooking." *Science and Nature: Hot Topics.* http:// www.bbc.co.uk/science/hottopics/cooking/ (accessed on May 21, 2008). Clear explanations, animations, and video of many cooking food science topics.

*Eating for Health.* Vol. 3. Chicago: World Book Inc., 1993. Part of the "Growing Up" series, this volume provides thorough, interesting information about carbohydrates, vitamins, and minerals as well as metabolism, eating disorders, and processing.

Exploratorium. *Science of Cooking.* http://www.exploratorium.edu/cooking/ (accessed on May 21, 2008). Recipes, illustrations and clear explanations of the science behind many foods, including pickles, candy, bread, and meat.

Kids Health. *Food and Nutrition.* http://www.kidshealth.org/kid/nutrition/ index.html#All_About_Food (accessed on May 22, 2008). Series of easy-to-read articles on food and nutrients.

Planet Science. *The Planet Science Diner.* http://www.planet-science.com/ outthere/index.html?page=/outthere/diner/index.html (accessed on May 22, 2008). Clear information on many aspects of kitchen chemistry.

Wolke, Robert L. *What Einstein Told His Cook: Kitchen Science Explained.* New York: W. W. Norton and Co., 2002. Answers to common questions about cooking and food science in a simple, clear style.

# 37

# Food Spoilage

When food has spoiled it is usually noticeable to your senses of smell and sight. Spoilage is when food has taken on an undesirable color, odor, or texture. Eating spoiled food can result in food poisoning, which can cause vomiting, nausea, and more severe symptoms. There are two main causes of natural food spoilage: microscopic organisms and chemical changes.

*Attack of the microbes* Leave food out on the kitchen countertop and within seconds it can become the home of microorganisms that are floating by in the air. When these microbes land on a suitable environment, they settle down and begin to grow. Many foods present an ideal environment.

The three main types of microbes that cause food spoilage are yeasts, molds, and bacteria. Bacteria are single-celled organisms that grow under a wide range of conditions. Yeasts and molds are both types of fungi, a large grouping of organisms that have both plant and animal characteristics. These microorganisms cause beverages to sour, fuzz to grow, slime to form, and the color and smell of foods to change.

Microorganisms are everywhere: in the air, water, soil, homes, and people. The majority of microorganisms are harmless or helpful to humans and all life on Earth. When they start living on food items though, they can quickly cause the food to spoil. The amount and rate of food spoilage increases as the number of microorganisms rise. And microorganisms grow, meaning they reproduce, at a speedy rate. Bacteria, for example, can reproduce once every twenty minutes under ideal conditions. That means, if there are no limitations, a food product that starts off with one bacterium will multiply to over five billion in about ten hours. If bacteria grew at this rate in real life they would soon overtake the planet. Fortunately, once too many bacteria live in one area, their food runs out and eventually they start dying.

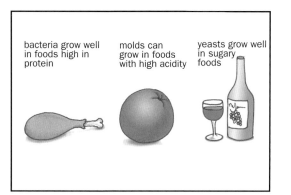

bacteria grow well in foods high in protein

molds can grow in foods with high acidity

yeasts grow well in sugary foods

*Each type of microorganism has its own unique requirements for growth.* GALE GROUP.

*The leftover that became a home* Each type of microorganism has its own unique requirements for growth, but there are general conditions that most food-munching microbes need:

- Food: Each type—and species—of microbe thrives on different nutrients. Many bacteria thrive on proteins, such as meat; the fungi mold commonly grows on sugars and bread; and yeasts like simple sugars.

- Moisture or water: Yeasts, molds, and bacteria all need water; some need more than others. Molds, for example, grow at lower levels of water than most bacteria.

- Suitable temperature: Many microbes grow well at warm temperatures roughly equal to the inside of the human body.

- Exposure to air: Yeasts and molds need air to grow. Most bacteria that cause food spoilage also need air to grow. One exception is the *Clostridium* bacterium, which is a common cause of canned food spoilage because it does not need air to live.

- Suitable acidity level: Bacteria generally prefer mid- to low-acid foods such as vegetables and meat. Certain yeasts and molds grow in fruits that can tolerate a high-acid environment.

- Time to grow: Even though bacteria can reproduce quickly, they still need time to grow. If food is consumed immediately after it is prepared, the bacteria won't have time to cause spoilage.

*Slowing spoilage* Long before people knew about microorganisms, ancient civilizations developed methods to prevent their food from spoiling. These techniques prevented microorganisms from living on the food in some way—either by making living conditions unpleasant or deadly, or by preventing the microorganisms from ever settling down on the food.

Any substance added to food to give it a desired quality is called an additive. Preservatives are a type of additive that causes food to last longer without spoiling. There are both synthetic and natural preservatives. Natural preservatives were one of the earliest methods used to prevent spoilage. Spices are natural preservatives people have long valued. When Italian explorer Christopher Columbus (1451–1506) set sail for the New World, one of the items he was searching for was spices. Other natural preservatives include vinegar, salt, and Vitamin C. Some foods contain a high concentration of these items, giving them a natural resistance to microbial growth.

Antioxidants are substances that prevent spoilage by reducing the food's exposure to air. Vitamin C and Vitamin E are natural antioxidants.

Dehydration involves removing the water from food. When food is dehydrated, microorganisms no longer have the moisture they need to live. Ancient peoples dried strips of meat and other foods out in the sun. Dried snacks, such as fruits and raisins, are common dehydrated foods.

Salting is another ancient method of preventing spoilage that combines the techniques of adding preservatives and dehydrating. Salt lowers the amount of water in the food and also removes water from the microbial cells, making it a harsh environment for organisms to live. Using salt to preserve food remains widespread in modern day. Pickles, meat, and fish are commonly salted. While salting can make food last longer, it also increases the sodium in food.

Canning was another major breakthrough in food preservation. In the 1700s French leader Napoleon Bonaparte was searching for a method that would preserve foods for his troops. He offered a large cash prize to anyone who could develop a preservation method. In response a French candy maker came up with the idea of sealing foods in cans. Although the technique has changed over time, the basic process remains the same. The food is placed in a can, heated, and the can is quickly sealed. Modern canning techniques suck the air from the can before it is sealed.

Chilling/heating: Microorganisms do not like it too hot or too cold. Temperatures that are outside the microorganisms' living requirements will cause their growth to slow. Extreme hot and cold temperatures will kill the microbes. Before the refrigerator was invented, people

*Dried snacks, such as fruits and raisins, are common dehydrated foods.* COPYRIGHT © KELLY A. QUIN.

*Jars of home-canned vegetables.* © CRAIG LOVELL/CORBIS.

gentle heating over time kills most organisms

covering keeps new microbes out, refrigerating slows growth

*Pasteurization is a preservation technique that destroys most microbes by heating a liquid, then placing it in an airtight container.* GALE GROUP.

wrapped foods in snow and ice. Refrigerators and freezers will slow or stop the growth, yet the low temperatures will not kill the microorganisms. When the food item is returned to a suitable environment the microorganisms will again start to grow. There are even bacteria that grow well in the cool refrigerator air. Boiling is another method of destroying microorganisms, yet boiling can change the taste and nutritional value of the food. Cooking food thoroughly also destroys microorganisms.

French chemist Louis Pasteur (1822–1895) was the first person to demonstrate that microorganisms in the air produce food decay. In 1865, he developed a gentle heating method to destroy microorganisms in liquids and cause little change in the taste. After heating the liquid to 131°F (55° Celsius), he placed the liquid in an airtight container. This process is known as pasteurization and in modern day, it uses slightly higher temperatures. Pasteurization destroys almost all the microorganisms without altering the composition, flavor, or nutritional value of the liquid. Most milk is treated this way.

*All by themselves* Spoilage also can occur from natural chemical changes within the food without any help from microorganisms. Rancidity occurs when fats in the food break down, producing undesirable flavors and smells. For example, rancidity gives butter a strong, bitter taste. Salt in butter helps prevent the butter from turning rancid. Food can also decay on its own from natural proteins that begin to decompose or break down the food.

## WORDS TO KNOW

**Additive:** A chemical compound that is added to foods to give them some desirable quality, such as preventing them from spoiling.

**Antioxidants:** Used as a food additive, these substances can prevent food spoilage by reducing the food's exposure to air.

**Bacteria:** Single-celled microorganisms that live in soil, water, plants, and animals that play a key role in the decay of organic matter and the cycling of nutrients. Some are agents of disease.

**Canning:** A method of preserving food using airtight, vacuum-sealed containers and heat processing.

**Control experiment:** A setup that is identical to the experiment, but is not affected by the variable that acts on the experimental group.

**Dehydration:** The removal of water from a material.

**Fungi:** The kingdom of various single-celled or multicellular organisms, including mushrooms,

molds, yeasts, and mildews, that do not contain chlorophyll.

**Hypothesis:** An idea in the form of a statement that can be tested by observation and/or experiment.

**Pasteurization:** The process of slow heating that kills bacteria and other microorganisms.

**Preservative:** An additive used to keep food from spoiling.

**Rancidity:** Having the condition when food has a disagreeable odor or taste from decomposing oils or fats.

**Spoilage:** The condition when food has taken on an undesirable color, odor, or texture.

**Spore:** A small, usually one-celled, reproductive body that is capable of growing into a new organism.

**Variable:** Something that can affect the results of an experiment.

## EXPERIMENT 1

## Preservatives: How do different substances affect the growth of mold?

**Purpose/Hypothesis** Mold is a type of fungi that reproduces via spores. Spores are similar to plant seeds except they are microscopic. They move about in the air and when they land on a food source with a comfortable environment, they begin to grow. Once spores begin to grow, the mold releases more spores and the cycle continues. There are thousands of different kinds of molds.

*Bread can get moldy very quickly.* COPYRIGHT © KELLY A. QUIN.

## What Are the Variables?

Variables are anything that might affect the results of an experiment. Here are the main variables in this experiment:

- the type of bread
- the temperature
- the amount of light
- the additive
- the amount of the additive
- the quantity of the preservative in the additive

In other words, the variables in this experiment are everything that might affect the mold's growth. If you change more than one variable at the same time, you will not be able to tell which variable had the most effect on inhibiting mold growth.

In this experiment you will examine how additives can act as preservatives for the bread. You will use different types of possible preservatives: vinegar, salt, vitamin C, and lemon juice. Molds grow well in a moist environment. You will spray the liquid preservatives on the bread to dampen the bread. For the salt, you will dampen the bread with water before you apply the salt.

Before you begin, make an educated guess about the outcome of this experiment based on your knowledge of molds and spoilage. This educated guess, or prediction, is your hypothesis. A hypothesis should explain these things:

- the topic of the experiment
- the variable you will change
- the variable you will measure
- what you expect to happen

A hypothesis should be brief, specific, and measurable. It must be something you can test through further investigation. Your experiment will prove or disprove whether your hypothesis is correct. Here is one possible hypothesis for this experiment: "All the preservatives will inhibit the growth of fungi to some degree; salt will inhibit it the most."

In this case, the variable you will change is the substance sprayed on the bread. The variable you will measure is the amount of mold growth.

Conducting a control experiment will help you isolate each variable and measure the changes in the dependent variable. Only one variable will change between the control and your experiment. For your control in this experiment you will spray plain water on the bread. At the end of the experiment you can compare the control and the experimental results.

**Level of Difficulty** Moderate.

**Materials Needed**

- water
- 5 slices of nonpreservative white bread

*Step 10: Place each damp slice of bread in its labeled bag and seal.* GALE GROUP.

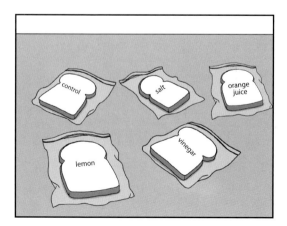

- spray bottle, such as one used to water plants
- 5 plastic bags
- graph paper marked in 0.05-inch or 1.0-millimeter increments
- transparent paper
- preservatives: white vinegar, lemon juice, table salt, nonpulp orange juice high in vitamin C (you can also select other, or additional, items to test)
- marking pen
- microscope or magnifying glass (optional)

**How to Experiment Safely**

When conducting experiments with microorganisms, treat them all as if they could cause disease. Do not touch the mold or try to smell the bread. Never taste or ingest any of the bread.

**Approximate Budget** $10.

**Timetable** 1 hour, 20 minutes setup; about 15 minutes daily for about 6 to 9 days.

**Step-by-Step Instructions**

1. Lay out five slices of bread.
2. Label each of the bags with the name of one preservative; label one bag "Control."
3. Prepare the preservatives by making sure each of the liquids flows easily through the spray bottle. If not, try to get a bottle with wider holes or dilute the liquid.

**Surface Area Growth**

| Bread | 1 day | 2 days | 3 days | 4 days | 5 days | 6 days |
|---|---|---|---|---|---|---|
| control | | | | | | |
| vinegar | | | | | | |
| orange juice | | | | | | |
| salt | | | | | | |
| lemon | | | | | | |

*Data chart for Experiment 1.*
GALE GROUP.

## Troubleshooter's Guide

Below are some problems that may arise during this experiment, some possible causes, and some ways to remedy the problems.

**Problem:** Mold did not grow on any of the breads.

**Possible cause:** Make sure the bread you purchased has no preservatives in it. You may want to buy fresh bread from a bakery. Once you have bread that has no preservatives, repeat the experiment.

**Possible cause:** You may have saturated the bread, not giving the fungi an environment that promotes growth. Repeat the experiment, lowering the number of sprays for each of the liquids to make sure the bread is only dampened.

**Problem:** Mold grew at the same rate on the Control slice as on one of the slices with the preservative.

**Possible cause:** There may not have been enough of the preservative in the additive, such as if you used a juice that did not have a high percentage of vitamin C or an imitation lemon juice. Make sure the additive contains the preservative you want to test, and repeat the experiment.

**Possible cause:** If you added water to the additive, you may have diluted the additive too much. Repeat the experiment, using another liquid additive or a spray bottle with wider holes as opposed to diluting the liquid.

4. Pour a small amount of vinegar in the spray bottle. Spray the vinegar on a piece of bread to dampen it, counting the number of sprays it takes to dampen. Do not soak it.

5. Rinse the spray bottle thoroughly with water and repeat the process for the lemon juice and orange juice, rinsing the bottle out in between. Use the same number of sprays for each.

6. Rinse out the sprayer and fill with water.

7. Spray the same number of sprays on the two remaining pieces of bread.

8. On one piece of bread sprinkle salt lightly over the damp bread.

9. Allow the breads to sit on the counter for one hour.

10. Place each piece of bread in the appropriate bag; put the water bread in the "Control" bag. Seal the bags.

11. Set the bags in a dim area, such as in a drawer.

12. Either trace or copy the graph paper on a clear piece of transparency.

13. Every day at roughly the same time, examine each piece of bread for mold. Do not remove the bread from the bag. If there is any mold, lightly place the transparent graph over the bread and determine the surface area of the mold by counting the number of squares. Note the results on a chart.

14. Continue examining each of the breads until mold has covered at least one of the slices.

15. If you have a magnifying glass or microscope, examine the mold(s) up close and note their descriptions.

16. After you have completed the summary, throw away the breads in their bags.

**Summary of Results** Graph your data, labeling "Days" on the X-axis and "Surface Area" on the Y-axis. Use a different color pen or type of line for each of the substances on the bread, and mark the graph clearly. What was the substance that prevented mold growth for the greatest number of days? Once mold did begin to grow, how did the rate of growth compare to the first few days when there was no growth? If the growth rate increased rapidly, theorize why you think this occurred. Describe the mold or types of mold on the breads. Common types of molds that grow on bread are bluish-green or green molds; black or brown-black molds; and reddish or pink molds. By examining the molds and referring to a reference source you may be able to identify them.

**Change the Variables** In this experiment you can change the variables in several ways:

- change the temperature, higher or lower
- change the type of bread, using bread with preservatives or comparing brands
- leave the breads out in both light and dark areas and compare growth
- use a different growth substance, such as a type of fruit instead of bread

## What Are the Variables?

Variables are anything that might affect the results of an experiment. Here are the main variables in this experiment:

- the temperature of the milk
- the milk's exposure to heat
- the amount of light
- the type (wholeness) of the milk
- the type of milk

In other words, the variables in this experiment are everything that might affect the growth of bacteria. If you change more than one variable at the same time, you will not be able to tell which variable had the most effect on the spoilage of the milk.

# EXPERIMENT 2

## Spoiled Milk: How do different temperatures of liquid affect its rate of spoilage?

**Purpose/Hypothesis** The two main groups of bacteria in milk are Lactic acids and Coliforms. Lactic acid is the natural bacteria present in milk and dairy products. Coliforms are the main reason for milk spoilage. Pasteurization kills almost all of the bacteria, but some of the bacteria that cause milk to spoil still remain. If these bacteria are given an environment that promotes growth, they will rapidly multiply.

## How to Experiment Safely

When conducting experiments with microorganisms, treat them all as if they could cause disease. Do not touch the milk and, if you do, wash your hands thoroughly. Do not taste or ingest any of the milk. Be careful when working at the stove.

In this experiment, you will be conducting two mini-trials in which you will determine how temperature affects the rate of milk spoilage. You will examine the environmental temperatures that affect milk by allowing glasses of milk to sit in cool, warm, and room-temperature environments. You will also determine how the temperature of the milk affects spoilage. One cup of milk will be boiled, then left in a room-temperature environment. After three days, you will examine each of the milks. When milk spoils it changes in consistency, appearance, and smell. Spoiled milk also undergoes a chemical change. As the milk spoils, the bacteria produce acid. It is the acid that causes the milk to clot. You can compare the acidity of the test milks by using indicator strips.

Before you begin, make an educated guess about the outcome of this experiment based on your knowledge of spoilage. This educated guess, or prediction, is your hypothesis. A hypothesis should explain these things:

- the topic of the experiment
- the variable you will change
- the variable you will measure
- what you expect to happen

A hypothesis should be brief, specific, and measurable. It must be something you can test through further investigation. Your experiment will prove or disprove whether your hypothesis is correct. Here is one possible hypothesis for this experiment: "The milk in the warm area will spoil the quickest; the milk that was boiled will take the greatest amount of time to spoil."

In this case, the variable you will change is the temperature of the milk. The variable you will measure is the relative amount of spoilage of each milk.

Conducting a control experiment will help you isolate each variable and measure the changes in the dependent variable. Only one variable will change between the control and your experiment. For the control for the boiled milk at room temperature, use the unboiled milk at room temperature. To compare milk spoilage among the test milks choose a standard among them, such as the milk at room temperature. Use the data from this standard to gauge the spoilage of the other test milks.

**Level of Difficulty** Easy to Moderate.

**Materials Needed**

- whole milk
- refrigerator
- heat lamp, such as one used for plants
- 4 tall heat-resistant glasses
- plastic wrap
- 4 rubber bands
- pot
- spoon
- hot plate or stove
- measuring cup
- acid/base indicator strips
- masking tape
- marking pen

*Steps 6 and 7: Place a rubber band around the plastic wrap and then place in its designated environment.* GALE GROUP.

**Approximate Budget** $3 (not including lamp).

**Timetable** 20 minutes setup; about 10 minutes daily for 4 to 5 days.

**Step-by-Step Instructions**

1. Label each of the cups: "Cold," "Warm," "Room Temp/Control," and "Boiled."
2. Measure out 1 cup of milk and pour it in the glass labeled "Cold." Pour another cup in the glass labeled "Warm," and another cup in the "Room Temp/Control."
3. Pour 1 cup in the pot and bring the milk to a low boil.
4. Stir continuously while letting the milk boil for one minute.
5. Pour the hot milk in the glass labeled "Boiled."
6. Immediately, place plastic wrap over each of the glasses.
7. Wrap a rubber band around the plastic wrap to secure it to the glass.
8. Set the "Cold" glass in the refrigerator; the "Warm" glass near the heat lamp; and the remaining two glasses in an undisturbed area at room temperature.
9. Describe how each glass of milk appears each day for four to five days. Do not remove the plastic wrap or shake the glass.

## Troubleshooter's Guide

Below is a problem that may arise during this experiment, a possible cause, and a way to remedy the problem.

**Problem:** After several days, the milk at room temperature appeared to have the same amount of spoilage as the milk in the refrigerator.

**Possible cause:** The room may be at a cool temperature and the bacteria could need longer to grow. Continue the experiment for several more days.

10. At the end of the experiment, when at least one of the milks has separated, place an indicator strip in each glass and note the results—acid, base, or neutral—by comparing the color of the wet strips with the chart provided with the indicator strips.

**Summary of Results** Examine your results and note the acidity level of the milk(s) that spoiled at the fastest rate. How did the control milk compare to the boiled milk? Compare the appearance of the milk at the warm environment to the cool environment. How did the spoiled milk's appearance change daily? When acid causes milk to curdle it forms solids called curds, and a liquid, called whey. Which of the test milks formed curds and whey? In an analysis of this experiment summarize what conclusions you can draw about the environment(s) that promote bacterial spoilage.

After you keep the milk clot for a while, the clot shrinks and a yellow fluid (whey) is released. You can make this happen more quickly by squeezing a little lemon juice (acid) into a small amount of milk. The curds are the white caseins, or milk proteins, and they are sticky (people once used them as glue). If you touch them, remember to wash your hands.

**Change the Variables** In this experiment you can change the variables in several ways. You can change the fat content of the milk by comparing skim milk, whole milk, 2% milk, and other types. You can add a substance to the milk, such as sugar or chocolate, that may alter the speed of bacteria growth. Another way to change the experiment is to vary how much light the milk is exposed to by leaving the same type of milk out in a bright and dark area. You could also alter the food substance by using different beverages or solid foods instead of milk.

## Design Your Own Experiment

**How to Select a Topic Relating to this Concept** Food spoilage is a common problem, with many possible project ideas. You could examine spoilage among different types of foods. You can also examine the steps taken to prevent spoilage, both in terms of additives and food handling. Check the Further Readings section and talk with your science teacher to learn more about spoilage. You could also talk with a microbiologist for details on the microorganisms involved in spoilage.

When experimenting with food, do not taste or ingest any of the food items, and make sure to mark the item clearly to keep others away. Aside from causing food poisoning, some microorganisms that are attracted to food can cause diseases that are potentially deadly. If you conduct an experiment with food in the home, make sure you tell an adult.

**Steps in the Scientific Method** To conduct an original experiment, you need to plan carefully and think things through. Otherwise, you might not be sure what question you are answering, what you are or should be measuring, or what your findings prove or disprove.

Here are the steps in designing an experiment:

- State the purpose of—and the underlying question behind—the experiment you propose to do.
- Recognize the variables involved and select one that will help you answer the question at hand.
- State your hypothesis, an educated guess about the answer to your question.
- Decide how to change the variable you selected.
- Decide how to measure your results.

**Recording Data and Summarizing the Results** Your data should include charts and graphs such as the one you did for these experiments. They should be clearly labeled and easy to read. You may also want to include photographs and drawings of your experimental setup and results, which will help other people visualize the steps in the experiment.

If you are preparing an exhibit, you may want to display your results, such as any experimental setup you designed. If you have completed a nonexperimental project, explain clearly what your research question was and illustrate your findings.

**Related Projects** Projects related to spoilage are numerous, inexpensive, and waiting in the kitchen. You could conduct a project examining the uses of synthesized versus natural preservatives. Foods spoil at different rates and under different environments. You could test different foods, all with the same main ingredient, for variables that affect the rate of spoilage. You could also examine how spoilage poses a serious health threat by examining potential diseases and illnesses from spoiled food.

You could group certain foods together and determine if the rate of spoilage changes, depending on what the food is near. You could also examine expiration dates and conduct an experiment that tests how accurate the date is to when it begins to spoil. When working with food, make sure not to taste or ingest any of the food, and to always label it clearly as an experiment. Spoiled food contains microorganisms, some of which could be extremely harmful.

## For More Information

Dalton, Louisa. "What's that Stuff?: Food Preservatives." *Chemical & Engineering News,* November 11, 2002. http://pubs.acs.org/cen/science/8045/8045sci2.html (accessed on March 6, 2008). Information on various food preservatives.

D'Amico, Joan, and Karen Eich Drummond. *The Science Chef Travels Around the World: Fun Food Experiments and Recipes for Kids.* New York: John Wiley, 1996. Food experiments and recipes from around the world.

"Food: Nutrition, Safety and Cooking." *University of Nebraska Lincoln.* http://lancaster.unl.edu/food/myths-ss/index.htm (accessed on March 8, 2008). Quiz and common myths on food safety.

"From Farm to Table." *www.foodsafety.gov.* http://www.foodsafety.gov/~fsg/fsgkids.html (accessed on March 8, 2008). Links to government sites on food safety and spoilage.

"Kids World: Food safety." *N.C. Department of Agriculture and Consumer Services.* http://www.ncagr.com/cyber/kidswrld/foodsafe/index.htm (accessed on March 8, 2008). Food safety facts and interactive question on spoilage.

# 38

# Forces

A force causes or changes an object's motion: It is a push or pull on an object. Forces have both a size and a direction. Forces also work in pairs: In order for a force to occur there must be an interaction between two objects. For example, when throwing a boomerang a person applies a force to the object that makes it move. Weightlifting exerts a force on the weight to pull it upward. These are forces that occur by physical contact between the two objects.

Yet forces also occur upon a person who is standing still. Forces are, in fact, occurring on everyone and everything on Earth, along with celestial objects. In these forces, two interacting objects exert a push or pull with no physical contact between them. An example of this force is gravity. Gravity is the force of attraction between any two objects in the universe.

*Guiding principles* While there have been numerous contributors to people's knowledge of forces, English scientist Isaac Newton (1642–1727) formulated the laws of motion, the rules that explain how forces work. As he was working on the laws of motion, Newton also explained the effect of gravity throughout the universe. In 1687 Newton published his landmark work *Philosophiae Naturalis Principia Mathematica (Mathematical Principles of Natural Philosophy),* which gave people a new understanding of the universe and laid the foundation for the development of physics.

Newton developed three laws of motion to explain forces:

First law of motion: With no force, an object at rest will stay at rest, and an object moving in a certain direction and speed will remain moving in that same path and velocity. Velocity is the speed of an object in a particular direction. This resistance of an object to change its motion is called inertia. The greater the mass of an object is, the more force is needed for the object to overcome its inertia. For example, a toy train

*Newton's second law of motion: acceleration. For example, if someone throws two balls with equal force, the ball with the lower mass will have greater acceleration.* GALE GROUP.

*Newton's third law of motion: Forces always work in pairs. For example, when stepping off of a boat there are multiple forces at work.* GALE GROUP.

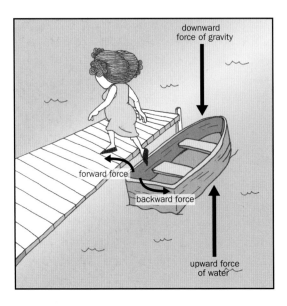

moving around a track would require relatively little force to make it move compared with the push a real train would need.

Second law of motion: When a force acts upon an object it will accelerate. Acceleration is the rate of change in velocity. The acceleration of an object depends upon the size of the force and the mass of the object. The relationship between these variables in mathematical terms is: Force (F) = Mass of Object (m) x Acceleration of Object (a), or $F = ma$, which can also be written $a = F/m$. As the force increases, the acceleration will also increase. The more mass an object has, the lower the rate of acceleration.

An example of this law is evident when comparing the force needed to throw two objects, such as two balls. If Ball 1 has 10 times the mass as Ball 2 and a pitcher throws the balls with equal force, then Ball 1 will accelerate at one-tenth the acceleration of the lighter ball. To make the two balls accelerate at the same rate, the pitcher will need to use ten times more force on Ball 1 than on Ball 2.

Third law of motion: For every action, there is an equal and opposite reaction. This law states that forces always work in pairs. When one force moving in a certain direction acts upon another force, then there must be a force of equal strength moving in the opposite direction.

There is usually more than one force at work. For example, when a boat is sitting still at the dock the force of gravity pulls with a downward force and the water responds with an equal and opposite upward force. A person who boards the boat and pushes it away from the dock exerts another force. The push starts the boat moving gradually away from the dock due to its inertia. Yet once moving, the boat will need that same amount of force to stop it. When the boat stops and the boater steps back onto the dock, that is another force. As the person steps off the boat with a push, the boat will move back in the opposite direction.

***Round and round we go*** Newton's laws explain both straight motion and circular motion. A force that causes an object to follow a circular path is called centripetal force. The word centripetal comes from the Latin words *centrum* and *petere,* meaning center seeking. (This force is often confused with centrifugal force, meaning center fleeing. Centrifugal force is not considered a true force, as there is no force acting upon the object; it is only the tendency of the object to continue in a straight line. See Ocean chapter.) Anytime there is a circular movement around a central point, then centripetal force is at work.

*In centripetal force, the inward force pulls the object or body away from its straight path to form a circular movement.*
GALE GROUP.

Centripetal force is based on Newton's first law of motion that states an object will travel along a straight path with constant speed unless a force acts upon it. Thus, for a circular motion to occur, there must be a constant force pulling the object towards the center of the circle. This force is always directed inward. For a planet orbiting the Sun, the force is gravity; for a ball twirling on a string, the force is the tension in the string; for a loop in a roller coaster ride, the force is applied by the curved track.

An object moving in a circle is constantly accelerating because it is continuously changing its direction. This is true even if the object is moving at a uniform speed. (Acceleration is a change in velocity and velocity is the speed of an object in a particular direction.) The amount of centripetal force needed to keep an object moving in a circular path depends upon its acceleration, along with its mass.

When the centripetal force is taken away, the object follows Newton's first and third laws: Its inertia causes the object to move in a straight line and the force by which it moves outward is equal in strength and opposite in direction.

## EXPERIMENT 1

### Newton's Laws in Action: How do water bottle rockets demonstrate Newton's laws of motion?

Purpose/Hypothesis The laws of motion explain how force affects the movement of an object. Many objects such as trains, airplanes, and theme park rides demonstrate these laws. In this experiment, you will work with a water bottle rocket to observe Newton's laws. After constructing a basic launcher you will use a plastic two-liter bottle and water to measure the

## WORDS TO KNOW

**Acceleration:** The rate at which the velocity and/or direction of an object is changing with respect to time.

**Centripetal force:** A force that pushes an object inward, which causes the object to move in a circular path.

**Control experiment:** A setup that is identical to the experiment, but is not affected by the variable that acts on the experimental group.

**First law of motion (Newton's):** An object at rest or moving in a certain direction and speed will remain at rest or moving in the same motion and speed unless acted upon by a force.

**Force:** A physical interaction (pushing or pulling) tending to change the state of motion (velocity) of an object.

**Gravity:** Force of attraction between objects, the strength of which depends on the mass of each object and the distance between them.

**Hypothesis:** An idea in the form of a statement that can be tested by observation and/or experiment.

**Inertia:** The tendency of an object to continue in its state of motion.

**Second law of motion (Newton's):** The force exerted on an object is proportional to the mass of the object times the acceleration produced by the force.

**Third law of motion (Newton's):** For every action there is an equal and opposite reaction.

**Variable:** Something that can affect the results of an experiment.

**Velocity:** The rate at which the position of an object changes with time, including both the speed and the direction.

force required to lift the rocket. By adding water to the rocket, you will increase its mass.

A rocket exhibits all three of Newton's laws of motion. Newton's first law states that an object at rest will stay at rest, and an object in motion continues in motion. When the rocket is sitting on the launcher it is an object at rest. Once a force is applied to the rocket and it is in motion, it continues in motion. Newton's second law explains that when a force acts upon an object it causes the object to accelerate. This is seen when force—in this case, the pressure of the air pumped in the bottle by the tire pump—is exerted on the rocket. The rocket launches and accelerates in upward motion. Newton's third law refers to reactions, stating that for every action there is an equal and opposite reaction. When the rocket lifts, the air and water that filled the bottle are forced out of the spout in the opposite direction while propelling the rocket higher.

The rocket will be your object, either at rest or in motion. The force is the pressure of the air pumped inside the launcher. As the rocket propels forward, the water will escape and cause the mass to change.

Before you begin, make an educated guess about the outcome of this experiment based on your knowledge of rockets and Newton's laws of motion. This educated guess, or prediction, is your hypothesis. A hypothesis should explain these things:

- the topic of the experiment
- the variable you will change
- the variable you will measure
- what you expect to happen

A hypothesis should be brief, specific, and measurable. It must be something you can test through further investigation. Your experiment will prove or disprove whether your hypothesis is correct. Here is one possible hypothesis for this experiment: "The greater the amount of water in the rocket (bottle), the more air pressure (force) is required for launching."

In this case, the variable you will change is the mass (the amount of water in the rocket). The variable you will measure is the force (the air pressure in the rocket) required for liftoff.

*A rocket exhibits all three of Newton's laws of motion. (1) When the rocket is sitting on the launcher it is an object at rest. (2) Once a force is applied to the rocket and it is in motion, it continues in motion. (3) When the rocket lifts, propellants in the rocket are forced out in the opposite direction while propelling the rocket higher.*
AP/WIDE WORLD

**Level of Difficulty** Difficult.

**Materials Needed** To build launcher:
- 5 feet (1.5 meters) of ¾-inch CPVC pipe (available in the plumbing section of home improvement or hardware stores). It is generally a yellowish color and is sold in 10-foot (3-meter) lengths. Use a saw or PVC cutters to cut.
- 7 inches (18 centimeters) of ½-inch CPVC pipe
- T-joint fitting with ¾-inch ends and a ½-inch center for CPVC pipe
- 45-degree elbow with ¾-inch ends for CPVC pipe
- 90-degree elbow with ¾-inch ends for CPVC pipe

## What Are the Variables?

Variables are anything that might affect the results of an experiment. Here are the main variables in this experiment:

- the amount of water in the bottle
- the air pressure in the bottle
- the tightness of the seal between bottle and launcher
- thickness of the bottle
- preciseness of gauge on tire pump

In other words, the variables in this experiment are everything that might affect the mass of the rocket and the force applied by the compressed air inside. If you change more than one variable, you will not be able to tell which variable impacted the rocket liftoff.

- two end caps for ¾-inch CPVC pipe
- PVC primer (minimal amount)
- PVC glue/cement (minimal amount)
- roll of masking tape (½- or ¾-inch wide)
- 2 inches (5 centimeters) of ⅝-inch inner diameter clear vinyl tubing (available at hardware or home improvement store)
- tire valve stem (ask at a local tire store and explain it's for a science experiment; it may be possible to get a donation)
- saw or PVC cutting tool
- drill
- paring knife
- expandable pipe wrench; it needs to have the capacity to hold the ¾-inch cap
- scrap wood block
- safety goggles
- protractor

For launch:

- water
- bike tire pump with pressure gauge. Make sure it is a full-size pump. Small pumps that fit in a backpack may not create enough force.
- measuring cup
- 2-liter plastic soda bottle
- permanent marker
- paper towels or a drying rag
- tape measure
- open space
- partner and adult present when using tools

**Approximate Budget** $18 (not counting the bicycle pump).

**Timetable** 1 hour to build; 30 minutes to dry; 30 minutes for experiment.

**Step-by-Step Instructions** To build the launcher:

1. From the 5-foot (1.5-meter) piece of the ¾-inch pipe cut two 6-inch (15-centimeter) pieces and one 2-inch (5-centimeter) piece.

The remaining piece should be approximately 46 inches (117 centimeters) long.

2. One person will clamp one of the ¾-inch end caps with the wrench. Rest the cap on the scrap wood block to avoid drilling through the workspace. Have the helper drill a hole in the center of the PVC cap. The hole needs to be large enough for the tire stem to come part way through, approximately $\frac{1}{4}$ inch. Check to ensure the tire valve is able to be pushed partway through the hole. It may be necessary to trim away part of the rubber around the valve stem. This may be done with a paring knife.

3. Glue the end cap to the 2-inch length of pipe: Push the valve stem partway through the 2-inch (5-centimeter) tube. Apply primer to the outside of the 2-inch (5-centimeter) pipe, the inside of the end cap, and a small amount to the base of the valve stem. Next, apply the glue over the primer. (Note: PVC glue dries very quickly and makes a lasting bond. Once the two pieces of CPVC touch, you have only a few seconds before they are connected forever.)

4. Hold the valve stem partway out of the 2-inch (5-centimeter) piece of pipe and place it through the hole on the end cap. The valve stem should stick out of the hole in the cap. Pull firmly and slightly twist the valve stem, making sure it is secure. Wipe away excess glue.

5. Connect the 46-inch (117-centimeter) piece of pipe to the 2-inch (5-centimeter) piece with the 45-degree elbow. Apply the primer and glue to the inside of the elbow and the outside of the long piece. Insert the pipe into the elbow. Next, apply to the other side of the elbow and the outside of the 2-inch piece. Firmly press the elbow on the 2-inch piece of pipe. Wipe away excess glue. Set aside to dry.

6. Cut a 7-inch (18-centimeter) length of the ½-inch pipe. This will become your launching post.

7. Connect the launching post to the T-joint fitting. Glue the two ¾-inch CPVC pieces to the ends of the T-joint fitting. First apply the primer, then the glue again to the inside of the connector and

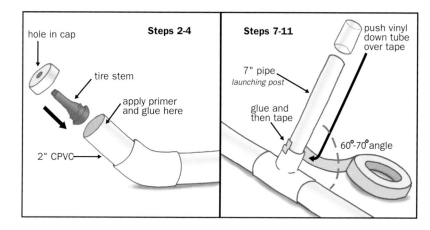

hole in cap

tire stem

apply primer
and glue here

2" CPVC

7" pipe
launching post

glue and
then tape

push vinyl
down tube
over tape

60°-70° angle

*Steps 2 to 4 and Steps 7 to 11:*
*Constructing the launcher.*
GALE GROUP.

the outside of the pipe. The 7-inch piece of ½-inch CPVC is then glued into the empty hole of the T-joint fitting.

8. Tape masking tape around the connection of the 1/2 in PCVC post and the T. It will be necessary to make several wraps and tapering the tape slightly (about an inch or two) up the post. Next, push the 2-inch piece of clear vinyl tubing down the tube and over the tape. Use an extra piece of the ¾-inch PCVC to assist in pushing the tubing down snugly over the tape. The tape and tubing will create a stopper for the bottle to fit on.

9. Using your bottle, test to see if the tape and tubing will create a tight seal. If the seal is not tight, remove the tubing and add more tape.

10. Glue the 90-degree elbow to the long piece made in the first five steps.

11. Use your protractor to glue the T post to the 90-degree elbow. The post should create between a 70-degree and 60-degree angle with the ground, pointing away from the valve stem end of the launcher. Do not angle the post less than 45 degrees.

12. Allow launcher to sit about 30 minutes to dry.

To launch:

1. In an open area, fill the 2-liter bottle with 2 cups (about 0.5 liter) of water.

2. Place the launch post in the bottle and push for a snug fit. Mark this spot with a permanent marker. (It works best to turn the launcher slightly on its side, and gently "roll" it back to its

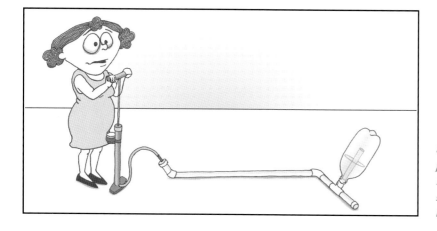

*Steps 3 and 4: Pump the tire pump to fill the bottle with air. Keep pumping at a slow and steady pace until the rocket launches.* GALE GROUP.

standing position with the bottle on top. This way the water will not come out of the bottle.)

3. Attach the tire pump to the valve nozzle.

4. Pump the tire pump to fill the bottle with air. Keep pumping at a slow and steady pace until the rocket launches. The helper should note the gauge and record the pressure required for liftoff.

5. Repeat launch for two more trials, noting the force (air pressure) and distance for each trial.

6. Fill the 2-liter bottle with 3 cups (about 0.75 liter) of water.

7. Repeat Steps 2 through 5.

8. Fill the 2-liter bottle with 4 cups (about 1.0 liter) of water.

9. Repeat Steps 2 through 5.

**Summary of Results** Examine your results to determine which amount of water required the greatest amount of force for liftoff? Was your hypothesis correct? Hypothesize what would happen if you changed the bottle size, and maintained the water amount. What would occur if a cone top and wings were attached to the rocket? Write a brief summary of the experiment and your analysis.

*Step 5: Data chart for rocket launch.* GALE GROUP.

**Change the Variables** There are several ways you can modify the experiment by changing the variables. You can change the sizes of the bottle and maintain the water amount. Another approach could include using various bottle

| Data for Rocket Launch (averages) | | |
|---|---|---|
| | Pressure/Force | Distance |
| 2 cups water | | |
| 3 cups water | | |
| 4 cups water | | |

## Troubleshooter's Guide

Below is a problem that may arise during this experiment, a possible cause, and a way to remedy the problem.

**Problem:** The rocket will not take off.

**Possible cause:** Make sure your seal is tight. Wipe the stopper off after each launch. Check the tire pump to determine if it is attached appropriately. The pump may be too weak to perform the launch.

sizes and filling each bottle to half of capacity, rather than a uniform water amount. If you have access to a football field, you could perform the experiment on the field and attempt to measure the distance of each launch. It may be beneficial to prop the launcher on a block of wood to create more of an angle (do not go less than 45 degrees).

**Modify the Experiment** You can also explore Newton's laws by conducting a simpler version of the rocket experiment. You will need a piece of wire several feet long. Gather together a balloon, tape measure, string, wide straw and masking tape. Slip the straw onto the wire so that it moves about freely, and securely tie the wire to two objects, such as two chairs.

Blow up the balloon, place a straw in it and tape the straw so that no air escapes. Bending the straw will help keep the air from escaping. Place a piece of masking tape on the end of the straw to seal the air inside. Tape the straw to the balloon. As you look at your experimental setup, think

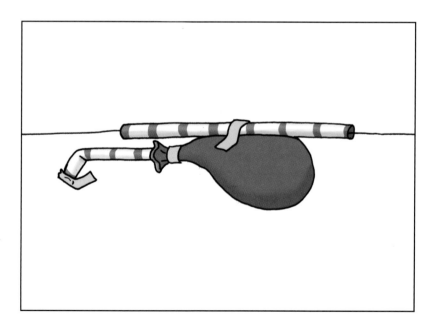

*Slip the straw onto the wire so that it moves about freely, and securely tie the wire to two objects, such as two chairs.*
ILLUSTRATION BY TEMAH NELSON.

about all the forces. The air, for example, is a force acting on the outside of the balloon.

Now take the tape off the end of the straw. What happens as the air escapes? Newton's third law of motion states that for every action force there is an equal and opposite reaction force. The air is the action and the movement of the straw is the opposite reaction. Measure how far your balloon moved along the wire. How can you make the straw move a shorter distance? How can you make it move farther? Experiment with blowing up the balloon different amounts. After each trial, write down the distance the straw moved.

## EXPERIMENT 2

## Centripetal Action: What is the relationship between distance and force in circular motion?

Purpose/Hypothesis Centripetal force is any force that acts on an object at a right angle to its path of motion. The constant right angle force results in the object moving in a circular path. In this experiment, you will examine how altering the force and radius will affect the acceleration of an object. Radius is the distance from the center to the outer point of a circle. The object's mass will stay the same.

A piece of string will have a mass attached to one end and washers creating the force attached to the other end. You will first alter the radius, and then alter the force. For a more accurate measure of how many times the mass completes a circle or revolution, you will count how many times it revolves in 30 seconds. That number will then be divided by 30 to give its revolutions per second. Another way to increase accuracy is to complete three trials of each experimental trial.

Comparing the results to a control experiment will help you isolate each variable and measure the changes in the dependent variable. In this experiment there will be two variables that you will change, one at a time. Only one variable will change between the control and the experimental setup each time. In the first part, the distance will change when the radius increases. In the second part, the force will change. At the end of the experiment you can compare each of the results to the standard experiment.

Before you begin, make an educated guess about the outcome of this experiment based on your knowledge of centripetal force. This educated

## What Are the Variables?

Variables are anything that might affect the results of an experiment. Here are the main variables in this experiment:

- the force
- the radius
- the mass

In other words, the variables in this experiment are everything that might affect the acceleration of the mass. If you change more than one variable at the same time, you will not be able to tell which variable had the most effect on centripetal force.

guess, or prediction, is your hypothesis. A hypothesis should explain these things:

- the topic of the experiment
- the variable you will change
- the variable you will measure
- what you expect to happen

A hypothesis should be brief, specific, and measurable. It must be something you can test through further investigation. Your experiment will prove or disprove whether your hypothesis is correct. Here is one possible hypothesis for this experiment: "The greater the force, the greater the acceleration; the greater the radius; the lower the acceleration."

In this case, the variable you will change is the force and the distance, one at a time. The variable you will measure is the acceleration of the mass.

**Level of Difficulty** Easy to Moderate.

**Materials Needed**

- spool of thread with narrow hole
- ruler
- ten metal washers of equal size
- 3 feet (90 centimeters) of string
- masking tape
- watch with second hand
- bobbin, small spool of thread, rubber stopper or other lightweight object that can be easily tied
- helper

**Approximate Budget** $2.

**Timetable** 30 minutes.

**Step-by-Step Instructions**

1. Slide the string in the large spool of thread and move the spool up 2 feet (0.6 meters).

2. On the long side of the string, attach four metal washers (this is the force) to the end and secure with a knot.

3. Tie the bobbin or rubber stopper to the end of the short side of the string. This is the mass.

4. Wind a piece of tape about 1 inch (2.5 centimeters) below the spool to make sure it does not slide down and change the radius. Mark the string at the point above the tape.

5. Hold the washers with one hand and begin to swing the mass until it is moving parallel to the floor. Practice swinging at a steady rate.

6. While you are swinging, have your helper time 30 seconds and count the number of revolutions the bobbin makes.

7. Repeat Step 6 two more times so that you have three trials. This is your standard experiment.

8. Remove the tape and slide the spool down 1 foot (0.3 meters) towards the washers. Reattach the tape about 1 inch (2.5 centimeters) below the spool.

9. Again, time the number of revolutions in a 30-second period, then repeat for two more trials. Note the results.

10. Return the spool to its beginning position, reattaching the tape at the marked point on the string.

11. Double the number of washers to eight. Support the washers until you have a steady swing and then have your helper time 30 seconds while you count the revolutions. Repeat two more times and note the results.

**Summary of Results** Determine the time for each revolution per second by dividing the total revolutions by 30. Once you have the revolutions per second for each trial, average the three trials. Make a chart of your data. Compare how long it took to complete a full circle when the radius lengthened. How much force would it take to have the revolutions of different radiuses

**How to Experiment Safely**

Be careful when swinging the mass and check to ensure the knot is tight. Make sure you are working in an open area.

*Steps 5 and 6: Count the number of revolutions of the mass in 30 seconds.* GALE GROUP.

## Troubleshooter's Guide

Below is a problem that may arise during this experiment, a possible cause, and a way to remedy the problem.

**Problem:** The radius looked like it was changing.

**Possible cause:** The paperclip might have slid loose. Use a tight paperclip and make sure it is attached firmly, then repeat the experiment.

be the same. Look at how the increased force compares with the acceleration of the lesser force? What would happen to the acceleration if you halved the force? Hypothesize how the force and/or radius would need to change if the mass was doubled and you wanted to keep the acceleration equal.

**Change the Variables** You can continue to experiment on changing the variables in this experiment in new ways and new combinations. Try to halve the force and halve the radius. Look at what occurs if the radius is tripled and the force remains constant. You can also change the mass of the object, making it lighter or heavier. Make sure you secure the mass tightly to the string and try to work in an open area.

## Design Your Own Experiment

**How to Select a Topic Relating to this Concept** Force is a broad topic that has many possible experiments. To gather ideas on force, you can observe how force is applied in daily life. Look at sporting events and playground rides to see the application of Newton's laws and centripetal force. You could also research how celestial bodies in the universe apply centripetal force.

Check the Further Readings section and talk with your science or physics teacher to learn more about force.

**Steps in the Scientific Method** To conduct an original experiment, you need to plan carefully and think things through. Otherwise, you might not be sure what question you are answering, what you are or should be measuring, or what your findings prove or disprove.

Here are the steps in designing an experiment:

- State the purpose of—and the underlying question behind—the experiment you propose to do.

*A planet orbits a sunlike star. Astronomers depend on the principles of centripetal force to help them predict orbits and revolutions.* © AFP/CORBIS.

- Recognize the variables involved and select one that will help you answer the question at hand.
- State your hypothesis, an educated guess about the answer to your question.
- Decide how to change the variable you selected.
- Decide how to measure your results.

**Recording Data and Summarizing the Results** Your data could include charts and graphs to display your data. If included, they should be clearly labeled and easy to read. You may also want to include photographs and drawings of your experimental setup and results, which will help other people visualize the steps in the experiment.

If you are preparing an exhibit, you may want to display your results, such as any experimental setup you designed. If you have completed a nonexperimental project, explain clearly what your research question was and illustrate your findings.

**Related Projects** There are many possible projects related to force. You could construct simple machines to experiment with the amount of force required for work. These projects could explore how force varies with distance and mass. Astronomers depend on the principles of centripetal force to help them predict orbits and revolutions. You could examine how the planets, suns, and moons each have their own unique orbits due to the principles behind centripetal force. You could also explore the force of gravity with everyday objects.

## For More Information

Christianson, Gale E. *Isaac Newton and the Scientific Revolution.* New York: Oxford University Press, 1998. The personal life story of Newton and his work.

Clark, John O. E. *Physics Matters!* Danbury, CT: Grolier Education, 2001. Provides a clear explanation of the science of physics with pictures and applications.

"Newton's Laws of Motion." *NASA Glenn Research Center.* http://www.grc.nasa.gov/WWW/K-12/airplane/newton.html (accessed on February 3, 2008). Explanations and illustrations of Newton's laws of motion presented with different details for different grade levels.

"Skateboard Science." *The Exploratorium.* http://www.exploratorium.edu/skateboarding (accessed on February 3, 2008). A look at the science of skateboarding and how it relates to centripetal force.

# 39

# Forensic Science

Who, what, where, and when? At a crime scene, these are the pieces of information forensic scientists work to piece together. Forensic science is the application of science to the law. Often called forensics, it covers many areas of the sciences, included microbiology, physical science, and chemistry. Advances in the field of forensic science have shifted the way people solve crimes and the justice system.

Evidence left at the crime scene includes the physical (such as a scrap of clothing or footprint) and biological (such as DNA). In many cases the evidence may be invisible to the naked eye. Fibers and strands of hair are examples. It took the development of high-powered microscopes in the nineteenth century to bring forward this area of forensics. Once crime solvers could see the object, they could study and compare it to possible suspects. Analysis techniques on blood, materials, and biological evidence have also revolutionized the field of forensics.

*Fingering the evidence* Hundreds of years ago people noticed that humans all have unique fingerprints. This observation was put to use officially in the late 1800s by Scottish doctor Henry Faulds. Credited with the first fingerprint identification, Faulds became interested in fingerprinting after noticing fingerprints on ancient clay pottery. Soon afterwards, his hospital was broken into. Faulds identified the thief from a greasy fingerprint on a surgical alcohol bottle.

Fingerprints have become an important piece of criminal evidence. Over the years, technologies to analyze fingerprints have improved, but the basic idea of fingerprint analysis remains the same. People are all born with a unique fingerprint pattern—including identical twins. The pattern stays the same over the course of a person's life, whether you are nine or 90 years old.

There are three basic patterns used to categorize fingerprints: the loop, arc, and whorl. As its name says, the loop has a loop pattern, where the print starts and ends on the same side of the finger. An arc pattern rises

**507**

*People are all born with a unique fingerprint pattern.*
ED BOCK/CORBIS.

and falls slightly, from one side of the finger to the other. The whorl forms circles around a central point.

*Looking at blood* Blood found at a crime scene can provide key pieces of information to piece together how the crime happened. One forensic technique is called blood pattern or blood spatter analysis. A blood pattern can help investigators reconstruct the angle the blood came from, what direction it was traveling, and its velocity (speed).

The shape and size of the blood spatter provides clues as to the surface it landed on. Droplets that strike a hard surface, such as glass, will have a smooth circle. Blood droplets that hit wood spatter outwards. The direction of blood can trace the blood's angle of origin. When a blood droplet strikes a surface straight down, perpendicular to the floor, it forms a clean circle. Blood that strikes a surface at an angle, such as 60 degrees, will have a tear drop shape. By knowing both the length and width of the blood drop investigators can calculate the impact angle.

Even when there is no visible sign of blood, investigators can spot blood by spraying a substance called luminol. When luminol comes into contact with blood, it reacts with the iron in the blood. The reaction produces a blue glow that last for seconds before it fades. Investigators turn the lights off and look for the glow.

*Fiber evidence* If a piece of material or thread is left at a crime scene, analyzing the fiber can help investigators identify where it came from. The fiber can come from a rug, clothing, or handbag.

There are many types of fibers and each has its own characteristics. For example, each fiber will burn in a slightly different way. Some common types of fibers and their properties include:

- Cotton: A plant fiber; the individual plant fibers that make up the yarn are relatively short compared to other fibers. When ignited, it burns with a steady flame and smells like burning leaves.

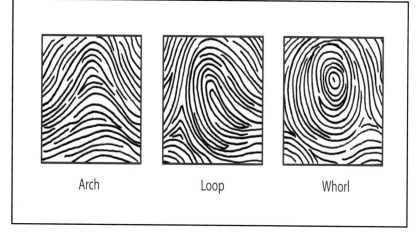

Arch        Loop        Whorl

*There are three basic patterns used to categorize fingerprints: the loop, arc, and whorl.*
ILLUSTRATION BY TEMAH NELSON.

- Linen: A plant fiber; the individual fibers that make up the yarn are relatively long. Linen takes longer to ignite than cotton.
- Silk: A natural protein fiber made from worms. When burned, it burns quickly and smells like burning hair.
- Wool: A protein fiber that comes from the fur of sheep. When burned, the flame is steady.
- Acetate: Produced from cellulose (wood fibers). Acetate burns quickly with a flame that is relatively hard to put out.
- Nylon: A synthetic (manmade) fiber made from petroleum products. Nylon melts and burns rapidly. It smells like burning plastic.
- Polyester: A synthetic fiber, polyester melts and burns at the same time. The smoke from polyester is black with a sweetish smell.
- Rayon: A synthetic fiber made from wood pulp, rayon burns rapidly and leaves only a slight ash. The burning smell is close to burning leaves.

*The direction of blood can trace the blood's angle of origin.*
ILLUSTRATION BY TEMAH NELSON.

*High tech evidence* In the last half of the twentieth century, scientific findings have led to key advances in forensics. DNA fingerprinting, developed in 1984, is now a commonly used technique in forensics. All people have unique DNA—except identical twins—that is in almost every cell in the body. DNA fingerprinting identifies sequences of DNA unique to each person.

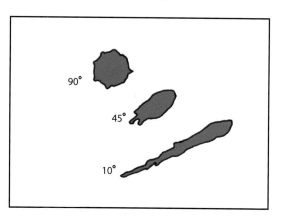

90°

45°

10°

# WORDS TO KNOW

**Blood pattern analysis:** The study of the shape, location, and pattern of blood in order to understand how it got there.

**Control experiment:** A setup that is identical to the experiment, but is not affected by the variable that acts on the experimental group.

**Deoxyribonucleic acid (DNA):** Large, complex molecules found in the nuclei of cells that carry genetic information for an organism's development; double helix. (Pronounced DEE-ox-see-rye-bo-noo-klay-ick acid)

**DNA fingerprinting:** A technique that uses DNA fragments to identify the unique DNA sequences of an individual.

**Forensic science:** The application of science to the law and justice system.

**Hypothesis:** An idea in the form of a statement that can be tested by observation and/or experiment.

**Luminol:** A compound used to detect blood.

**Variable:** Something that can affect the results of an experiment.

Investigators need only a tiny amount of DNA to analyze it. The DNA evidence can come from a hair root, saliva, or sweat. A DNA fingerprinting test can determine if the DNA from a crime scene matches the DNA of a suspect. It can also show if the DNA samples are from the same person or different people, and if the different people are related.

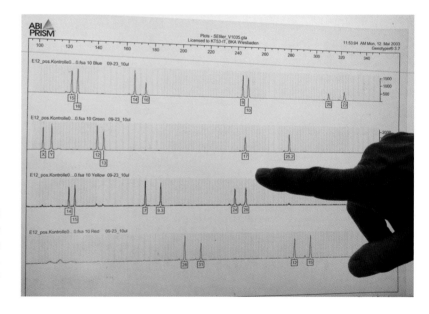

*An example of a DNA fingerprint from the forensic department at the German Federal Police in Wiesbaden, central Germany.* AP PHOTO/ MICHAEL PROBST.

There are many other techniques forensic scientists use. In the following experiments you will learn more about the forensic science techniques involved in fiber and blood pattern analyses.

## EXPERIMENT 1

### Fiber Evidence: How can scientific techniques be used to identify fiber?

Purpose/Hypothesis What if a tiny piece of material is found at a crime scene? How would you identify it? In this experiment you will conduct several techniques to examine the properties of three to four fiber samples. You will first examine the fibers the materials are made out of with a microscope, magnifying glass, or from a digital photograph. You will then conduct a burn test on the fibers.

On material samples, you will examine how each material absorbs water and if it dissolves in acetone (most fingernail polish removers contain acetone). Acetate dissolves in acetone; other fabrics do not. A fabric that contains acetate will partly dissolve.

After you examine the properties of each type of fiber, you will identify a material sample from a "crime scene."

Before you begin, make an educated guess about the outcome of this experiment based on your knowledge of forensic science and the fiber. This educated guess, or prediction, is your hypothesis. A hypothesis should explain these things:

- the topic of the experiment
- the variable you will change
- the variable you will measure
- what you expect to happen

### What Are the Variables?

Variables are anything that might affect the results of an experiment. Here are the main variables in this experiment:

- the cleanliness of the fiber
- the type of fiber
- the coating on the fiber
- the length of the fiber
- the environmental condition

In other words, the variables in this experiment are everything that might affect the identification of the fiber.

*Watch how the acetone effects the fabric.* ILLUSTRATION BY TEMAH NELSON.

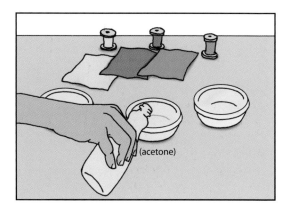

(acetone)

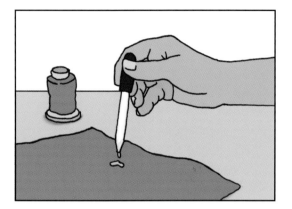

*Water absorption step 1: Drop two drops of water on each fabric sample.* ILLUSTRATION BY TEMAH NELSON.

A hypothesis should be brief, specific, and measurable. It must be something you can test through further investigation. Your experiment will prove or disprove whether your hypothesis is correct. Here is one possible hypothesis for this experiment: "Fibers each have different properties, and if the properties of each sample are known, the sample can be identified."

In this case, the variable you will change is the type of fiber. The variable you will determine is the type of material.

**Level of Difficulty** Difficult.

**Materials Needed**

- 1 to 2 spools of natural threads (cotton, linen, silk, or wool)
- 1 to 2 spools of synthetic threads, which include acetate and either nylon or polyester (acetate can be 50% acetate; you can rip the acetate thread from the fabric)
- fabric swatches that match the type of threads used, and which includes acetate; about 3 inches (7.6 centimeters) square (acetate can be 50% acetate)
- candle in a holder
- match
- eyedropper
- scissors
- fingernail polish remover that contains acetone
- 3 to 4 small plastic or glass containers
- long tweezers, about 12 inches (30 centimeters) or longer (available at science supply sources or some hardware stores)
- high-powered magnifying glass or microscope, or digital camera
- sink
- helper
- aluminum foil

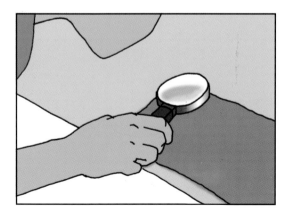

*Water absorption step 2: Note if the water absorbs into the fabric or stays bubbled on the*

Approximate Budget $15 (assuming you can obtain a microscope or magnifying glass from another source).

Timetable 2 hours.

Step-by-Step Instructions Magnification:

1. Look at the material pieces under the microscope or magnifying glass. If you have a high-resolution digital camera, you can take a photograph and magnify the pictures.
2. Note any features in a chart, such as loose threads, if the threads are short or long; if there is a twist in the threads, the weave of the material; and if there are holes in the weave. Draw or sketch your observations.

The Burn Test:

1. Wrap one thread around your closed hand five times and cut. Remove the clustered thread from around your hand and hold the two clusters together. The thread should be about 5 inches (13 centimeters) in length.
2. Use the tweezers to grasp one end of the thread cluster.
3. Light the candle and place it in sink. Set a piece of aluminum foil next to the sink. (If you do not have access to a sink you could conduct the test over a pan of water.)
4. Carefully, place the bottom of the thread into the candle flame. Observe it burn. Note if the flame is steady and how fast the flame moves. When the thread has finished burning, note any odor.
5. Conduct another trial with the same thread to make sure you have consistent results.
6. Repeat Steps 3–7 for each of the other threads.

Water Absorption:

1. Fill an eyedropper with water and lay out the fabric samples.

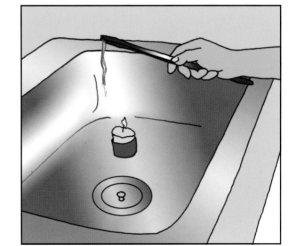

*The burn test.* ILLUSTRATION BY TEMAH NELSON.

## Troubleshooter's Guide

Below are some problems that may arise during this experiment, some possible causes, and some ways to remedy the problem.

**Problem:** The threads burn too quickly to identify anything.

**Possible cause:** The threads may be too short. Wrap the threads around your hands another two to three times. You also may need to conduct the burn test several times for each thread, to compare how each thread burns relative to the others.

**Problem:** I can't see much detail through the magnifying glass.

**Possible cause:** The magnification in your magnifying glass is not strong enough. You should be able to see the weave with a magnifying glass, or with your naked eye. Try to use a higher-powered magnifying glass if you want to see more detail, and repeat this test.

2. Drop two drops of water on each fabric sample. For each fabric sample, note if the water absorbs into the fabric or stays bubbled on the top.

Dissolve in Acetone:

1. Fill three small plastic or glass containers about half full with acetone. (If you have four fabric samples you will need four containers, or to wait until one is completed.)

2. Cut about a half-inch square of fabric from each material sample. Drop one fabric sample into each of the containers of acetone. Wait 10 minutes.

3. Use the tweezers to remove the fabric onto the aluminum foil. Note if any of the materials partly dissolve.

Material Matching:

1. Have a helper cut a small piece of a mystery fabric from one of the leftover swatches. Don't look at which piece of fabric it is!

2. Repeat all the tests, pulling a piece of string from the material for the burn test. You can also have your helper hand you the matching string.

**Summary of Results** Could you match the mystery material to one of the tested fabrics? Did any of the tests not fit the properties you identified? You can try matching other fabrics, or having a helper try to match a fabric. Consider how these tests would be helpful in solving a crime. You may want to write up your results, including any pictures or drawings.

**Change the Variables** If you want to change the variables in this experiment you can use different fabrics. You could also use different types of fiber, such as threads from carpets or furniture materials.

# EXPERIMENT 2

## Blood Patterns: How can a blood spatter help recreate the crime?

**Purpose/Hypothesis** The impact of blood on an object leaves forensic clues in its pattern and shape. This experiment focuses on investigating the angle of moving blood. You will test dropping artificial blood from different angles and evaluate the shape and pattern of the blood droplets. You will then use this knowledge to piece together where a "mystery" blood spatter came from.

To begin this experiment, use what you know about forensic science and blood spatters to make an educated guess about how blood spatters can help reconstruct a crime. This educated guess, or prediction, is your hypothesis. A hypothesis should explain these things:

- the topic of the experiment
- the variable you will change
- the variable you will measure
- what you expect to happen

A hypothesis should be brief, specific, and measurable. It must be something you can test through observation. Your experiment will prove or disprove whether your hypothesis is correct. Here is one possible hypothesis for this experiment: "Blood that moves at an angle will have longer droplets than blood traveling straight up and down."

In this case, the variable you will change is the angle of the blood and then the direction of the moving blood, and the variable you will measure is the blood droplet shape.

**Level of Difficulty** Moderate.

**Materials Needed**

- brown paper rolls (available from craft store); you can also tape paper together if rolls are not available
- eye dropper

## What Are the Variables?

Variables are anything that might affect the results of an experiment. Here are the main variables in this experiment:

- the artificial blood
- the surface the blood lands on
- the force with which blood is spurted out
- the height the blood is dropped from

In other words, the variables in this experiment are everything that might affect the blood spatter. If you change more than one variable, you will not be able to tell which variable most affected the pattern of the blood.

## How to Experiment Safely

There are no safety hazards but this experiment has splattering, and it can be messy. You may want to wear old clothes.

- small hand scrubber
- white corn syrup
- ketchup or tomato paste
- bowl
- measuring cup
- stirring spoon
- protractor
- tape measure
- pencil
- tape
- wooden board or other object with a flat bottom, such as the back of a long pan, about 24 inches (61 centimeters) high
- large flat working space outside
- helper

**Approximate Budget** $10.

**Timetable** Approximately one hour.

**Step-by-Step Instructions**

*Step 5a: Hold the eyedropper at the 90 degree mark and squeeze out a drop.* ILLUSTRATION BY TEMAH NELSON.

1. Lay the roll of paper down on a flat surface about 3 feet (91 centimeters) in length.

2. In a bowl, add $\frac{1}{2}$-cup of corn syrup and about 2 teaspoons of ketchup until it appears red. Stir. The "blood" should be thick enough to fall slowly from the spoon.

3. Tape the protractor to the flat board or object, approximately 10 inches (25 cm) above the ground. The 90 degree mark should be perpendicular to the ground. You can dangle the tape measure or a piece of string to the ground to make sure the 90 degree mark is perpendicular.

4. Fill up the eyedropper with the artificial blood.

5. Have the helper hold the board flat on the paper. Hold the eyedropper at the 90

degree mark and squeeze out a drop. Label the drop 90 degrees.

6. Move the eye dropper to the 60 degree mark. Squeeze out a drop of blood. You may need to squeeze several spurts to get a good drop. Label the drop 60 degrees. Move the object holding the protractor slightly back on the paper so the drop will not mix with the previous drop. Hold the dropper at the 30 degree mark and shoot out several drops. Label the drops 30 degrees.

*Step 5b: Label the drops.* ILLUSTRATION BY TEMAH NELSON.

7. Repeat Step 6, moving the eye dropper to the opposite angle, at the 120 degree and 150 degree mark. You may need to fill up the eyedropper again and move the board with the protractor forward and backwards on the paper. Label each drop.

8. Continue dropping blood at different angles until you can sketch the shape of a drop at each angle. Note its shape and characteristics.

9. Wet the bristles of the hand brush with the artificial blood.

*Step 10: Use the bristles of the hand brush to splatter the blood at a specific angle.* ILLUSTRATION BY TEMAH NELSON.

10. Move the protractor holder to a clean area of paper. Stand back and turn away. Have your helper select an angle and splatter the blood at a specific angle. Your helper may choose to drop the blood from a greater height.

11. Compare the splatter with the test splatters to reconstruct what angle the blood was moving.

12. You may also want to move the brush back and forth to see if you can determine the direction pattern of the blood spatter.

**Summary of Results** Compare all the droplets and spatter marks. Consider the tools that forensic specialists would use to collect and analyze the blood. Sketch the patterns of blood and summarize your results in writing.

## Troubleshooter's Guide

Here is a problem that may arise in this experiment, a possible cause, and a way to remedy it.

**Problem:** The artificial blood does not squirt out of the eye dropper.

**Possible cause:** The opening for the dropper is too small for the liquid. If you cannot find a larger eyedropper, you can make the liquid thinner by adding more ketchup or water.

## Design Your Own Experiment

**How to Select a Topic Relating to this Concept** Forensic science covers a broad ranges of fields and uses a wide range of techniques. Many of the techniques used by forensic investigators draw upon relatively new scientific advances. The techniques have opened up new forms of forensic evidence and improved the traditional types, such as eyewitness recognition.

If you are interested in investigating forensics, you may want to first explore all the different ways evidence is gathered. When you read or watch a mystery, consider the evidence at the crime scene and how forensic scientists could use it. Check the Further Readings section and talk with your science teacher to start gathering information on forensics that interest you.

**Steps in the Scientific Method** To do an original experiment, you need to plan carefully and think things through. Otherwise, you might not be sure what question you are answering, what you are or should be measuring, or what your findings prove or disprove. Here are the steps in designing an experiment:

- State the purpose of—and the underlying question behind—the experiment you propose to do.
- Recognize the variables involved, and select one that will help you answer the question at hand.
- State a testable hypothesis, an educated guess about the answer to your question.
- Decide how to change the variable you selected.
- Decide how to measure your results.

**Recording Data and Summarizing the Results** Your experiment can be useful to others studying the same topic. When designing your experiment, develop a simple method to record your data. This method should be simple and clear enough so that others who want to do the experiment can follow it.

Your final results should be summarized and put into simple graphs, tables, and charts to display the outcome of your experiment.

Related Projects Experiments in forensics can cover collecting and analyzing physical and biological evidence. You may want to investigate evidence collection to determine how training can help people see "crime" details they might have previously missed.

Face recognition is another area of forensics you can investigate. Footprints, tire tracks, and hand prints are other experiment ideas. There are also many experiments in fingerprinting, which can cover the best way to collect ("lift") fingerprints and analyze them. For a research project, you can explore how advances in chemistry, microbiology, and other sciences have changed forensic science.

## For More Information

Gardner, Robert. *Forensic Science Projects with a Crime Lab You Can Build.* Berkeley Heights, NJ: Enslow, 2008. Projects related to forensic science.

Harris, Tom. "How Luminol Works." *Virtual Museum of Canada.* "Virtual Exhibit on Forensic Science." http://www.virtualmuseum.ca/Exhibitions/Myst/en/index.html (accessed on May 19, 2008). Detailed overview, timeline, and a game on forensic science.

*Human Genome Project Information.* "DNA Forensics." http://www.ornl.gov/sci/techresources/Human_Genome/elsi/forensics.shtml (accessed on May 19, 2008). Basic information on DNA fingerprinting.

Layton, Julia. "How Crime Scene Investigations Works." *HowStuffWorks.* http://science.howstuffworks.com/csi4.htm (accessed on May 19, 2008). Information on a range of forensic evidence.

Rainis, Kenneth G. *Hair, Clothing, and Tire Track Evidence: Crime-Solving Science Experiments.* Berkeley Heights, NJ: Enslow, 2006. Science experiments related to forensic science.

# 40

# Fossils

From dinosaurs to prehistoric humans, fossils provide a glimpse into Earth's past events, environment, and life forms. Fossils are the remains or traces of ancient organisms. Fossils can range in age from a mere ten thousand years to several billion years old. They can be microscopic or hundreds of feet long. From the Latin word *fossilis,* meaning something dug up, fossils are found on every continent. Scientists who study fossils are called paleontologists.

Studying fossils has revealed a wealth of data about Earth's 4.6 billion-year-old history, including its past geography, weather, animals, plants, biodiversity, and how life has changed over time. Fossils can provide information on past environmental conditions. Different types of plants, for example, require specific temperature, acidity, and amounts of water to live. By studying fossils, scientists can also determine an ancient animal's age, health, eating habits, and movements. Unearthing 3.5 billion-year-old bacteria fossils led to theories on when life began and how it impacted the development of future life. Other fossil evidence shows how continents have shifted over time. Fossils can also create an understanding of modern Earth and how people can best preserve the planet.

Until about two centuries ago, fossils were mysterious objects that cultures explained in varying ways. Some theorized that fossils were weapons left behind from the gods; others believed they were the seeds of adult animals, or the remains of animals that did not make it onto Noah's ark. In the 1800s, scientists began turning up fossils of strange animals by the thousands: the giant reptilian *ichthyosaur,* the 40-foot (12-meters)-long *Megalosaurus,* and teeth from the immense plant-eating *Iguanodon.* People began to understand what fossils were and, in the late 1800s, fossil hunting began in earnest.

*Ancient rock formations* The vast majority of living organisms live, die, and decay without leaving behind any physical trace of their existence. Paleontologists estimate that only about 1 to 2% of all life forms ever become fossils. In order for a fossil to form, a number of conditions must occur simultaneously. Where an organism settles after death and its surroundings are the main factors that determine fossil formation.

Fossils occur in rocks. The majority of fossils are found in a type of rock called sedimentary rock. Sedimentary rock forms when sediment particles—such as mud, sand, and gravel—settle and form rock. The sediments build up in layers. Thus, the oldest rocks normally lie on the bottom layer and the youngest at the top. Sedimentary rock is the type of rock most exposed at Earth's surface. Shale, limestone, and sandstone are examples of sedimentary rock.

One common fossilization process, called permineralization, creates a three-dimensional replica of the remains when minerals replace some or all of the organic matter. The first step in permineralization is for a dead organism to become buried in sediment quickly, before it is eaten or decomposed by other organisms. Over the next several hundred thousand years, layers of sediments cover the dead organism.

The quicker a dead organism is covered with layers of sediment the greater its chance of being preserved. How quickly sediment covers a dead life form also determines the degree of preservation. Organisms are made up of soft parts, such as skin and tissue, which decompose quickly. Animals will eat them, microorganisms will break them down, and weather will erode them. In general, these parts decompose before they

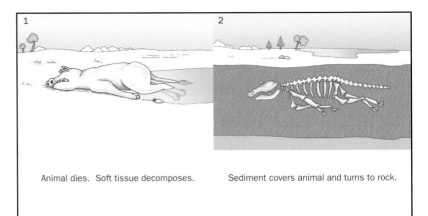

*Turning bone into rock: the fossilization process of permineralization.* GALE GROUP.

Animal dies. Soft tissue decomposes.

Sediment covers animal and turns to rock.

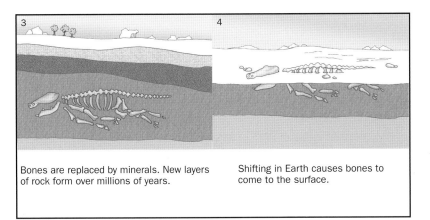

Bones are replaced by minerals. New layers of rock form over millions of years.

Shifting in Earth causes bones to come to the surface.

*Permineralization continues. When the organic matter is completely replaced by minerals it is called petrifaction.* GALE GROUP.

are protected by sediments, leaving only the hard parts of the dead organism, such as teeth, bones, and shells.

As the sediment turns into rock, minerals and water from the rock seep into the remains. Slowly, these minerals fill in the open pore spaces of the organism's remains. When the organic matter is completely replaced by minerals it is called petrifaction. The result is a duplicate of the structure made of rock. Petrifaction commonly occurs in wood. One of the largest examples of petrifaction is at the Petrified Forest National Park in Arizona, which holds acres of 200-million-year-old logs that have turned to stone.

Even after a fossil is formed, a set of circumstances still must occur before it can be found. Shifting landmasses, weather eruptions, and natural disasters can destroy the fossil. The rock must also move towards a top layer of Earth in order for it to be exposed. This may occur over millions of years as the rock is pushed to the surface, or human activity can expose it.

*Forming other fossils* Another type of fossil occurs when no part of the organism's body remains. A fossil mold is an imprint of a bone, shell, or other hard body part. A mold forms when the dead organism settles in sediment and then decays, leaving an outline of its shape. If the mold fills with minerals it is called a cast. The rock cast has the same outer three-dimensional shape as the organism. Paleontologists often create casts of fossil molds by filling them with liquids, such as plaster, that harden.

Body parts of ancient plants, insects, spiders, and other small animals are also found preserved in tree resin. Fossils form when one of these

*The imprint of a 200-million-year-old fossilized plant discovered in 2002.* AP/WIDE WORLD

creatures becomes trapped inside the sticky resin, which hardens to become a substance called amber. These life forms are often preserved with incredible detail. Some are so well preserved that scientists have attempted to extract the organism's genetic material, the deoxyribonucleic acid (DNA) molecule.

Fossils that are not part of the animal or plant are called trace fossils. Examples of trace fossils include footprints, tunnels, and dung. Trace fossils provide evidence of the organism's physical characteristics, eating habits, and activities. Examining fossilized droppings or dung, called coprolites, can supply evidence of where an animal lived and what it ate. A footprint can reveal an animal's weight, size, and whether it hopped, sprinted, or walked.

Because an animal sets down many hundreds of thousands of traces during its lifetime, but leaves only one body, paleontologists find trace fossils far more frequently than body fossils.

*The dating game* In order to piece together a timeline of life on Earth, scientists need to understand a fossil's age and how it relates to others. This information for all fossils is documented in the fossil record, a key source in understanding how species have evolved. Some organisms dominate the fossil record more than others because of certain physical characteristics. For example, fossils of animals without bones or shells are far more rare than those with hard parts. Marine animals are preserved more readily than land animals because they are more likely to be preserved in soft sediment. This is one reason why estimating the existence span of a species, its first appearance until its extinction, is one of the most challenging parts of the fossil record.

One way to date a fossil is to determine its relative age, or how old it is in relation to other fossils or rocks. Unless the rock layers were overturned, fossils found in lower rock layers would be older than those found in upper layers. Fossilized rock with similar features and different locations are compared and placed relative to each other in the fossil record.

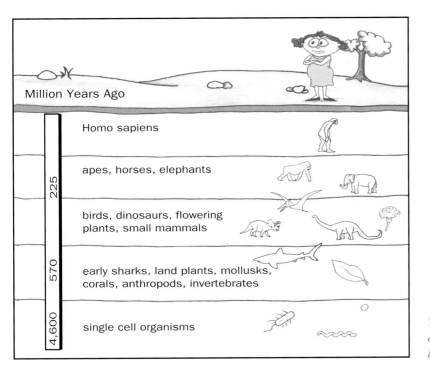

Million Years Ago

Homo sapiens

apes, horses, elephants

225

birds, dinosaurs, flowering plants, small mammals

570

early sharks, land plants, mollusks, corals, anthropods, invertebrates

4,600

single cell organisms

*The fossil record traces organisms through Earth's history.* GALE GROUP.

Absolute dating is a more precise approach that determines how many years old the fossil is from the current year. These methods were developed in the twentieth century with the findings of the known rate of decay of certain radioactive elements. Each element decays at its own constant and unique rate. Radioisotope dating techniques measure the amount of a certain element in nearby rocks to date the fossil.

While relatively precise, absolute dating provides only an approximate date for the organism, accurate to hundreds of thousands of years. One type of absolute dating method examines the amount of the element carbon 14 found in the rock. All plant and animal life absorb carbon 14, and its rate of decomposition is known. This method is useful on material that is less than about 50,000 years old, which includes many human remains but excludes most fossils. For older fossils, scientists measure the amount of other radioactive elements left in rock, such as potassium, thorium, and uranium.

*Discovered in the European nation of Georgia and dated by scientists at 1.7 million years, these partial human-like skulls are the oldest human ancestral fossils ever found outside of Africa.* AP/WIDE WORLD

## WORDS TO KNOW

**Absolute dating:** The age of an object correlated to a specific fixed time, as established by some precise dating method.

**Cast:** In paleontology, the fossil formed when a mold is later filled in by mud or mineral matter.

**Coprolites:** The fossilized droppings of animals.

**Control experiment:** A setup that is identical to the experiment, but is not affected by the variable that acts on the experimental group.

**Fossil:** The remains, trace, or impressions of a living organism that inhabited Earth more than ten thousand years ago.

**Fossil record:** The documentation of fossils placed in relationship to one another; a key source to understand the evolution of life on Earth.

**Hypothesis:** An idea in the form of a statement that can be tested by observation and/or experiment.

**Mold:** In paleontology, the fossil formed when acidic water dissolves a shell or bone around which sand or mud has already hardened.

**Paleontologist:** Scientist who studies the life of past geological periods as known from fossil remains.

**Permineralization:** A form of preservation in which mineral matter has filled in the inner and outer spaces of the cell.

**Petrifaction:** Process of turning organic material into rock by the replacement of that material with minerals.

**Radioisotope dating:** A technique used to date fossils, based on the decay rate of known radioactive elements.

**Relative age:** The age of an object expressed in relation to another like object, such as earlier or later.

**Sediment:** Sand, silt, clay, rock, gravel, mud, or other matter that has been transported by flowing water.

**Sedimentary rock:** Rock formed from compressed and solidified layers of organic or inorganic matter.

**Variable:** Something that can affect the results of an experiment.

## EXPERIMENT 1

## Making an Impression: In which soil environment does a fossil most easily form?

Purpose/Hypothesis Paleontologists have found fossils on every continent, yet some areas contain more fossils than others. One of the key factors leading to fossil formation is the type of sediment or material in which a dead organism settles. (Most organisms settle where they die; in some cases a river, wind, or animals can carry the organism to another location.) Scientist use fossils to study and determine the lifestyles and adaptations of plants and animals. The more details found in a fossil, the more information the scientists gain.

In this experiment, you will determine how the soil makeup of different geographical areas impacts the number of fossil casts formed. You will make three fossil casts in three soils of varying moisture content. One of the soils will be dry sand. Sand is made up of large particles and does not hold moisture. A second type of soil will be a mixture between sand and moist topsoil, which is made up of smaller soil particles that retain water. The third soil will be a wet topsoil.

These soils will be the foundation layer for a plaster of paris cast. Using one object, a shell, you will first press the organism into each soil to equal depths. The plaster of paris will form a cast from this mold. This cast will be the fossil.

## What Are the Variables?

Variables are anything that might affect the results of an experiment. Here are the main variables in this experiment:

- the soil makeup
- the consistency of the plaster of paris
- the object/organism
- the depth the object is pressed

In other words, the variables in this experiment are everything that might affect the ability of the object to make an impression. If you change more than one variable at the same time, you will not be able to tell which variable had the most effect on the impression.

To begin this experiment, make an educated guess about the outcome of the experiment based upon your knowledge of fossils and sediment. This educated guess, or prediction, is your hypothesis. A hypothesis should explain these things:

- the topic of the experiment
- the variable you will change
- the variable you will measure
- what you expect to happen

A hypothesis should be brief, specific, and measurable. It must be something you can test through further investigation. Your experiment will prove or disprove whether your hypothesis is correct. Here is one possible hypothesis for this experiment: "The moist soil will make the best fossil impression; the dry material will not be firm enough to cause a fossil to form."

Once you have gathered your soil bases you need to make your impressions. It is best to use a seashell with distinguishing qualities such as scallops, ridges, and possibly an erosion hole or chip.

The variable you will change will be the soil. The variable you will measure will be the general shape and amount of detail of the impression. The item you use to make the impression should stay the same.

## How to Experiment Safely

Be careful when removing your fossil casts; plastic containers may break.

**Level of Difficulty** Easy to Moderate.

**Materials Needed**

- plaster of paris (available at craft stores)
- shell, preferably one with identifiable features such as a hole, chip, or alternate mark
- 3 small disposable containers, such as a butter dish, large enough to fit the shell
- water
- disposable spoons
- measuring spoon
- ruler
- straw
- tweezers
- marking pen
- bowl
- 3 cups (0.75 liters) of sand (available at garden store)
- 3 cups (0.75 liters) of moist, organic topsoil (available at garden store)

**Approximate Budget** $5 to $10.

**Timetable** 1 hour for the experiment; overnight for the plaster of paris to harden.

**Step-by-Step Instructions**

1. Make a sketch of your shell, noting the width, depth, and any identifiable features.
2. In a bowl, mix 1 cup (about 0.25 liters) of moist topsoil with 1 cup (about 0.25 liters) of sand. This is the moist soil.
3. Mix 2 cups (about 0.5 liters) of topsoil with 8 tablespoons (about 120 milliliters) water. This is the wet soil.
4. Label each container with the type of soil and place each soil type into the appropriate container. The soil should be at

*Step 6: Push the straw down until the mark on the straw is level with the soil.* GALE GROUP.

least 2 inches (5 centimeters) deep. Even out the surface of the soil.

5. Use the ruler to mark a line on the straw at 0.8 inches (2 centimeters).

6. Place your shell in the soil with the ridges facing down. Gently place the straw in the center of the shell. Push the straw down with your pointer finger until the mark on the straw is level with the soil.

7. Using tweezers, carefully remove your shell.

8. Wash and dry the shell. Repeat Step 6 for the other two soil samples.

9. Mix enough plaster of paris to make a 1-inch-deep (2.5-centimeters) layer in each container. The plaster should be the consistency of thick pudding.

10. Pour a layer of plaster of paris into each container.

11. Allow plaster to harden overnight.

12. Remove your fossil casts by slipping a butter knife or similar thin object in the side between the soil, fossil, and container. It may be necessary to break the plastic containers.

13. Make sketches of each cast. (If a digital camera or Polaroid is available, you could take pictures.) Include any measurements of width and depth you are able to determine from your fossil cast.

---

## Troubleshooter's Guide

Below is a problem that may arise during this experiment, a possible cause, and a way to remedy the problem.

**Problem:** You have no fossils, only a lump of plaster.

**Possible cause:** All of your soil samples may have been too loose. It may be necessary to choose a soil sample that has a more solid consistency.

---

**Summary of Results** Review the sketches of the casts compared to that of the shell. Which soil type is best for making fossils? What qualities did you compare to determine the best soil? Note on the sketch or photograph where any information can be observed on the fossil. For example, a shell may have a hole in one point that can indicate erosion. What type(s) of environments do you feel are most suitable for fossils to form? From your conclusions, how would the environment impact the study of species through fossils?

**Change the Variables** To change the variable in this experiment, you could use different objects to make the cast. Try both heavier and lighter objects. You could also change the soil type, creating a wet mud soil and comparing that to the dry sand. Another way to alter the experiment is to vary the thickness of the soil layer.

## What Are the Variables?

Variables are anything that might affect the results of an experiment. Here are the main variables in this experiment:

- the hardness of the organism
- the definable shape of the organism
- the flexibility of the organism
- force applied to make mold
- placement of the object on clay base

In other words, the variables in this experiment are everything that might affect the organism's imprint. If you change more than one variable at the same time, you will not be able to tell which variable had the most effect on the physical characteristics of each organism's mold.

## EXPERIMENT 2

## Fossil Formation: What are the physical characteristics of an organism that make the best fossils?

Purpose/Hypothesis Organisms vary from the microscopic and jelly-bodied to the mammoth and skeletal. The physical characteristics of the organism and its environment are two key factors in forming a fossil. Dating back about 3,500 million years, the fossil record does not represent all types of organisms equally. Paleontologists theorize that many groups of animals and plants have left no fossil remains. There are some types of organisms that are more dominant in the record than others. There are some organisms that have hard parts, some with only soft parts, and many with both. Examples of hard parts include bones, teeth, and wood; examples of soft parts include skin, muscle, and internal organs.

In this experiment, you will examine how an organism's characteristics determine the fossil remains left behind. You will create a fossil mold out of four different types of organisms or parts from organisms.

You will begin by preparing a clay base for each of the items you are going to fossilize. Clay is a soft, moist substance similar to the watery sediment that preserves many fossils. You will first select four organisms to observe from four different categories: an exoskeleton, meaning skeletal bones on the outside; an endoskeleton, meaning an internal skeleton; an organism without a skeleton; and a plant. Examples of these four categories are a shell (exoskeleton), chicken bone (endoskeleton), feather (lacking a skeleton), and a leaf (plant).

Each organism has physical characteristics that you can note before forming its imprint. Characteristics include if the organism has hard or soft parts, its shape, width, height, and any distinguishing features. To form an imprint you will drop a heavy book from the same height to make sure you use the same amount of pressure for each organism. After making an imprint of each organism, you can then compare the characteristics of the organism and the fossil imprint it makes.

Before you begin, make an educated guess about the outcome of this experiment based on your knowledge of fossilization. This educated guess, or prediction, is your hypothesis. A hypothesis should explain these things:

- the topic of the experiment
- the variable you will change
- the variable you will measure
- what you expect to happen

A hypothesis should be brief, specific, and measurable. It must be something you can test through further investigation. Your experiment will prove or disprove whether your hypothesis is correct. Here is one possible hypothesis for this experiment: "The feather will produce a poor fossil that is difficult to identify because it has no specific shape or form; the chicken bone will produce the best fossil imprint."

In this case, the variable you will change is the organism. The variable you will measure is the physical characteristics of the mold created by the organism.

Level of Difficulty Moderate.

Materials Needed

- modeling clay
- plant (leaf, fern)
- chicken bone, or another small bone
- shell (or other object to represent an endoskeleton)
- feather (or other object lacking a skeleton)
- heavy book
- ruler
- pencils
- magnifying lens
- wax paper
- tape
- four pieces of cardboard

Approximate Budget $8.

Timetable 60 to 90 minutes.

|  | shell | bone | feather | fern |
|---|---|---|---|---|
| hard/softness of organism |  |  |  |  |
| sketch of organism's shape |  |  |  |  |
| sketch of mold's shape |  |  |  |  |
| features of organism |  |  |  |  |
| features of mold |  |  |  |  |
| height & width of organism |  |  |  |  |
| height & width of mold |  |  |  |  |

*Step 1: Data chart for Experiment 2.* GALE GROUP.

*Step 6: Drop a heavy object from the same height onto each organism.* GALE GROUP.

### Step-by-Step Instructions

1. Create a data chart, listing the organisms across the top columns and the observable characteristics down the sides. Make the chart boxes large enough to illustrate your observation and include descriptive words.

2. Feel each organism prior to making the fossil mold and note whether it is hard, soft, or both.

3. Draw a sketch of your organism. Measure the height and width and include in the sketch.

4. Cover each piece of cardboard with a sheet of wax paper, and then create four clay bases. Make the bases of equal size and thickness. The base should be about twice as high as the highest organisms, and be at least 1 inch (2.5 centimeter) larger in diameter than the largest object.

5. Gently place the first organism in the center of the first clay base. Do not apply pressure.

6. Place the clay base against a wall (or any flat, vertical object) and tape the ruler against the wall perpendicular to the base. Hold the book about 2 inches (5 centimeters) above the clay base with the organism on it, and drop the book. The height of the book above the organism does not have to be exactly 2 inches (5 centimeters); however, whatever the height is, use that same height for all organisms.

7. Remove the book and gently remove the organism.

8. Repeat Steps 5 through 7 for each organism.

9. Use the ruler to reexamine the same physical characteristics that you noted for the organism and note the results on your chart. Use the magnifying glass to observe any distinguishing features in the mold.

**Summary of Results** Examine your chart. Which qualities are the most varied among your organisms? Which mold provides the most accurate information? How does the detail of the mold relate to whether the organism is hard or soft? What are some other characteristics on the organism that the mold does not convey? Hypothesize what would occur to each material if you used a lighter book. Analyze what would happen to each organism if it was turned over and the imprint was made of the other side. Write a brief summary of the experiment and your analysis.

> ## Troubleshooter's Guide
>
> Below is a problem that may arise during this experiment, a possible cause, and a way to remedy the problem.
>
> **Problem:** There was no imprint on any or most of the objects.
>
> **Possible cause:** You may not have used enough force to press down on the object. Repeat the experiment, using a heavier book or raising the book to a higher measurement on the ruler.

**Change the Variables** There are several ways you can modify the experiment by changing the variables. You can change the organisms you use. Try several different samples from the same class; for example, in the plants you could use a flower, a leaf, and a cactus. You can also alter the substance that sets the imprint formation. You could try dough made of a mixture of used coffee grounds, cold coffee, flour, and salt. How would this moist base impact your experiment? Another way to alter the variable is to change the force used to press down on the object in the clay.

**Modify the Experiment** You can modify this experiment by filling the impressions with Plaster of Paris. The Plaster of Paris represents the mud or sediment that will fill the form. Follow the experiment, noting the characteristics each of the four organisms leaves in the clay.

Keep track of which clay model has which organism imprint. (It might be hard to tell them apart when they are covered with Plaster of Paris.) Mix up the Plaster of Paris, and spoon the plaster onto the clay until the impressions are filled. Allow the plaster to harden then carefully remove it from the clay. Use a magnifying glass to examine the mold. How do the imprints in the mold compare to the imprints in the clay?

## Design Your Own Experiment

**How to Select a Topic Relating to this Concept** Fossils open a window into Earth's life, geography, and environment that can reach back billions of years. To think of fossil-related projects, you can make a list of all ancient events and people you have learned about and consider how fossils could have been used to gather the data.

Check the Further Readings section and talk with your science teacher to learn more about fossils. You can also gather ideas for topics by visiting a natural history museum or science museum.

**Steps in the Scientific Method** To conduct an original experiment, you need to plan carefully and think things through. Otherwise, you might not be sure what question you are answering, what you are or should be measuring, or what your findings prove or disprove.

Here are the steps in designing an experiment:

- State the purpose of—and the underlying question behind—the experiment you propose to do.
- Recognize the variables involved and select one that will help you answer the question at hand.
- State your hypothesis, an educated guess about the answer to your question.
- Decide how to change the variable you selected.
- Decide how to measure your results.

**Recording Data and Summarizing the Results** In any experiment you conduct, you should look for ways to clearly convey your data. Your data

*Paleontologists excavating a fossil bed in Utah.* © JAMES L. AMOS/CORBIS.

should include charts and drawings such as the one you did for these experiments. They should be clearly labeled and easy to read. You may also want to include photographs and drawings of your experimental setup and results, which will help other people visualize the steps in the experiment.

If you are preparing an exhibit, you may want to display your results, such as any experimental setup you designed. If you have completed a nonexperimental project, explain clearly what your research question was and illustrate your findings.

Related Projects There are many project ideas that relate to fossils. If there is a museum or university in the area in which you can see fossils, you can compare the different types of preservation, including petrifaction and fossils preserved in amber (these are sold by several companies). For a research project, you could explore the environmental conditions of areas that are rich with fossils, both in the United States and other parts of the world. You can explore fossil molds and imprints by examining how the environment or other factors play a part in the fossilization process.

How paleontologists collect fossils is another area of study. Identifying and collecting fossils is a meticulous process that requires many skills. There are many organizations and companies that offer fossil hunts, complete with lessons on how to locate, unearth, and identify fossils. Dinosaurs are a popular topic for documentaries and movies. You can examine these films to look at how the filmmakers reached their representation of these creatures, how much of it was artistic freedom, and what was taken from the fossil record. For example, do paleontologists know that dinosaurs were certain colors? How do the more modern representations of dinosaurs differ from those made in the mid-1900s?

## For More Information

BBC. "Prehistoric Life" *Science and Nature: Prehistoric Life*. http://www.bbc.co.uk/sn/prehistoric_life/index.shtml (accessed on March 13, 2008). Radio, animations, and explanations of prehistoric life and fossil evidence.

"Fossil Gallery." *The Paleontology Portal*. http://www.paleoportal.org/index.php?globalnav=fossil_gallery&sectionnav=main (accessed on March 13, 2008). Choose a time period to see images of fossils.

Kittinger, Jo S. *Stories in Stone: The World of Animal Fossils*. New York: Franklin Watts, 1998. Photographs accompany information on various types of fossils and how they help people understand life on Earth.

"Rocks and Layers." *U.S. Geological Survey.* http://pubs.usgs.gov/gip/fossils/rocks-layers.html (accessed on March 13, 2008). Brief description of where fossils are found in rocks.

San Diego Natural History Museum. "Finding Fossils." *Dinosaur Dig.* http://www.bbc.co.uk/sn/prehistoric_life/index.shtml (accessed on March 13, 2008). Information on how to look for and identify fossils.

"Tour of geologic time." *University of California Museum of Paleontology.* http://www.ucmp.berkeley.edu/exhibits/geologictime.php (accessed on March 13, 2008). Information on the geologic time periods of Earth.

Trueit, Trudi Strain. *Fossils.* New York: Franklin Watts, 2003. What fossils look like, and how paleontologists use them to understand Earth.

# 41

# Fungi

As a way of organizing living things, scientists have created five main classifications called kingdoms (some scientists use more than five). Each kingdom breaks down into smaller and smaller classifications. Plants and animals, for example, are two of these kingdoms. Fungi form another kingdom.

There are thousands of types of fungi. They are both single-celled and multicelled; living on land and in water. They include the microscopic, such as yeasts, and the relatively mammoth, such as mushrooms. Scoop up a single teaspoon of topsoil and you will find about 120,000 fungi. One of the largest living organisms on Earth is a fungus. It is called the humongous fungus and extends about 3.5 miles (5.6 kilometers).

Fungi play a vital role in Earth's cycle of life. They decompose or break down dead bugs and plant material, such as leaves, converting their components into elements that living organisms can reuse. They are an essential source of food for plants and animals. Many plants depend on fungi for their nutrients. Fungi also have had a profound effect on human life. Take a look at a moldy fruit and you are observing a type of fungi that has transformed modern medicine. People eat fungi and use them to manufacture bread, wine, and flavorings. Fungi can also cause plant and animal diseases. In humans, dandruff and athlete's foot are two wide-spread examples of disease caused by fungi.

*It's a plant ... It's an animal ... It's a ...* People once classified fungi as part of the plant kingdom. Years later they thought these creatures were part of the animal kingdom. As scientists learned more about this varied group of life, they found all fungi share characteristics that make them a unique kingdom.

Fungi are eukaryotic (pronounced yoo-KAR-ee-ah-tic) organisms, meaning that their DNA or genetic material is enclosed in a nucleus. A nucleus is the round or oval structure inside a cell that is surrounded by a

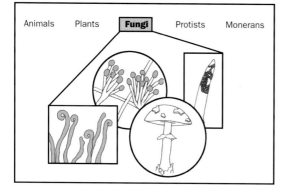

| Animals | Plants | **Fungi** | Protists | Monerans |

*Fungi are one of the five kingdoms that scientists use to classify living organisms.*
GALE GROUP.

*Some fungi are decomposers, breaking down dead organic matter as they draw nutrients from it. A fungus that grows on fallen leaves is an example of a decomposer.* © GARY BRAASCH/CORBIS.

protective envelope. Fungi need air, food, and water to live. They thrive in moist, warm environments, such as the underside of a rock or the space between a person's toes. Most types of fungi do not depend on sunlight for energy, as plants do. Because of this, they thrive in dark areas, such as caves and in soil.

Fungi do not manufacture their own food. To grow, fungi draw nutrients from the materials on which they live. Some fungi are decomposers, breaking down dead organic matter as they draw nutrients from it. A fungus that grows on a rotting tree or fallen leaves is an example of a decomposer.

Fungi that grow on living animals and plants are called parasites. Parasites take the materials from the creature, or host, sometimes harming the organism in the process. A fungus that lives on a plant's roots, for example, receives its food from the plant. Ringworm is an example of a human fungal parasite. Fruit that has mold on it, called a blight, is an example of a plant fungal parasite.

One unique type of fungi is the lichen. Commonly found on rocks, trees, and buildings, lichens are composed of fungi living in partnership with one or more other types of organism. One common lichen unites fungi with green algae. In this lichen, algae produce food for the fungi and fungi provide an outer layer of protection for the algae.

There are microscopic single-celled fungi, but the majority of fungi are more complex. Multicelled fungi string their cells together in long, threadlike strands called hyphae (pronounced HIGH-fee). The hyphae produce chemicals that break down the complex nutrients of its food source into simpler forms. These nutrients are absorbed through the walls of the hyphae, and flow between their cells. In search of food, hyphae spread outwards underneath the visible part of the fungi. The tangled mass of hyphae forms a network called a mycelium. Myceliums range in size from clumps of mold to systems that stretch for miles (kilometers). A fungus's mycelium can expand quickly, adding up to a kilometer of new hyphae per day.

*Reproducing styles* Most fungi reproduce by releasing tiny particles called spores. Usually composed of a single cell, spores are smaller than dust particles and float through the air. A spore contains all the chemicals needed to make its fungus. Wind and water are the two main ways spores spread. Animals can also carry the spores. For example, the stinkhorn fungi produce an odor that attracts flies and beetles, which then carry the spores away.

Spores can end up everywhere—they are in the air, on clothes, plants, and skin. When the spore encounters the right conditions it will grow and develop into the individual fungus.

*Fungi that grow on living animals and plants are called parasites. Fruit that has mold on it is an example of a plant fungal parasite.* COPYRIGHT © KELLY A. QUIN.

Fungi can also reproduce by growing and extending their hyphae. Hyphae grow as new cells form at the tips, creating ever-longer chains of cells. Many yeasts reproduce by budding. In budding, a parent yeast pushes out its cell to form a bud. In time, the bud pinches off and a new yeast cell is produced.

*Popular fungi* Fungi can cause diseases in plants and animals. Yet there are many types of fungi that humans commonly use, from tasty treats to medicines.

Mold: Mold is a type of fungi. It was a few of these stray mold spores that altered the treatment of bacterial diseases throughout the world. In 1928, British bacteriologist Alexander Fleming (1881–1955) was growing the *Staphylococcus* bacteria in his laboratory for study. Bacteria are a type of microscopic organism, some of which can cause disease. At that time, bacterial infections were sweeping throughout the world and killing millions of people.

*The tangled mass of hyphae forms a network called a mycelium.* GALE GROUP.

One day Fleming accidentally left a dish of bacteria uncovered on his lab bench before he took a vacation. When he returned Fleming noticed the dish was crowded with bacterial growth except for one clear area where a patch of mold was growing. The mold had produced a substance that stopped bacteria from growing. Fleming named the substance penicillin, after the *Penicillium* mold.

Years later during World War II (1939–1945) scientists Howard Florey and Ernst Chain continued Fleming's work. Bacterial infections were

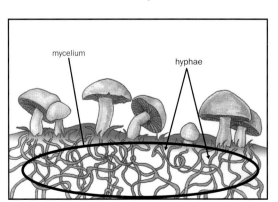

*Most fungi reproduce by releasing spores that float through the air and grow when they find the right environment.* GALE GROUP.

*Many yeasts reproduce by budding.* GALE GROUP.

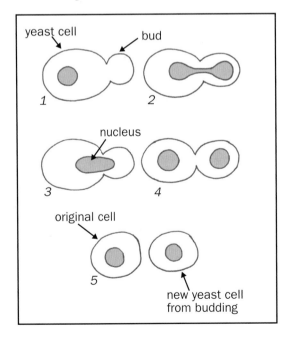

common in the war and were causing many soldiers to die. The scientists found penicillin effective against a wide range of harmful bacteria and they began to mass-produce it. Penicillin became the first antibiotic. Antibiotics weaken or destroy bacteria and other organisms that cause diseases. The success of penicillin led to the developments of many other antibiotics, such as streptomycin, that stop the spread of disease.

**Mushrooms:** Mushrooms are one of the most familiar types of fungi. They can grow in damp soil and rotting wood. Although some mushrooms are edible to humans, many of these fungi contain harmful poisons. Eating even a small bite of some types, such as the white destroying angel mushroom, can kill a healthy adult.

The common mushrooms found in grocery stores produce their spores from gills located under their umbrella-like cap. A single mushroom can produce about two billion spores. The main part of the mushroom, its hyphae, lives underground. Cup-shaped mushrooms are part of another fungi group and they carry their spores in tiny pouches. Types of these mushrooms are rare and highly valued, For example, truffles are delicacies that belong to this group. Truffles live completely underground. Truffle hunters use highly trained pigs and dogs to sniff out their location.

**Yeast:** Yeasts are single-celled fungi that belong to the same group as the truffles. These cells look like little round or oval blobs under a microscope. Clusters of yeast create a white powdery appearance. They are commonly found on leaves, flowers, soil, and fruits.

Bakers have long made use of a natural process in yeast called fermentation. Yeasts eat a form of sugar or starch. In fermentation, yeasts break down the sugars and starches into carbon dioxide gas and alcohol. The carbon dioxide gas bubbles, causing an expansion or rising of the material around it. People use yeast to make bread rise, and produce the alcohol in beer and wine.

## WORDS TO KNOW

**Antibiotic:** A substance produced by or derived from certain fungi and other organisms, that can destroy or inhibit the growth of other microorganisms.

**Control experiment:** A setup that is identical to the experiment, but is not affected by the variable that acts on the experimental group.

**Eukaryotic:** Multicellular organism whose cells contain distinct nuclei, which contain the genetic material. (Pronounced yoo-KAR-ee-ah-tic)

**Fermentation:** A chemical reaction in which enzymes break down complex organic compounds (for example, carbohydrates and sugars) into simpler ones (for example, ethyl alcohol).

**Fungi:** Kingdom of various single-celled or multi-cellular organisms, including mushrooms, molds, yeasts, and mildews, that do not manu-facture their own food.

**Hypha:** Slender, cottony filaments making up the body of multicellular fungi. (Plural: hyphae)

**Hypothesis:** An idea in the form of a statement that can be tested by observation and/or experiment.

**Kingdom:** One of the five classifications in the widely accepted classification system that designates all living organisms into animals, plants, fungi, protists, and monerans.

**Mycelium:** In fungi, the mass of threadlike, branching hyphae.

**Nucleus:** Membrane-enclosed structure within a cell that contains the cell's genetic material and controls its growth and reproduction. (Plural: nuclei.)

**Spore:** A small, usually one-celled, reproductive body that is capable of growing into a new organism.

**Variable:** Something that can affect the results of an experiment.

In the following two experiments, you will explore how yeast breaks down food and in what environment it grows best. For an experiment on food spoilage and the fungi mold, see the Spoilage chapter.

## EXPERIMENT 1

## Decomposers: Food source for a common fungi

Purpose/Hypothesis Decomposition is a critical part of Earth's cycle of life. In this experiment you will examine how fungi affect decomposition. You will use a banana as the food source for the fungi. This fruit provides a moist environment and other conditions that promote yeast growth. For the fungi you will use dry yeast that is used in cooking. The yeast

## What Are the Variables?

Variables are anything that might affect the results of an experiment. Here are the main variables in this experiment:

- the food source (fruit)
- the type of fungi
- environmental conditions, such as temperature and humidity
- exposure to air

In other words, the variables in this experiment are everything that might affect the decomposition of the fruit. If you change more than one variable at the same time, you will not be able to tell which variable had the most effect on the decomposition.

becomes activated when it is given a source of moisture. You will place the yeast on a banana and then observe how it affects the fruit. Changes to the fruit can include changes in color, breaks in the skin, and odor.

Before you begin, make an educated guess about the outcome of this experiment based on your knowledge of fungi and decomposition. This educated guess, or prediction, is your hypothesis. A hypothesis should explain these things:

- the topic of the experiment
- the variable you will change
- the variable you will measure
- what you expect to happen

A hypothesis should be brief, specific, and measurable. It must be something you can test through further investigation. Your experiment will prove or disprove whether your hypothesis is correct. Here is one possible hypothesis for this experiment: "Yeast will cause the banana to decompose more rapidly than it would without the yeast."

In this case, the variable you will change is the addition of yeast to the banana. The variable you will measure is the description of the banana.

Conducting a control experiment will help you isolate each variable and measure the changes in the dependent variable. Only one variable will change between the control and your experiment. For your control in this experiment you will use a plain banana. At the end of the experiment you can compare the control and the experimental results.

**Level of Difficulty** Easy.

**Materials Needed**

- dry yeast, about 1 tablespoon
- 1 banana
- 2 self-sealing plastic bags or plastic bags with twisty ties

## How to Experiment Safely

Be careful when handling the knife. Do not taste or ingest any food in this experiment.

- knife
- marking pen

**Approximate Budget** $3.

**Timetable** 15 minutes setup; five minutes daily for about a week.

**Step-by-Step Instructions**

1. Peel the banana and slice two pieces. (You may want to cut it in half first lengthwise.)
2. Place a slice of banana inside each plastic bag.
3. Sprinkle dry yeast on one slice.
4. Label the bag with the yeast "Yeast" and the bag without the yeast "Control."
5. Seal or tie both bags shut and leave them in a warm place.
6. Observe the bags daily for one week. Each day write a brief description of how each banana appears. On the final day, note the difference, if any, between the two banana pieces. Observe changes in color, breaks in the skin, odors, and physical changes in the shape, size, or consistency (hard, soft, mushy) of the fruit.

**Summary of Results** Look at the description of your results. Which banana slice shows the most and fastest decomposition? Was your hypothesis correct?

**Change the Variables** There are several ways to change the variables in this experiment. You can alter the fungi's food source by using another fruit, fruit skin, or other item. Make sure the food source contains some moisture to activate the yeast. You can also use another type of fungi. If necessary, you can purchase a specific fungi from a biological supply company. Another way is to change the environment of the fruit, such as by placing one piece in a dark area and one in a bright area.

## Troubleshooter's Guide

Below is a problem that may arise during this experiment, some possible causes, and some ways to remedy the problem.

**Problem:** The banana pieces decomposed at equal rates.

**Possible cause:** You may have used yeast that was dead. Check the expiration date of your yeast and, if necessary, purchase more. Repeat the experiment using the new yeast.

*Step 5: Seal or tie both bags and leave in a warm place.* GALE GROUP.

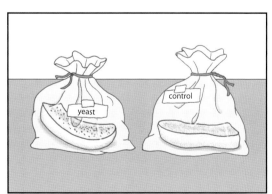

## EXPERIMENT 2

## Living Conditions: What is the ideal temperature for yeast growth?

Purpose/Hypothesis People have long taken advantage of the natural fermentation process of yeasts to produce foods, including alcohol and risen bread. (Ancient cultures' use of fermentation is one of the earliest uses of biotechnology, which applies living organisms for human use.) Bakers commonly use the *Saccharomyces cerevisiae* yeast to produce carbon dioxide, which causes bread to rise.

In this experiment you will examine in which conditions yeasts best live and grow. Yeasts kept in the most suitable living conditions will be the most active; those kept in less suitable conditions will not be as active. You will pour equal amounts of yeast into similar bottles and provide the yeast with water and a food source, sugar. Each bottle of yeast will be given a different growth environment: one warm and one cold. You will compare them to a third bottle kept at room temperature.

You will measure the activity of the yeast by measuring the amount of carbon dioxide the yeast releases. You can do this in two ways. To measure the carbon dioxide, you will seal the opening of the bottle with an empty balloon. The carbon dioxide gas produced will cause the balloon to inflate. Every twenty minutes you will measure the amount of gas produced by measuring the circumference of the balloon. Another way to measure the carbon dioxide is to measure the acidity of the yeast solution. Carbon dioxide mixes with water in the yeast solution to form a weak acid, called carbonic acid. The more carbon dioxide produced, the more acidic the solution. You will use acid/base indicator strips to check the level of acidity after you remove the balloon.

Before you begin, make an educated guess about the outcome of this experiment based on your knowledge of fungi. This educated guess, or prediction, is your hypothesis. A hypothesis should explain these things:

- the topic of the experiment
- the variable you will change
- the variable you will measure
- what you expect to happen

A hypothesis should be brief, specific, and measurable. It must be something you can test through further investigation. Your experiment will prove or disprove whether your hypothesis is correct. Here is one possible hypothesis for this experiment: "The yeast given the warmest environment will grow the most rapidly and produce the most carbon dioxide gas; the yeast in the coldest environment will grow the least rapidly and produce the least gas."

In this case, the variable you will change is the temperature of the yeast's environment. The variable you will measure is the amount of carbon dioxide produced.

Conducting a control experiment will help you isolate each variable and measure the changes in the dependent variable. Only one variable will change between the control and your experiment. The control you will use for this experiment is a room temperature environment (water) for the yeast. Before you introduce the yeast to its environment, you will measure the acidity of the plain sugar-water to have a control for the acidity level. At the end of the experiment you can compare the control results with the experimental results.

## What Are the Variables?

Variables are anything that might affect the results of an experiment. Here are the main variables in this experiment:

- temperature
- type of fungi (the yeast)
- quantity of the fungi
- type of food source (the sugar)
- quantity of the food source

In other words, the variables in this experiment are everything that might affect the amount of carbon dioxide produced from the yeast. If you change more than one variable at the same time, you will not be able to tell which variable had the most effect on the yeast's growth.

Level of Difficulty Moderate.

Materials Needed

- 3 identical small glass or plastic bottles with narrow mouths
- 3 balloons
- 3 packets of dry yeast (not rapid-rising)
- about 9 teaspoons of sugar
- string
- tape
- ice cubes
- hot water
- 3 cups
- 2 clear bowls or rectangular containers, at least half the bottles' height
- tape measure
- acid/base indicator strips
- measuring cup, with spout preferably

## How to Experiment Safely

Have an adult present when handling hot water. Do not taste or ingest any of the solutions in the experiment.

- measuring spoons
- funnel (optional)
- thermometer or temperature gauge, should range from 65–115° Fahrenheit (18–46°Celsius) (optional)
- marking pen

**Approximate Budget** $8

**Timetable** 1 hour allowing water to sit; 1 hour and 45 minutes for experiment.

**Step-by-Step Instructions**

1. To get room temperature water: In three separate cups, measure ¾ cup water. The water should not be hot or cold to the touch. Allow the water to sit for about one hour to reach room temperature. If you have a thermometer, the water should be at about 68–73.4°Fahrenheit (20–23°Celsius).
2. While waiting, label one bottle "Hot," one bottle "Cold," and one bottle "Control."
3. Add 3 teaspoons of sugar to each cup and mix thoroughly.
4. Dip an indicator strip briefly in one of the sugar–water solutions. Compare the indicator color to the color chart. An acid should turn the indicator red, a base should turn the indicator blue. Note the results.
5. Pour the sugar-water into the three bottles. You may need a funnel for this. Clean the cups for later use.
6. Prepare a warm-water bath and a cold-water bath. For the warm-water bath, fill one of the two clear bowls or rectangular containers with warm water from the kitchen sink faucet. Let the water run until it gets fairly warm to the touch, but not scalding hot (about 104–113°Fahrenheit [40–45°Celsius]). For the cold-water bath fill the other bowl or container with cold water from the kitchen sink faucet and add ice cubes until the water gets cool to the touch (about 41–59°Fahrenheit [5–15°Celsius]).
7. Add one packet of dry yeast to each of the three bottles.
8. Securely place a balloon over the top of each bottle opening. Tape each balloon to the bottle to ensure no gas can escape.
9. Swirl each bottle gently to mix the contents.

*Step 10: Place yeast in hot, cold, and room temperature environments.* GALE GROUP.

10. Place the bottle labeled "Hot" in the warm-water bath. Place the bottle labeled "Cold" in the cold-water bath. You may need to secure the bottles down with string and tape so that they sit firmly in the water and do not bob.

11. After 20 minutes, measure the circumference of each balloon. When you wrap the tape measure around the balloon make a small mark on the balloon with the pen above the measure to mark the spot. Note the results in a data chart.

12. Check to make sure the warm water is still warm. If it has cooled significantly, scoop some out and replace with fresh warm water. Add ice cubes to the cold water, if necessary

13. Continue measuring the balloons in 20-minute intervals until the balloons no longer expand. It should take about 60 minutes or more.

14. Remove the balloon from the "Cold" bottle and pour some of its contents into a clean cup. Dip an indicator strip briefly in the solution. Compare the indicator color to the color chart and note the results.

15. Repeat Step 14 for the bottles labeled "Hot" and "Control," making sure to pour the contents into a clean cup each time. Note the results of each indicator strip.

Summary of Results Examine the data chart and graph the results of the circumference for each environmental condition. Label the measurements on one axis and the time on another. How does the balloon circumference of the yeast grown in a room temperature environment compare to that of the yeast grown in the cold-water and warm-water bath? Which bottle showed the greatest increase in balloon circumference? Which bottle was the most acidic? What do the results of the indicator convey about the growth of the yeast in each environment? Can you construct a hypothesis about the environmental conditions for all fungi from these results? Write a brief summary explaining your results and any conclusions you can draw from them.

Change the Variables There are several ways to change the variable in this experiment. You can alter the type of fungi. You can change different environmental conditions, such as the light level on the yeast. By using varying concentrations of acidic foods, such as lemon juice or vinegar instead of sugar water, you can alter the acidity level of the yeast.

Modify the Experiment You can add to this experiment by examining the fungi you grew up close. You will need access to a microscope and you may need an adult to help you use it. After you identified the ideal temperature for yeast growth, place a drop of the yeast solution onto a slide and cover. Yeast are single-celled organisms that divide by a process called budding. A yeast cell can divide in about 20 minutes. Sketch what you see under the microscope.

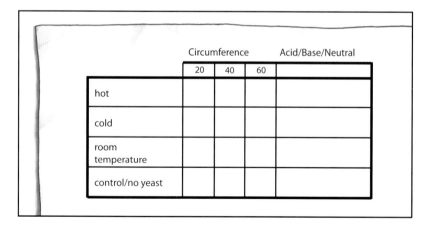

*Step 11: Note the circumferences of the balloons and acidity of the solutions in a data chart.* GALE GROUP.

| | Circumference | | | Acid/Base/Neutral |
|---|---|---|---|---|
| | 20 | 40 | 60 | |
| hot | | | | |
| cold | | | | |
| room temperature | | | | |
| control/no yeast | | | | |

If you do not have access to slides, you can purchase prepared yeast slides at a science supply store. You can also compare the reproduction rate of the yeast that was the most active to the yeast that was the least active. Does one divide slower than the other?

## Design Your Own Experiment

**How to Select a Topic Relating to this Concept** From the microscopic to the mammoth, fungi are a wide and diverse kingdom of life. There are numerous projects related to fungi, from basic observation to exploring their living requirements. You could also explore fungi's profound effect on Earth's life cycle and human life.

Check the Further Readings section and talk with your science teacher to learn more about fungi. While some fungi may appear edible, remember to never eat any mushroom or other fungus you find unless you have had it identified by an expert in fungi. The mushroom may be poisonous or you could be allergic to it.

**Steps in the Scientific Method** To conduct an original experiment, you need to plan carefully and think things through. Otherwise, you might not be sure what question you are answering, what you are or should be measuring, or what your findings prove or disprove.

Here are the steps in designing an experiment:

- State the purpose of—and the underlying question behind—the experiment you propose to do.
- Recognize the variables involved and select one that will help you answer the question at hand.
- State your hypothesis, an educated guess about the answer to your question.
- Decide how to change the variable you selected.
- Decide how to measure your results.

---

### Troubleshooter's Guide

Below are some problems that may arise during this experiment, some possible causes, and some ways to remedy the problems.

**Problem:** No balloons expanded and there was no indication of acidity in the solutions in the bottles labeled "Hot" and "Cold."

**Possible cause:** You may have used yeast that was no longer active. Check the expiration date of your yeast and, if necessary, purchase more. Repeat the experiment using this yeast.

**Problem:** The balloon on the bottle labeled "Hot" did not expand.

**Possible cause:** You may have used water that was too hot, causing the yeast to die instantly. Repeat the experiment, using warm water.

---

*Mushrooms are one of the most familiar types of fungi.* FIELD MARK PUBLICATIONS.

**Recording Data and Summarizing the Results** Your data should include charts and drawings such as the one you did for these experiments. They should be clearly labeled and easy to read. You may also want to include photographs and drawings of any fungi you worked with, the experimental setup, and results, which will help other people visualize the experiment.

If you are preparing an exhibit, you may want to display your results, such as any experimental setup you designed. You may also want to include specimens, in a closed container, so that others can observe what you studied. If you have completed a nonexperimental project, explain clearly what your research question was and illustrate your findings.

**Related Projects** Fungi are a broad kingdom filled with many possible experiments at hand because fungi grow on such a wide variety of sources. Different materials will grow different fungi. You could conduct a project on the differences among one group of fungi, such as molds. Most molds grow well on materials such as bread, used coffee-grounds, fruits, or other food items that are moist with no preservatives. You could isolate and grow the same type of fungi on a variety of food sources. Or you can keep the food source constant and grow different types of fungi on it.

You could also perform a project on the reproduction of fungi. Examine the spores of fungi and the different methods fungi use to reproduce. For a research project, you could look at how fungi have had an effect on humans, in both positive and negative ways. You could look at how food manufacturers protect food against certain types of fungi and how fungi are a natural part of many foods.

## For More Information

Darling, Kathy. *There's a Zoo on You!* Brookfield, CT: The Millbrook Press, 2000. A look at fungi, bacteria, viruses, and other microbes that affect humans.

Fogel, Robert. *Fun Facts About Fungi.* http://www.herbarium.usu.edu/fungi/FunFacts/factindx.htm (accessed on March 11, 2008). Fun facts and information on fungi.

Ho, David. "Alexander Fleming." *Time.com.* http://www.time.com/time/time100/scientist/profile/fleming.html (accessed on March 11, 2008). A profile of Alexander Fleming, who was one of the principal discoverers of the antibiotic penicillin.

*LichenLand: Fun with Lichens.* http://ocid.nacse.org/lichenland (accessed on March 11, 2008). Information and close-up photographs of a wide range of lichens.

Nardo, Don. *Germs.* San Diego, CA: KidHaven Press, 2002. Basic explanation of microbes.

Pascoe, Elaine. *Fungi.* New York: PowerKids Press, 2003. Simple introduction to fungi with many pictures.

Silverstein, Robert, Alvin, and Virginia. *Fungi.* New York: Twenty-first Century Books, 1996. Clear details on the fungi kingdom.

Volk, Tom. *Tom Volk's Fungi.* http://botit.botany.wisc.edu/toms_fungi (accessed on March 11, 2008). Information on fungi with links, pictures, and answers to frequently asked questions.

# 42

# Genetics

Your genes play a major role in who you are: your features and even some personality traits come from your genes. Many other characteristics are produced from a combination of your genes and the environment. Genes are the basic units of heredity. They are passed from parent to offspring, and are carried in almost every cell of the body. Genetics is the science of genes and understanding how traits are passed down from parent to child.

*A chunk of DNA* Genes are segments of DNA that are housed in the nucleus (center) of cells. DNA is short for deoxyribonucleic acid. It is a long molecule shaped like a twisted ladder, which is called a double helix. In organisms that have two parents, like humans, half the DNA in the body comes from the father and half from the mother. All our DNA is packed so tightly in every cell, that if you attached all the molecules together it would stretch thousands of miles.

What makes each person's DNA unique is the order of the four chemical "letters" that make up the molecule. The chemicals are A, G, C, T, for short. Much like the meaning of words, the sequence of the letters determines its meaning. The letters AGCCT may produce a different characteristic than the CGCCT sequence. DNA sequences contain instructions to make proteins. Every organism has many thousands of different proteins, and it is the proteins that carry out the instructions. Each section of DNA that provides the instructions to manufacture a protein is called a gene. A gene determines the protein, and the protein carries out its specific function.

In each cell, DNA is organized into structures called chromosomes. Species have different numbers of chromosomes. Humans have 23 pairs of chromosomes: 23 from the mother paired with 23 from the father, making a total of 46. Sperm and egg cells have 23 unpaired chromosomes. When the sperm and egg cells join, the child gets 23 chromosomes

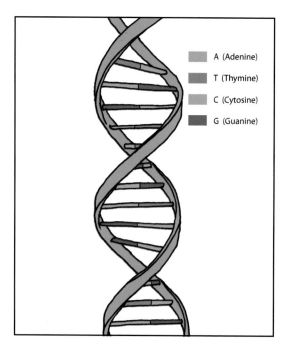

A (Adenine)

T (Thymine)

C (Cytosine)

G (Guanine)

*What makes each person's DNA unique is the order of the four chemical "letters" that make up the molecule.*
ILLUSTRATION BY TEMAH NELSON.

*When the sperm and egg cells join, the child gets 23 chromosomes from each parent, one of each.*
ILLUSTRATION BY TEMAH NELSON.

from each parent, one of each. That means, except for the sex cells, you have two copies of every chromosome and thus, every gene.

***It starts with a pea*** No one knew about genes or DNA when the curiosity of Gregor Mendel (1822–1884) led to a turning point in the study of genetics. Mendel was an Austrian monk who was interested in science and mathematics. He failed his teaching examination, moved to a monastery and continued studying science. He also enjoyed gardening.

Mendel wanted to understand the traits of pea plants, such as color and shape. Between 1856 and 1863 he bred numerous pea plants, carefully noting his experiments and the traits of each offspring. His results led him to several key genetic laws. One is the law of independent assortment, which says that parents's traits are passed to the offspring independently of one another.

Some scientists at the time theorized that traits were "blended" together, a mixture of both parents. In blending, the theory went, a pink flowering plant would spring from a cross between a red flowering and a white flowering plant. But Mendel showed that traits do not mix or blend. The red trait stays red and the white trait remains white. Parents pass down their traits intact.

Even if the offspring does not appear to have the parents's traits (a red or a white color, for example) they are still carrying these traits. The traits can appear in the next generation. Mendel showed this in his pea studies.

A plant with wrinkled peas bred to another plant with wrinkled peas produced a plant that has a quarter of its peas smooth. This led Mendel to the idea of dominant and recessive genes.

We have two forms of every gene: one from the mother and one from the father. These forms are called alleles. If a trait is dominant, you needs only one of the alleles for the trait to be visible, or "expressed." Dimples, for example, are a dominant trait. If a child inherits the dimple gene from only one parent the child will dimple. If a trait is recessive, you need both copies of the gene for it to be apparent. Red hair is a recessive trait. A child would need to inherit the red-hair gene from both the mother and father to be a red head.

After Mendel, many researchers have made findings that have helped us better understand genetics. The identification of mutations was another major finding. A mutation is a change in the DNA of a gene. There are many different ways mutations can occur. Sometimes a mutation is repaired before it causes a trait to be expressed. And there are many mutations that have no negative effect. But there are also mutations that can cause health disorders. The sickle cell disease, for example, is a blood disorder that can cause pain and serious health problems. The sickle cell gene is recessive, and it occurs from a single "letter" mutation in the DNA.

*Altering the genes* As researchers have learned how genes function and where they are located, it has led to techniques that recombine or modify genes. This technique is called genetic engineering or recombinant DNA technology. In simple form, genetic engineering first identifies a gene that expresses a desired trait. The gene is snipped out of the DNA and inserted into the DNA of another cell's DNA in another organism. The "new" trait is then expressed in this organism.

*Gregor Mendel used pea plants to experiment with genetics.* GETTY IMAGES.

The first genetically engineered medicine was, in 1982, the hormone insulin. The gene for insulin was isolated from a person and inserted into bacteria cells. The bacteria cells, which rapidly reproduced, began producing insulin. Genetic engineering is now commonly used in research to "track" or see activity in the body. Researchers often use a gene that produces bioluminescence. Organisms that carry this gene, such as the firefly and certain fish, give off natural light. The gene is attached to a specific gene or compound in the body, which allows researchers to follow the light and see its activity. Today, genetic engineering is commonly used in research, medicine, and industry.

There is ongoing research to learn more about what genes do and how they behave. In 2003, researchers finished a massive project to sequence the entire DNA of humans. This was called the Human

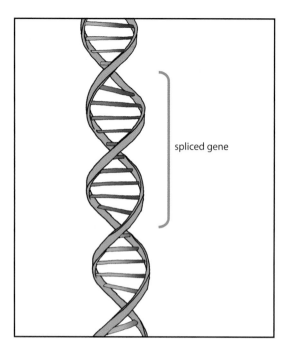

*Gene splicing is also called genetic engineering or recombinant DNA technology.* ILLUSTRATION BY TEMAH NELSON.

*The allele for widow's peak is dominant; straight hairline is recessive.* ILLUSTRATION BY TEMAH NELSON.

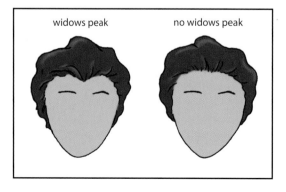

Genome Project. By studying and understanding what genes do and how they function, researchers hope to answer many questions related to development and disease. There is also ongoing research to sequence the DNA of many other organisms.

In the following experiment and project, you will explore more about genes and how they are inherited. If you want to learn more about DNA, see the DNA chapter.

## EXPERIMENT 1

### Genetic Traits: Will you share certain genetic traits more with family members than non-family members?

In appearances, there are many broad traits humans share. But it is the unique set of characteristics that distinguishes people. Some physical characteristics are more common than others. A trait that only needs one allele to appear is a dominant trait; and a trait that needs both alleles to appear is recessive. There are many characteristics, such as hair color, that are due to a combination of multiple genes. Other characteristics, such as height, relate to a combination of genes and the environmental influences. There are also characteristics that researchers have traced to one or only a handful of genes.

In this experiment, you will compare five genetic characteristics to family members and participants outside your family. You can then determine the percent of family members and non-family members who have the trait, and compare it to whether you have the trait. You will need a lot of family and non-family members. Try to observe the frequency of the following characteristics in at least five to ten people. These features are due to only one or a few genes.

- Widow's peak or straight hairline: A widow's peak gives the forehead hairline a downward dip, like a "V." If there is no widow's peak, the hairline is straight. The allele for widow's peak is dominant; straight hairline is recessive.

## WORDS TO KNOW

**Alleles:** One version of the same gene.

**Bioluminescence:** Light produced by living organisms.

**Base pairs:** In DNA, the pairing of two nucleotides with each other: adenine (A) with thymine (T), and guanine (G) with cytosine (C).

**Chromosome:** A structure of DNA found in the cell nucleus.

**Control experiment:** A setup that is identical to the experiment, but is not affected by the variable that acts on the experimental group.

**Dominant gene:** A gene that passes on a certain characteristic, even when there is only one copy (allele) of the gene.

**Deoxyribonucleic acid (DNA):** Large, complex molecules found in the nuclei of cells that carry genetic information for an organism's development; double helix. (Pronounced DEE-ox-see-rye-bo-noo-klay-ick acid)

**DNA replication:** The process by which one DNA strand unwinds and duplicates all its information, creating two new DNA strands that are identical to each other and to the original strand.

**Double helix:** The shape taken by DNA (deoxyribonucleic acid) molecules in a nucleus.

**Gene:** The basic unit of heredity; the genes contain a section of DNA that codes for a protein.

**Genetic engineering:** A technique that modifies the DNA of living cells in order to make them change its characteristics. Also called genetic modification.

**Hypothesis:** An idea in the form of a statement that can be tested by observation and/or experiment.

**Nucleus:** The central part of the cell that contains the DNA.

**Pedigree:** A diagram that illustrates the pattern of inheritance of a genetic trait in a family.

**Protein:** A complex chemical compound consisting of many amino acids attached to each other that are essential to the structure and functioning of all living cells.

**Recessive gene:** A gene that produces a certain characteristic only two both copies (alleles) of the gene are present.

**Variable:** Something that can affect the results of an experiment.

---

- Dimples versus no dimples: Dimples are from the dominant allele; no dimples is the recessive allele.

- Earlobes: Detached or not detached: If the earlobes hang free they are detached. Detached earlobes are a dominant allele; attached earlobes are recessive. Earlobes are the dominant allele and attached earlobes are recessive.

- Mid-finger hair: Hair on any of the middle-section of the fingers is a dominant allele. If the middle section of the fingers are hairless, it is from a recessive allele.

## What Are the Variables?

Variables are anything that might affect the results of an experiment. Here are the main variables in this experiment:

- the participants

To begin this experiment, make an educated guess about the outcome of the experiment based on your knowledge of genes and heredity. This educated guess, or prediction, is your hypothesis. A hypothesis should explain these things:

- the topic of the experiment
- the variable you will change
- the variable you will measure
- what you expect to happen

A hypothesis should be brief, specific, and measurable. It must be something you can test through further investigation. Your experiment will prove or disprove whether your hypothesis is correct. Here is one possible hypothesis for this experiment: "I will share at least 50% of my characteristics with my family members."

Variables are anything you can change in an experiment. In this case, the variable you will change are the participants. The variable you will measure will be whether participants have the specific trait.

**Level of Difficulty** Moderate (due to the number of participants needed).

**Materials Needed**

- about 10 non family-member participants
- family members, at least five
- notepad and pen

*Detached earlobes are a dominant allele; attached earlobes are recessive.*
ILLUSTRATION BY TEMAH NELSON.

**Approximate Budget** $0.

**Timetable** Varies widely depending upon the number of participants. Each participant should take about five to 10 minutes to document.

**Step-by-Step Instructions**

1. Make two charts of each trait you will be observing, one for family members and one for non-family members.
2. Note whether you have each of the characteristics.
3. Begin testing family members and non-family members. For each person that has

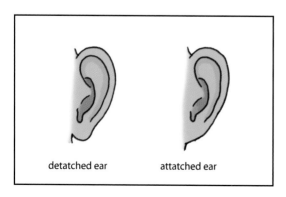

detatched ear            attatched ear

the characteristic, make a mark if it matches you. For example, if you have a widow's peak and your sister has a widow's peak, make a mark. If your sister does not have a widow's back, note the results separately.

4. When you have finished testing all participants, add up how many family members and non-family members you tested.

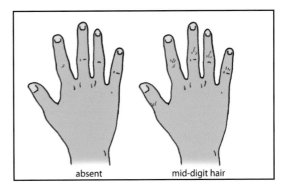

absent            mid-digit hair

*Hair on any of the middle-section of the fingers is a dominant allele.* ILLUSTRATION BY TEMAH NELSON.

**Summary of Results** For both the family and non-family member charts, divide the number of participants by the number of participants who share the same trait as you. This will give you what percent of people in each category share your traits. What percent do family members share your traits? Are there certain traits that you share equally or more with the people outside your family. You may want to graph your data, and write up a summary of your findings.

## PROJECT 2

### Building a Pedigree for Taste

**Purpose/Hypothesis** It is not always practical or possible to breed organisms the way Mendel did, and so scientists need other ways to understand how traits are passed down through the generations. A pedigree is a

|  | My Traits | Family | non-Family |
|---|---|---|---|
| widow's peak |  |  |  |
| dimples |  |  |  |
| earlobes detatched |  |  |  |
| mid-finger hair |  |  |  |
| % shared traits |  |  |  |

*Step 1: Make two charts of each trait you will be observing, one for family members and one for non-family members.* ILLUSTRATION BY TEMAH NELSON.

## Troubleshooter's Guide

This experiment is relatively straightforward and you should have no major troubles. The one problem you may have is to get enough participants to give you strong data. The number of family members and non-family participants does not have to be the same, but the more people you can collect data on for each group, the more accurate your data will be.

diagram that is similar to a family tree. The pedigree shows as many generations as possible and in genetics, it shows which family members have a particular trait. Looking at who inherits a trait over several generations helps predict if a trait is genetic and if it is recessive or dominant.

The purpose of this project is to construct a pedigree of one trait. The trait you will follow is if someone can taste or not taste PTC. PTC stands for phenylthiocarbamide. This compound gives foods like broccoli and coffee a bitter flavor. By constructing a pedigree, it will help you determine if the trait is dominant or recessive.

You will need three generations of family members for this project. For example, you and your siblings would be one generation; your parents would be another generation; and their parents would be a third generation. You do not need to use your family; you could make a pedigree of a friend's family.

All pedigrees have the same symbols. The basic symbols include:

- squares symbolize males
- circle symbolize females
- a line between male and female symbolizes mating
- individuals who show the trait have a dark circle or square
- individuals who do not show the trait have a white circle or square
- each generation is numbered to the left with Roman numerals
- Arabic numbers, from left to right, represent birth order

Level of Difficulty Easy/moderate (because of data collection).

Materials Needed

- PTC paper (available from hobby and science supply sources); see Note below.
- family members
- paper/pencil

Note: You could also construct pedigrees for other traits you are curious about; see Experiment 1 for other options.

Approximate Budget $5.

Timetable Varies widely depending upon finding family members.

### Step-by-Step Instructions

1. Use the symbols and the illustration as a guide to make a pedigree of the family you are going to analyze. Make sure to number and label the pedigree.

2. Have as many people as possible taste the PTC paper. If they can taste the PTC, color in the square or circle.

3. For any people you cannot test, place a question mark in the square or circle.

*Step 2: Have as many people as possible taste the PTC paper.* ILLUSTRATION BY TEMAH NELSON.

**Summary of Results** When you have finished testing all the family members, study your pedigree. If only one parent has the trait, how does it affect the offspring? If no parents can taste PTC, do any of the offspring? The ability to taste PTC is a dominant trait. Can you tell this from your pedigree? You might want to construct pedigrees of different families, especially if the family you tested was a non-PTC tasting family.

## Design Your Own Experiment

**How to Select a Topic Relating to this Concept** The study of genetics can reach into many different fields and areas. As researchers continue to understand genes, consider what answers genetics can give us. You may want to explore characteristics of certain animals, such as dogs, or how different animals are related to one another. You can also investigate technologies that scientists use to understand genetics. What are some ways that genes are manipulated, and how can this affect human life?

Check the Further Readings section and talk with your science teacher to start gathering information on genetics questions that interest you.

**Steps in the Scientific Method** To conduct an original experiment, you need to plan carefully and think things through. Otherwise, you might not be sure what question you are answering,

*A pedigree is a diagram that is similar to a family tree.* ILLUSTRATION BY TEMAH NELSON.

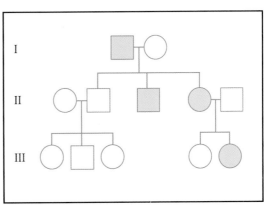

## Troubleshooter's Guide

There should be no major problems in this project. The main issue will be finding enough family members to test if they can taste PTC. You may have to mail family members the PTC test strips. If it is not possible in your family, you can conduct the project on another family.

what you are or should be measuring, or what your findings prove or disprove.

Here are the steps in designing an experiment:

- State the purpose of—and the underlying question behind—the experiment you propose to do.
- Recognize the variables involved and select one that will help you answer the question at hand.
- State your hypothesis, an educated guess about the answer to your question.
- Decide how to change the variable you selected.
- Decide how to measure your results.

**Recording Data and Summarizing the Results** Your data should include charts and graphs such as the one you did for these experiments. They should be clearly labeled and easy to read. As DNA is difficult to visualize, you may also want to include photographs and drawings of your experimental setup and results. This will help others visualize the steps in the experiment.

If you are preparing an exhibit, you may want to display your results, such as any experimental setup you designed. If you have completed a nonexperimental project, explain clearly what your research question was and illustrate your findings.

**Related Projects** There are several genetic techniques you can do that give more information on DNA and genes. Two commonly used techniques are gel electrophoresis and DNA fingerprinting. These techniques will require special equipment and help. (Check the Resources section for companies that sell kits.) You can also replicate an experiment of Mendel's with pea plants.

You can also focus on predicting genetic characteristics. There are some genetic traits that differ among males and females. The trait for color-blindness, for example, is carried on the female's sex chromosomes and affects mostly males. You can conduct color-blind tests in a certain population (classmates and family) and determine if your sample matches the overall population.

Advances in genetics and genetic manipulations has also brought many ethical questions and controversies. You could investigate one potential controversy, such as genetically manipulated food, and present different viewpoints.

# For More Information

Cells Alive. *Animal Cell Mitosis.* http://www.cellsalive.com/mitosis.htm (accessed May 22, 2008). Interactive animation of chromosomes dividing into two cells.

Cold Spring Harbor Laboratory. *DNA from the Beginning.* http://www.dnaftb.org/dnaftb/3/concept (accessed on June 2, 2008). Clear explanation of genetic concepts with illustrations, animations, and audio.

*DNA From the Beginning.* http://www.dnaftb.org/dnaftb (accessed on March 1, 2008). An animated introduction on the basics of DNA, heredity, and genetics.

National Institute of General Medical Sciences. *The New Genetics.* http://publications.nigms.nih.gov/thenewgenetics/index.html (accessed May 22, 2008). Comprehensive information with illustrations of how genes work.

Ridley, Matt. *Genome: The Autobiography of a Species in 23 Chapters.* New York: HarperColllins, 2000. Each chapter looks at one gene on a human's chromosome.

The Tech Museum of Innovation. *Understanding Genetics.* http://www.thetech.org/genetics (accessed on May 17, 2008). Online DNA exhibit includes images of cells and DNA.

The University of Utah, Genetic Science Learning Center. *Tour of the Basics.* http://learn.genetics.utah.edu/units/basics/tour (accessed May 22, 2008). Basic information with illustrations of DNA and genes.

# Germination

The first stage in the development of a seed, when it grows from seed to seedling, is germination. Like humans, seeds are equipped with their own growing mechanisms. An embryo and a supply of food exist within these tiny life starters. But until they are exposed to certain conditions of temperature, moisture, oxygen, and in some cases light, seeds remain dormant, or inactive, for days, months, or even hundreds of years. For example, scientists found a North American Arctic lupine seed that was about 10,000 years old. It was the oldest seed found so far, and it eventually grew into a plant similar to today's lupine. The seed waited 10,000 years and sprouted only when the right germination conditions were in place.

*Really old books about green things* Botany, the study of plant life, had its beginnings in ancient Greece. Theophrastus (c. 372–287 B.C.E.) wrote two large botanical works that were so revolutionary they guided scientists for the next 1,800 years. In his books *On the History of Plants* and *On Causes of Plants,* Theophrastus set down a theory of plant growth, plant structure analysis, and the relationship of agriculture to botany. He also identified, classified, and described 550 plants.

*Getting through the ground* Germination begins with a seed's activation underground and ends when the first leaves push through the soil. A seed may remain viable, that is, capable of germination, for many years. Temperature plays a big factor in germination. The most favorable temperature ranges from 59 °F to 100.4 °F (15 °C to 38 °C). Temperatures above or below this range slow down the germination rate.

Absorbing water is a seed's first activity. Every seed has a little helper called a micropyle, an opening that enables water to enter the seed more easily. Water kicks off the seed's life processes, including respiration. Respiration is the process of oxygen from the air entering the seed and helping the cell use its stored food as energy. Too much water can literally

*In the first stages of a seed's germination, the cotyledons start to use up stored food and its root system begins to grow.* PHOTO RESEARCHERS INC.

drown out the necessary oxygen, so water has to be available in the right amount.

The embryo, including one or two cotyledons, or seed leaves, starts to use up its stored food. Its cells begin to divide and grow, which causes the seed's coat, or testa, to burst open. The seed's root system, or radicule, starts to grow, threading its way through the testa into the soil.

The cotyledon develops into the shape we call a seedling. It has two parts. The upper part supports an embryonic shoot at the end. This eventually pushes through the soil as a stem and leaves. The lower part contains the roots. As seeds grow, the stem and leaves push up. Food reserves provide the enormous energy they need to heave their way through soil. Seedlings have been known to push through tarred roads. Once they are above ground, chlorophyll usually begins to form in the leaves and stems.

Germination is the process a dormant seed goes through when it wakes up to begin the growing process. Our lives depend on plants. Conducting germination experiments will take the mystery out of this important life process.

## EXPERIMENT 1

*As they grow, seedlings use up much energy. As a result, they can actually push through tarred roads while growing.* PHOTO RESEARCHERS INC.

### Effects of Temperature on Germination: What temperatures encourage and discourage germination?

Purpose/Hypothesis In this experiment you will investigate the ideal temperature needed to awaken a seed and stimulate it to grow. Before you begin, make an educated guess about the outcome of this experiment based on your knowledge of seed growth. This educated guess, or prediction, is your hypothesis. A hypothesis should explain these things:

- the topic of the experiment
- the variable you will change
- the variable you will measure
- what you expect to happen

## WORDS TO KNOW

**Botany:** The branch of biology involving the scientific study of plant life.

**Chlorophyll:** A green pigment found in plants that absorbs sunlight, providing the energy used in photosynthesis, or the conversion of carbon dioxide and water to complex carbohydrates.

**Cotyledon:** Seed leaves, which contain the stored source of food for the embryo.

**Dormant:** The condition of a seed when its growing processes are inactive.

**Embryo:** The seed of a plant, which through germination can develop into a new plant.

**Germination:** The beginning of growth of a seed.

**Hypothesis:** An idea in the form of a statement that can be tested by observation and/or experiment.

**Micropyle:** Seed opening that enables water to enter easily.

**Radicule:** Seed's root system.

**Respiration:** The physical process that supplies oxygen to an animal's body. It also describes a series of chemical reactions that take place inside cells.

**Seedling:** A small plant just starting to grow into its mature form.

**Testa:** A tough outer layer that protects the embryo and endosperm of a seed from damage.

**Variable:** Something that can affect the results of an experiment.

**Viable:** The capability of developing or growing under favorable conditions.

A hypothesis should be brief, specific, and measurable. It must be something you can test through observation. Your experiment will prove or disprove whether your hypothesis is correct. Here is one possible hypothesis for this experiment: "Temperatures near or below freezing and those over 100°F will prevent germination."

In this case, the variable you will change is the temperature, and the variable you will measure is the number of seeds that germinate. You expect those seeds stored in very hot and very cold temperatures will not germinate.

**Level of Difficulty** Easy/moderate.

### What Are the Variables?

Variables are anything that might affect the results of an experiment. Here are the main variables in this experiment:

- the temperature of the surrounding air
- the amount of water provided
- the type of soil used

In other words, the variables in this experiment are everything that might affect the germination of the seeds. If you change more than one variable, you will not be able to tell which variable had the most effect on the seeds' germination.

## How to Experiment Safely

The lamp can cause fires when not handled properly. Ask an adult to help you set it up.

### Materials Needed

- 15 seeds (Lima beans, kidney beans, and lentils are good seed choices; use only one variety.)
- water
- 3 sponges
- 3 plastic trays big enough to hold a sponge
- 3 napkins big enough to hold a sponge
- 3 thermometers (Fahrenheit or Celsius)
- access to a refrigerator
- a lamp with a 40-watt bulb

**Approximate Budget** $10. (The seeds may be purchased at a supermarket as dried beans or you may find them in your family's kitchen. Try to borrow thermometers to reduce the cost.)

**Timetable** 20 minutes to set up the experiment; one to two weeks to complete it.

### Step-by-Step Instructions

1. Place a sponge into each of the plastic trays.
2. Place five seeds on top of each sponge.

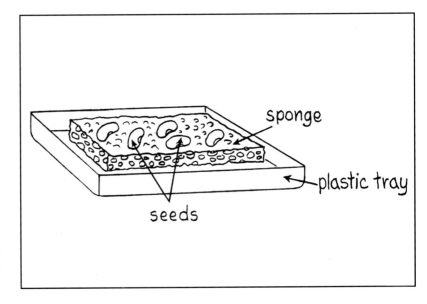

*Steps 1 and 2: Set-up of plastic tray with sponge and five seeds on top of sponge.* GALE GROUP.

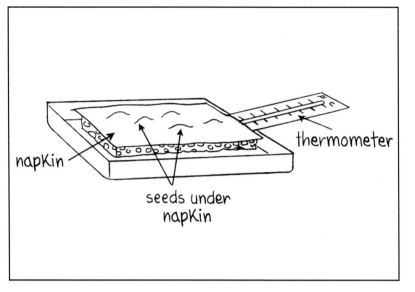

napkin

thermometer

seeds under
napkin

*Steps 3 to 5: Set-up of plastic
tray with napkin over seeds and
thermometer.* GALE GROUP.

3. Pour water over the seeds and the sponge so that water collects in the tray. Do not pour too much. The seeds should not sit in the water.

4. Place a napkin over the seeds to keep them from drying out.

*Step 7: Placement of third tray
underneath the lamp.* GALE
GROUP.

5. Place one tray indoors, away from a window or door. Place a thermometer under the napkin to record temperature.

6. Place another tray with seeds in the refrigerator. Again, place the thermometer under the napkin to record the temperature.

7. Place the third tray 10 to 12 inches (25 to 30 centimeters) away from the lamp and turn it on.

8. After about an hour, begin to record the temperature and condition of the seeds. Make up a data sheet with the headings Room Temperature and Location. Underneath add Date, Temperature, and Seed Activity. Then fill it in daily. Lift the napkin and diagram the changes in the seeds.

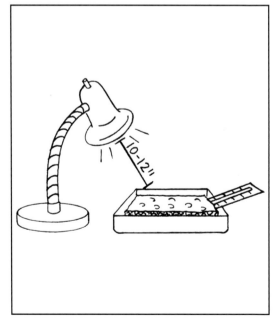

10-12"

9. Make sure the sponge stays wet at all times and the seeds are not under water. Check on the seeds daily.

**Summary of Results** Compare the data on your chart and summarize your findings. Did the results support your hypothesis? Which tray of seedlings grew the most? Which tray of seedlings did not grow at all?

**Change the Variables** To further explore how temperature affects germination, you can vary the experiment in the following ways:

- Use different types of seeds and see if one type of seed is more tolerant of high or low temperatures than others.
- Try growing seeds at different temperatures without watering them. Do any sprout?
- Try growing seeds in the dark at different temperatures. Cover the seed trays to block all light from reaching the seeds. Does light seem to be a factor in germination?

## EXPERIMENT 2

## Comparing Germination Times: How fast can seeds grow?

**Purpose/Hypothesis** Each seed type has an average germination time. The seed waits for the correct conditions to occur. For example, if a seed emerged after the first warm day in spring, it might get caught by a late frost and die. So the seed may wait for consistent conditions that are ideal for growth.

In this experiment, the goal is to compare the germination time for two different varieties of seeds. Before you begin, make an educated guess about the outcome of this experiment based on your knowledge of seed growth. This educated guess, or prediction, is your hypothesis. A hypothesis should explain these things:

- the topic of the experiment
- the variable you will change
- the variable you will measure
- what you expect to happen

A hypothesis should be brief, specific, and measurable. It must be something you can test through observation. Your experiment will prove or disprove whether your hypothesis is correct. Here is one possible hypothesis for this experiment: "When two different varieties of seeds are exposed to the same growing conditions, one group will consistently germinate before the other."

In this case, the variable you will change is the type of seed, and the variable you will measure is the time it takes to germinate. You expect one type of seed to germinate before the other.

**Level of Difficulty** Easy/moderate. (Daily attention is required during the two-week experiment.)

**Materials Needed**

- 12 seeds—two different varieties; six lima bean seeds and six radish seeds
- 2 to 3 cups of potting soil
- egg carton (dozen size)
- water in a spray bottle
- tray big enough to hold the egg carton
- fork

**Approximate Budget** $2 for seeds; borrow the spray bottle if possible.

**Timetable** 15 minutes to set up and two weeks to run the experiment.

**Step-by-Step Instructions**

1. Use the fork to poke holes in the bottom of the wells in the egg carton. This will allow drainage. Label the wells with the numbers one to 12—one to six along the back row and seven to 12 along the front row.
2. Place the six lima bean seeds in the back row (wells one to six) and the six radish seeds in the front row (wells seven to 12).
3. Fill the wells with soil to the top. (Each seed should have the same amount of soil in the well.) Place the egg carton on the tray.

## What Are the Variables?

Variables are anything that might affect the results of an experiment. Here are the main variables in this experiment:

- the types of seeds used
- the temperature of the surrounding air
- the amount of water provided
- the type of soil used

In other words, the variables in this experiment are everything that might affect the time it takes for the seeds to germinate. If you change more than one variable, you will not be able to tell which variable had the most effect on the germination time.

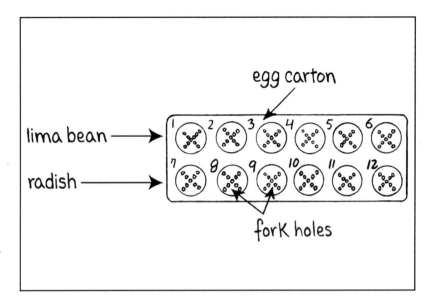

*Steps 1 and 2: Set-up of drainage holes and seeds in the egg carton.* GALE GROUP.

4. Using the spray bottle, water each well with the same number of squirts. Make sure all the soil is wet.

5. Place the egg carton/tray on a window sill in a warm room.

6. Water daily, making sure the soil stays wet.

7. Perform a daily inspection of your seedlings. Record the results on a chart with your observations. Number across the top from one to 12, with columns underneath. Then number the days down the far left of the chart, from one to 10. Use symbols illustrated to depict the stage of germination that is occurring.

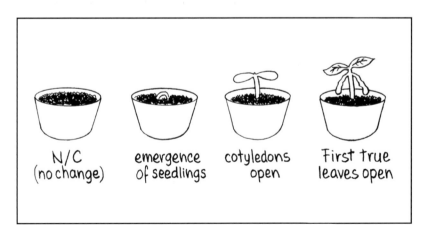

*Step 7: Four views of egg carton wells as the seeds grow: no change, emergence of seedling, cotyledons open, and first true leaves open.* GALE GROUP.

**Summary of Results** The goal of this experiment is to compare the average time of germination (from beginning to emergence of the first true leaves) for each seed species. Look at your results chart and determine the average number of days it took for the first true leaves to appear for each seed type. Which seeds germinated faster? Did one group consistently germinate before the other?

**Change the Variables** To further explore seed germination times, change the environmental conditions under which you try to sprout the seeds. In separate experiments, vary the amount of water, sunlight, or warmth provided for one type of seed, such as radish seeds. Do radish seeds sprout more quickly under certain environmental conditions? Then repeat the experiments with seeds of another type, such as bean seeds. Or you might expose identical trays of radish seeds and bean seeds to the same harsh environmental conditions (little water, cold temperatures) to see which seeds sprout first.

> ## Troubleshooter's Guide
>
> Here is a problem that may arise in your experiment, a possible cause, and ways to remedy it.
>
> **Problem:** The seeds have not done anything for two weeks.
>
> **Possible cause:** They may need more water. Try increasing the water and storing them in a warmer location. If that does not work, replace the seeds with new ones.

## EXPERIMENT 3

## Seed Scarification: Does breaking the seed shell affect germination time?

**Purpose/Hypothesis** There are some plants that go through a period of inactivity, called dormancy. Dormancy can protect the seed from harsh

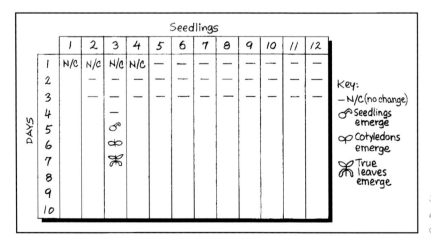

*Step 7: Sample seedling growth chart for Experiment 2.* GALE GROUP.

## What Are the Variables?

Variables are anything that might affect the results of an experiment. Here are the main variables in this experiment:

- the types of seeds
- the temperature of the surrounding air
- the amount of water
- the amount of light
- the type of soil used

In other words, the variables in this experiment are everything that might affect the time it takes for the seeds to germinate. If you change more than one variable, you will not be able to tell which variable had the most effect on the germination time.

environmental conditions, such as cold. To help the seed stay dormant, some seeds have developed a hard, thick seed coat. The coat keeps out water and nutrients.

Scarification is the process of cracking or opening the seed coat. In nature, seed scarification can happen several ways, such as the seed falling from a tree or thawing after freezing. People can cause seed scarification by hand. In this experiment, you will look at how seed scarification affects germination. Using the same type of seeds, you will slightly nick open several of the seed coats. With another group of seeds, you will nick the seed coat and then allow the seeds to soak in water. You can compare the germination time of these experimental seeds to a group of control seeds.

Before you begin, make an educated guess about the outcome of this experiment based on your knowledge of what a seed needs to germinate and seed coats. This educated guess, or prediction, is your hypothesis. A hypothesis should explain these things:

- the topic of the experiment
- the variable you will change
- the variable you will measure
- what you expect to happen

*Step 3: Gently make one or two nicks in the seed shell. Do not cut the seed too hard or it could injure the inner seed.* ILLUSTRATION BY TEMAH NELSON.

A hypothesis should be brief, specific, and measurable. It must be something you can test through observation. Your experiment will prove or disprove whether your hypothesis is correct. Here is one possible hypothesis for this experiment: "The group of seeds that are scarified will consistently germinate before the seeds not scarified."

In this case, the variable you will change is changing the seed shell, and the variable you will measure is the time it takes to germinate. You expect one type of seed to germinate before the other.

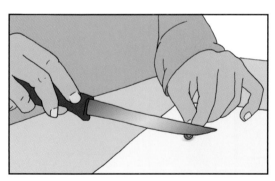

Level of Difficulty Moderate.

Materials Needed

- 12 seeds—of the same type; sweet peas, moonflowers, or morning glories work well (the seeds should be relatively large with a thick outer shell)
- 1 10-section peat pellet or similar type starter pot, with a cover (available at gardening stores); you can replace this with 2 to 3 cups of potting soil and an egg carton
- water
- 3 plastic bags
- paper towel
- plant labels
- knife

Approximate Budget $10.

Timetable 30 minutes to set up over 24 hour period; four to 10 days for germination.

Step-by-Step Instructions

1. Follow the direction for the peat pellet or add soil to the sections in the egg carton.
2. Separate the seeds into three groups, with two to four seeds in each group. Place one group of seeds into a plastic bag labeled "Control." Place the second group of seeds into the bag labeled "Scarification," and set the last group in a bag labeled "Scarification/Moisture."
3. With the Scarification group, have an adult help you take a knife and gently make one or two nicks in the seed shell. Do not cut the seed too hard or it could injure the inner seed. Return the seeds to its plastic bag.
4. Repeat this same process with the Scarification/Moisture group.

## How to Experiment Safely

Have an adult help you cut the seeds. Because the seeds are small, your adult helper will need to handle the knife extremely carefully.

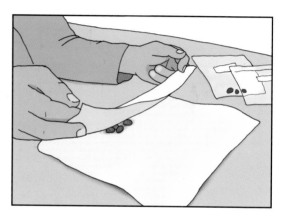

*Step 5: Wrap Scarification/ Moisture group of the seeds in a wet paper towel.* ILLUSTRATION BY TEMAH NELSON.

*Step 7: Cover the peat pellet (or carton) and set aside in a warm environment.* ILLUSTRATION BY TEMAH NELSON.

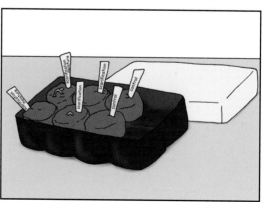

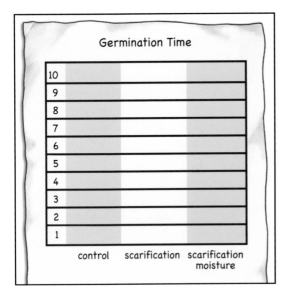

Germination Time

control  scarification  scarification moisture

*Step 9: Sample graph to mark when each of the seeds germinate.* ILLUSTRATION BY TEMAH NELSON.

5. Wrap Scarification/Moisture group of the seeds in a wet paper towel. Wrap the seeds in the towel and place it in a plastic bag labeled Scarification/Moisture. Allow these seeds to sit overnight

6. Plant each group of seeds separately. Place about two to three seeds in each section. Dig a small well in the soil, plant and water. Label a marker with the type of seed and insert. Repeat this with the other two groups of seeds. Each of the seeds should have the same amount of water.

7. Cover the peat pellet (or carton) and set aside in a warm environment.

8. Check daily, making sure the soil stays moist.

9. Set up a graph (see illustration) to mark when each of the seeds germinate.

**Summary of Results** Take a look at your chart. Which group of seeds germinated faster? Did the seeds that were soaked in moisture geminate faster or slower than the seeds that were only nicked? Write a summary of your results.

## Design Your Own Experiment

**How to Select a Topic Relating to this Concept** Since germination is dependent on so many variables, looking at variables may be the best place to start. For instance, cotyledons are the stored source of food for the growing embryo. What would happen if one cotyledon was removed? Or what would happen if a seed was cooked in boiling water for a minute? What would happen if the seed coat was removed before germination? Choose an aspect that interests you, then proceed with the research.

Check the Further Readings section and talk with your science teacher or school or community media specialist to start gathering information on germination questions that interest you.

**Steps in the Scientific Method** To do an original experiment, you need to plan carefully and think things through. Otherwise, you might not be sure what question you are answering, what you are or should be measuring, or what your findings prove or disprove.

Here are the steps in designing an experiment:

- State the purpose of—and the underlying question behind—the experiment you propose to do.
- Recognize the variables involved, and select one that will help you answer the question at hand.
- State a testable hypothesis, an educated guess about the answer to your question.
- Decide how to change the variable you selected.
- Decide how to measure your results.

**Recording Data and Summarizing the Results**
As a scientist investigating a question, you must gather information and share it with others. Bring all the data together and write a conclusion. Simplify the data into charts or graphs for others to understand easily.

**Related Projects** When dealing with seeds, you can take many different routes. You can try growing experiments or your investigation can be about seed anatomy, seed type (monocot or dicot), or methods of spreading the seeds.

## Troubleshooter's Guide

Here is a problem that may arise in your experiment, a possible cause, and ways to remedy it.

**Problem:** The seeds are not germinating, even after 10 days.

**Possible cause:** They may need more water or the soil might not have any nutrients. Make sure you have nutrient-rich soil. You can purchase it at a gardening store. Give the seeds water and repeat.

**Problem:** The seeds that were nicked with a knife did not germinate.

**Possible cause:** You may have cut and damaged the inside of the seed. Repeat the experiment, taking care to only nick the seeds.

**Problem:** There was no difference in any of the seeds' germination.

**Possible cause:** Not all seeds need scarification. You may have used a type of seed that did not. Try to purchase one of the recommended seed types, or ask for a recommendation at a gardening store for a type of seeds that needs scarification.

## For More Information

Andrew Rader Studios. "Plant Basics." *Rader's Biology4kids.com.* http://www.biology4kids.com/files/plants_main.html (accessed on February 8, 2008). Information on plant biology and structures.

Burnie, David. *Plant.* London: Dorling Kindersley, 1989. Includes chapters on plant life processes such as "A Plant Is Born," which covers germination.

Missouri Botanical Garden. *Biology of Plants.* http://www.mbgnet.net/bioplants/ (accessed on February 6, 2008). Basic information about plant biology and life.

United States Department of Agriculture. *Plant's Database.* http://plants.usda.gov (accessed on February 6, 2008). Provides a list of plants in every state, along with images of many plants.

*The Visual Dictionary of Plants.* London: Dorling Kindersley, 1992. Offers an in-depth overview of plants and their activities through text and clear, detailed photos.

## 44

# Gravity

Earth orbits the Sun. The Moon orbits the Earth. But how do the planets stay in the sky? How do we stay on Earth's surface? Englishman Sir Isaac Newton (1642–1727) figured out the answers to these questions while watching an apple fall in his orchard. Newton reasoned that the force that pulls the Moon into its curved path around Earth instead of a straight line was the same force that pulled the apple to the ground. Newton was a scientist and mathematician, and he wrote his theory on a scrap of paper, something he did with all his thoughts and formulas. The falling apple initiated his famous universal law of gravity, which states that the attracting force between any two bodies is directly proportional to the product of their masses and inversely proportional to the square of the distance between them. It was published in his book *Principia* in 1687.

*Well, how do they stay up there?* Danish scientist Tycho Brahe (1571–1630) developed a theory of planetary motions. Then, in 1609, Johannes Keppler used Brahe's theory when he said that the planets orbited elliptically rather than in a circle. An elliptical orbit is a curved path similar to the shape of an egg. Newton's laws unlocked many answers to questions scientists had been struggling with as they tried to figure out, among other things, what kept the planets orbiting in the first place.

The planets orbit and position themselves according to a balanced set of natural laws. One law is called inertia, the tendency of objects to continue whatever motion is affecting them. In other words, a rotating planet continues to rotate; a stationary book remains sitting on a desk. These objects continue to do what they do until a force causes an acceleration or change in their state of motion. This was part of Newton's First Law. In Newton's Second Law, he said the greater the force, the greater the acceleration. He also introduced the concept of mass, the

*Sir Isaac Newton developed the theory of gravity as he watched an apple fall.* LIBRARY OF CONGRESS.

amount of atoms, in an object. The relationship between an object's mass, acceleration, and the forces exerted on it was defined in his Second Law.

Newton's Third Law addressed gravity. For example, both the Moon and Earth are attracted to each other. But Earth has a much bigger mass, so it has a more powerful gravitational attraction that pulls the Moon into a curved path, or orbit, around Earth. The Sun exerts pulling forces as well. This attracting, pulling relationship exists between all the planets, moons, and stars. It keeps everything in the universe moving in an orderly fashion.

*High tide* The gravitational forces of the Moon and Sun pull on Earth's surface water, causing tides, or water surges, twice a day. The Moon has a stronger gravitational pull because it is closer to Earth than the Sun. Twice a month, when the Sun, Moon, and Earth are aligned, the force of their gravitational pull causes the highest tides, called spring tides. When the Sun and Moon are at right angles, they pull in different directions and have a weaker gravitational pull. Then lower tides, called neap tides, take place.

*What about me and the apple?* What keeps your feet on the ground is Earth's gravitational force pulling you down. The amount of gravitational force Earth exerts on an object, in this case you, depends on your mass. Earth has a very large mass, so its gravitational force is very strong. That is why we are not falling into space. You exert an attracting gravitational force on Earth as well, but the pull is very weak.

If *you* are being pulled to the ground, it is easy to understand why Earth's gravitational force also pulled Newton's apple to the ground. Gravitational forces have a great effect on our lives. Conducting experiments makes us aware of their presence and influence, from keeping us from falling off the planet to allowing us to launch rockets.

**Acceleration:** The rate at which the velocity and/or direction of an object is changing with the respect to time.

**Elliptical:** An orbital path which is egg-shaped or resembles an elongated circle.

**Hypothesis:** An idea in the form of a statement that can be tested by observation and/or experiment.

**Inertia:** The tendency of an object to continue in its state of motion.

**Mass:** Measure of the total amount of matter in an object. Also, an object's quantity of matter as shown by its gravitational pull on another object.

**Universal law of gravity:** The law of physics that defines the constancy of the force of gravity between two bodies.

**Variable:** Something that can affect the results of an experiment.

**Weight:** The gravitational attraction of Earth on an object; the measure of the heaviness of an object.

## EXPERIMENT 1

## Gravity: How fast do different objects fall?

**Purpose/Hypothesis** In this experiment, you will determine the effect that mass has on the gravitational pull exerted on a falling object. You will drop three pencils taped together at the same time as you drop a single pencil to see whether the heavier group falls faster. You will also drop two objects of about the same weight (a pencil and a Ping-Pong ball) but with different shapes to see which falls faster.

According to the laws of physics, the falling rate for all objects is the same. Gravity does pull harder on objects with more mass. However, objects with more mass also have more inertia. Inertia causes objects to continue whatever motion is affecting them. That means objects at rest tend to stay at rest—they resist moving. The more mass an object has, the more inertia it has. The amount of force needed to overcome inertia balances out the pull of gravity, so objects with more mass fall at the same rate as objects with less mass.

Falling rates can also be affected by air resistance, the force that air exerts on a moving object. Air resistance pushes up on a falling object, while

*The planets in the Andromeda Galaxy, M31, follow an elliptical orbit.* PHOTO RESEARCHERS INC.

## What Are the Variables?

Variables are anything that might affect the results of an experiment. Here are the main variables in this experiment:

- the weight of each pencil
- whether the pencils are dropped in a vertical or a horizontal position
- the distance from which all objects are dropped
- the amount of force used when the objects are dropped

In other words, the variables in this experiment are everything that might affect the mass and shape of the objects. If you change more than one variable, you will not be able to tell which variable had the most effect on the speed with which the objects hit the floor.

*Step 1: Tape three of the pencils together tightly.* GALE GROUP.

Grouping of Pencils

gravity pulls down. The more surface an object has, the more air resistance it has and the more slowly it will fall. You can test this by crumpling a sheet of paper into a ball and dropping it at the same time as you drop a flat sheet of the same paper. The flat sheet has more air resistance and will fall more slowly.

Before you begin the experiment, make an educated guess about the outcome based on your knowledge of gravity. This educated guess, or prediction, is your hypothesis. A hypothesis should explain these things:

- the topic of the experiment
- the variable you will change
- the variable you will measure
- what you expect to happen

A hypothesis should be brief, specific, and measurable. It must be something you can test through observation. Your experiment will prove or disprove your hypothesis. Here is one possible hypothesis for the pencil experiment: "The group of pencils and the single pencil will fall at the same rate." For the Ping-Pong ball experiment, your hypothesis might be this: "The Ping-Pong ball will fall more slowly than the pencil because its shape gives it more air resistance."

In this case, the variable you will change is the mass (pencils) and the shape (pencil and Ping-Pong ball) of the objects. The variable you will measure or observe is the time when each object hits the floor.

Level of Difficulty Easy/moderate.

Materials Needed

- 4 wooden pencils, unsharpened
- masking tape
- 1 Ping-Pong ball
- 6-foot (1.8 m) step ladder

**Approximate Budget** $5 for pencils, tape, and Ping-Pong ball.

**Timetable** 20 minutes.

**Step-by-Step Instructions**

1. Tape three of the pencils together tightly.
2. Place the taped pencils and the single pencil on the top of the ladder.
3. Ask your adult helper to climb the ladder.
4. Position yourself flat on the floor, about 6 feet (1.8 m) from the ladder so you can observe the pencils hitting the floor.
5. Have the adult pick up the taped pencils in one hand and the single pencil in his or her other hand.
6. Have the adult hold both sets of pencils at the same height from the floor, in a vertical position, and drop them. Your helper should not use any force, but simply let them both go at the same time.
7. Ask the adult to help you repeat this procedure with different groupings of pencils. Record your observations in a table similar to the one illustrated.

## How to Experiment Safely

Ask an adult to climb the ladder so you can lie on the floor and observe when the objects hit the floor. No one should ever stand on the top step of a ladder.

Dropping the Pencils

*Steps 3 to 6: Adult drops pencils from ladder; student positioned for observation.* GALE GROUP.

Results Chart

| Pencil Grouping | Falling Rate |
|---|---|
| 3 grouped pencils and 1 pencil | same |
| 2 grouped pencils and 2 loose pencils | |
| 4 loose pencils | |

*Step 7: Results chart for*
*Experiment 1.* GALE GROUP.

8. Have the adult repeat the procedure, dropping a single pencil, held vertically to reduce air resistance, and the Ping-Pong ball. Observe which object hits the floor first.

Summary of Results Study the observations on your table and decide whether your hypotheses were correct. Did the taped pencils and the single pencil hit the floor at the same time? If not, how would you explain the difference? (The larger group of pencils would have slightly more air resistance than the single pencil, even when dropped in vertical positions.)

Did the single pencil hit the floor before the Ping-Pong ball? Why is that? Write a paragraph summarizing your findings and explaining whether they support your hypothesis.

Change the Variables Here are some ways you can vary this experiment:

- Vary the distance from which you drop the objects. Can you observe a difference in falling rates when the distance is longer or shorter?

- Try dropping other objects with different amounts of mass or the same mass but different shapes. See how these changes affect their falling rates.

## PROJECT 2

## Measuring Mass: How can a balance be made?

**Purpose/Hypothesis** A useful measurement for science is not the weight but the mass of an object. The mass is the amount of atoms that make up an object. Here is your hypothesis: "By creating a balance with counterweights, you will cancel out the effects of gravity and calculate the mass of an object."

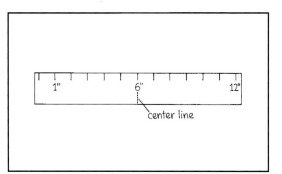

*Step 2: Mark the ruler in the middle.* GALE GROUP.

The materials used as a counterweight can be varied if the mass is known. The balance you will create is accurate only for low-mass objects. Do not exceed 0.9 ounces (25 grams) or accuracy will diminish.

**Level of Difficulty** Moderate.

**Materials Needed**

- 2 5-ounce (148-ml) cups
- plastic ruler, 1 foot (30 cm) long
- dried beans
- quarter, penny, nickel
- 30 small metal paper clips
- pencil
- Optional: dried split peas, Popsicle sticks

**Approximate Budget** $4 for the beans and wood.

**Timetable** Approximately 30 minutes.

**Step-by-Step Instructions**

1. Place the pencil on a level desk. If the pencil rolls, the desk is not level.
2. Mark the ruler in the middle.
3. Place the ruler over the pencil at right angles, as illustrated.
4. At each end of the balance place the 5-ounce (148 milliliter) paper cups. Draw rings to mark their positions.
5. Make sure the ruler is level, and neither side is touching the tabletop.

6. If a side is touching, very *slightly* move the ruler as it rests on the pencil. Try to balance it perfectly.
7. As a test material, place a quarter (0.19 oz or 5.5 grams) in one cup.
8. Place 1 nickel (0.175 oz. or 5 grams) and one paper clip (0.018 oz. or 0.5 grams) in the other cup. The balance should be level.
9. Continue to test other combinations of materials to determine which have equal mass.

Below is a list of common materials and their mass:

nickel: 0.175 oz. (5 grams)
dime: 0.08 oz. (2.3 grams)
penny: 0.087 oz. (2.5 grams)
quarter: 0.19 oz. (5.5 grams)
wooden Popsicle stick: 0.05 oz. (1.5 grams)
one paper clip: 0.018 oz. (0.5 grams)
dried split pea: 0.003 oz. (0.1 gram)

**Summary of Results** You now have made an instrument of measurement. It is important that you keep a record of the standard measurements and items for counterweights. Illustrated is a chart that you can make to keep track of the mass of tested objects.

**Modify the Experiment** For a more in depth look at gravity and how air pressure impacts gravity, you can do some simple experiments that will illustrate the relationship between these two forces.

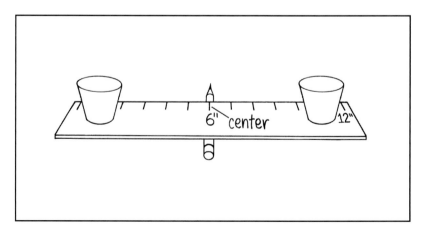

*Steps 3 and 4: Place the ruler over the pencil at right angles. At each end of the balance place the 5-ounce paper cups.* GALE GROUP.

In Experiment 1, you learned that air resistance, the force that air exerts on a moving object, affects the rate at which an object falls. Experiment with this idea further by using a plastic soda bottle and water. Using what you know about gravity and air resistance, predict what would happen if you added water to a soda bottle with holes and then change the air resistance in the bottle. What would happen to the water? How could air resistance prevent the water from spilling out of the holes?

Carefully poke small holes in the bottom of a plastic bottle. Fill the bottle with water and twist on the cap. Hold onto the bottle cap and lift it above a sink, while making sure you are not squeezing the bottle. What happens?

Now remove the cap and lift the bottle above the sink. What is happening to the water? How do the results show how air resistance can work against the force of gravity?

## Troubleshooter's Guide

Below are some problems that may occur during this project, possible causes, and ways to remedy the problems.

**Problem:** When you tested the quarter, it did not balance.

**Possible cause:** The balance is not accurate to the 0.5 gram point. The actual mass of the quarter is 5.6 grams. Try adding one or two split peas to counter the weight.

**Problem:** The balance keeps tipping and it does not seem to level out.

**Possible cause:** Try using a pencil that has flattened sides to decrease sensitivity.

## Design Your Own Experiment

How to Select a Topic Relating to this Concept Gravity is a force of nature that can be examined and studied in many different ways. Pretend to be Newton and make observations about what happens around you. Notice common events. Why does a coin fall through water more slowly than through air? Is gravity the same in water as it is in air? The study of gravity will lead you into other areas of physics such as friction, buoyant force, and acceleration.

Steps in the Scientific Method To do an original experiment, you need to plan carefully and think things through. Otherwise, you might not be sure what question you are answering, what you are or should be measuring, or what your findings prove or disprove.

*Recording chart for Experiment 2.* GALE GROUP.

| Object | Counterweights | Total mass |
|--------|----------------|------------|
|        |                |            |
|        |                |            |
|        |                |            |
|        |                |            |
|        |                |            |
|        |                |            |
|        |                |            |
|        |                |            |

*Air resistance working against the force of gravity.*
ILLUSTRATION BY TEMAH NELSON.

Here are the steps in designing an experiment:

- State the purpose of—and the underlying question behind—the experiment you propose to do.
- Recognize the variables involved, and select one that will help you answer the question at hand.
- State a testable hypothesis, an educated guess about the answer to your question.
- Decide how to change the variable you selected.
- Decide how to measure your results.

**Recording and Summarizing Results** It is important to be able to share your results with others. Put any data you collect into charts or graphs. Even Newton wrote down his measurements in journals.

When summarizing the results, reflect on your question or purpose and describe how it was answered or proven. Look at your hypothesis and see if your initial idea was correct. Plot the results on graphs and charts. Make them easy for others to understand or follow.

**Related Projects** One type of experiment that would be fun might be a scale to measure weight. All you need is a spring, hook, and some cardboard. By hanging objects on the hook and hanging them on the spring, you can measure the pull of gravity on a mass.

## For More Information

Allaby, Michael, et al. *The Visual Encyclopedia of Science.* New York: Kingfisher, 1994. Includes illustrated science text and colorful photos that explain the gravity concept.

Asimov, Isaac. *Asimov's Chronology of Science and Discovery.* New York: Harper & Row, 1989. Offers a clear, direct explanation of gravity.

Magill, Frank N. *The Great Scientists.* Danbury, CT: Grolier Education Corp., 1989. Contains a good background chapter about Isaac Newton, his discovery of gravity, and other scientific theories he introduced.

# 45

# Greenhouse Effect

In 1827, a French mathematician named Jean-Baptiste-Joseph Fourier came up with an interesting theory. He said Earth's atmosphere protected its inhabitants against the freezing temperatures of space. Fourier pointed out that Earth's atmosphere acted as an insulator, an effect similar to what happens when heat is trapped within the glass walls and roof of a greenhouse. He called his theory the greenhouse effect.

Today we know that the greenhouse effect takes place when sunlight passes through the atmosphere and is absorbed by land and water. The energy in the sunlight is converted to heat energy to warm the surface of Earth. Some of this heat energy is re-radiated out into the atmosphere in the form of infrared radiation. The infrared radiation has a longer wavelength than the sunlight and is absorbed by certain gases in the atmosphere, such as carbon dioxide. This traps the heat, keeping Earth's surface warm. The greenhouse effect is actually a good thing. Without it, we would experience an average temperature of −2.2°F (−19°C), and we would all freeze.

*Perfecting a theory* Two scientists in the nineteenth century expanded Fourier's theory. In 1861, English physicist John Tyndall said that certain atmospheric gases, such as carbon monoxide and water vapor, warmed Earth's surface. In 1896, Swedish scientist Svante Arrhenius made the greenhouse theory clearer in a scientific article. He stated that increased carbon dioxide levels in the atmosphere could trap more of the heat energy rising from Earth. More trapped heat energy meant warmer temperatures on Earth's surface. Arrhenius was the first to understand the concept of global warming and climate changes because of the greenhouse effect.

*We are all affected by the greenhouse effect* The greenhouse effect has been in the news a lot lately. Why? Carbon dioxide levels began to rise during the late 1700s when machines began doing work that had

*A greenhouse traps the Sun's heat within its glass walls and roof, just as carbon dioxide does in Earth's atmosphere.* PETER ARNOLD INC.

*Global warming, caused by the greenhouse effect, causes polar ice caps and glaciers to melt faster.* PHOTO RESEARCHERS INC.

previously been done by humans and animals. The machines needed fuel to work, and fossil fuels, such as coal and wood, were used. Fossil fuels contain carbon. Burning these fuels releases the carbon, which combines with the oxygen in air to form carbon dioxide. Back in the 1700s, this was not a big problem because there were not as many people or machines. But today, burning fossil fuels such as gasoline has caused a critical situation.

Besides being used in vehicles—including cars, trucks, and planes—fossil fuels are used to produce electricity. Burning these fossil fuels releases billions of tons (metric tons) of carbon dioxide into the air every year. At the same time, many of the forests, which absorb carbon dioxide from the air, have been cut down. All of these factors increase the volume of heat-trapping carbon dioxide gas in our atmosphere.

In addition, water vapor in the air and about thirty other gases also trap Earth's heat, including gases from nitrogen-based fertilizers and methane emissions from decomposing vegetation.

## WORDS TO KNOW

**Atmosphere:** Layers of air that surround Earth.

**By-products:** Something produced in the making of something else.

**Combustion:** Any chemical reaction in which heat, and usually light, are produced. The most common form of combustion is when organic substances combine with oxygen in the air to burn and form carbon dioxide and water vapor.

**Fossil fuels:** A fuel such as coal, oil, gasoline, or natural gas that was formed over millions of years from the remains of plants and animals.

**Global warming:** Warming of Earth's atmosphere as a result of an increase in the concentration of gases that store heat, such as carbon dioxide.

**Greenhouse effect:** The warming of Earth's atmosphere due to water vapor, carbon dioxide, and other gases in the atmosphere that trap heat radiated from Earth's surface.

**Greenhouse gases:** Gases that absorb infrared radiation and warm the air before the heat energy escapes into space.

**Hypothesis:** An idea in the form of a statement that can be tested by observation and/or experiment.

**Infrared radiation:** Electromagnetic radiation of a wavelength shorter than radio waves but longer than visible light that takes the form of heat.

**Insulation:** A material that is a poor conductor of heat or electricity.

**Microclimate:** A unique climate that exists only in a small, localized area.

**Troposphere:** Atmospheric layer closest to Earth where all life exists.

**Variable:** Something that can change the results of an experiment.

These greenhouse gases absorb heat energy from Earth before it escapes into space. According to scientists, these heat-trapping gases will cause an average temperature rise of 3–8 °F (16–13 °C) in the next 60 years, which could cause destructive weather changes.

Conducting experiments and projects on how the greenhouse effect works will help you become aware of the delicate natural balance that maintains Earth's environment as we know it. We have already experienced some of the problems caused by an overload of greenhouse gases, including air pollution, which causes respiratory problems. Being more aware of the greenhouse effect may make you want to help reduce these gases and help our planet.

*Nitrogen-based fertilizers contribute to the greenhouse effect.* PHOTO RESEARCHERS INC.

## What Are the Variables?

Variables are anything that might affect the results of an experiment. Here are the main variables in this experiment:

- the amount of sunlight reaching the greenhouse
- the amount of sunlight that passes through the glass or plastic
- the amount of wind or rain
- the color of the material under the greenhouse

In other words, the variables in this experiment are everything that might affect the temperature inside the greenhouse. If you change more than one variable, you will not be able to tell which variable had the most effect on temperature.

## EXPERIMENT 1

## Creating a Greenhouse: How much will the temperature rise inside a greenhouse?

Purpose/Hypothesis In this experiment you will measure the temperature inside a greenhouse. A greenhouse is a small enclosure that maintains a microclimate that is warmer than the climate outside it. A greenhouse is often used for growing plants in cold weather. It is made of plastic or glass that allows the Sun's light energy to pass through. When the light energy is absorbed by the soil and plants inside, it warms them. Some of this energy is then re-radiated out into the greenhouse in the form of infrared radiation, or heat energy. Because the heat energy has a longer wavelength than the entering light energy, most of the energy is absorbed and trapped by the plastic or glass of the greenhouse walls and roof, just as the greenhouse gases in our atmosphere absorb and trap the heat energy from Earth. Although a small portion of the heat energy escapes, most of it is reflected or re-radiated back into the greenhouse to warm the air.

Before you begin, make an educated guess about the outcome of this experiment based on your knowledge of greenhouses and the greenhouse effect. This educated guess, or prediction, is your hypothesis. A hypothesis should explain these things:

- the topic of the experiment
- the variable you will change
- the variable you will measure
- what you expect to happen

A hypothesis should be brief, specific, and measurable. It must be something you can test through observation. Your experiment will prove or disprove whether your hypothesis is correct. Here is one possible hypothesis for this experiment: "The more sunlight that shines on the greenhouse, the higher the inside temperature compared to the outside temperature."

In this case, the variable you will change (or let nature change) is the amount of sunlight that reaches the greenhouse, and the variable you will measure is the temperature inside the greenhouse compared to the outside temperature. If the difference between the inside temperature and outside temperature is greater on days when more sunlight reaches the greenhouse, you will know your hypothesis is correct.

## How to Experiment Safely

Goggles and adult supervision are required when hammering the nails. Wear gloves when handling the glass.

**Level of Difficulty** Easy/moderate.

**Materials Needed**

- 2 thermometers
- 4 wooden boards, roughly 1 x 6 x 20 inches (2.5 x 15 x 50 centimeters)
- One 24 x 24-inch (60 x 60-centimeter) piece of transparent plastic or glass, 0.25 inch (0.5 centimeter) thick
- Eight 2-inch (5-centimeter) nails
- hammer
- goggles
- gloves

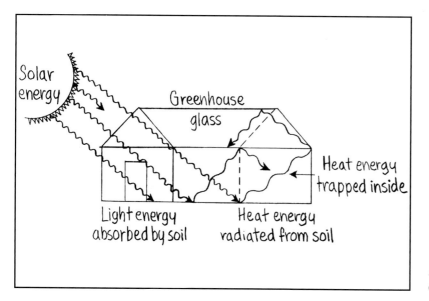

*How a greenhouse works.* GALE GROUP.

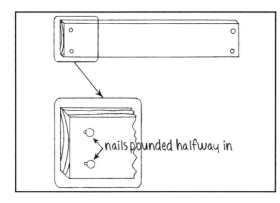

Step 1: Carefully hammer two nails through each end of a piece of wood. GALE GROUP.

**Approximate Budget** $10. (Use any lumber that is cost-effective.)

**Timetable** One week. (This experiment requires a half-hour to assemble and one week to monitor.)

**Step-by-Step Instructions**

1. Hammer two nails through each end of a piece of wood, as illustrated. Repeat with a second piece of wood. Place the wood into a square with the two pieces with nails opposite each other.

2. Hold the wood in position and assemble the box by carefully driving the nails into the ends of the two remaining pieces of wood.

| Greenhouse WEATHER CONDITIONS | DAY 1 | DAY 2 | DAY 3... |
|---|---|---|---|
| MORNING TEMP. | 65 | 65 | 63 |
| AFTERNOON TEMP. | 75 | 76 | 76 |
| EVENING TEMP. | 65 | 65 | 66 |

| Outside WEATHER CONDITIONS | DAY 1 | DAY 2 | DAY 3... |
|---|---|---|---|
| MORNING TEMP. | 59 | 62 | 55 |
| AFTERNOON TEMP. | 65 ☁ | 67 ⛅ | 69 ☀ |
| EVENING TEMP. | 58 🌧 | 59 | 59 |

KEY TO WEATHER CONDITIONS

☀ Sunny   ☁🌧 Rainy

⛅ Partly Sunny   ☁ Windy

☁ Cloudy

Step 6: Sample recording chart for Experiment 1. GALE GROUP.

3. Place the piece of plastic or glass over the wood box. Be sure it completely overlaps the wood box so there are no gaps around the edges.

4. Place the greenhouse outside in a sunny spot. Put one thermometer inside the greenhouse and one outside the greenhouse close by.

5. Record the temperature inside and outside at the same time in the morning, afternoon, and evening for seven days. Record for a longer period if three or more days are mostly cloudy, windy, or rainy.

6. Record the general weather conditions during each day. See the results chart illustrated.

**Summary of Results** Review the data collected at the same time of day. Graph this data so you can compare temperatures inside and outside of the greenhouse. Note the general weather conditions for each day on the graph. Do your results confirm your hypothesis? Was the temperature inside the greenhouse higher on days when there was more sunshine? Was it consistently higher than the temperature outside? Was the difference between the inside temperature and the outside temperature greatest when there was more sunshine?

---

## Troubleshooter's Guide

Here are some problems that may arise during this experiment, possible causes, and ways to remedy the problems.

**Problem:** The temperature inside the greenhouse is going up too high, for example, 110°F (43°C).

**Possible cause:** If you conduct this experiment during the warm summer months, the temperature inside the greenhouse will soar. Try placing a large piece of thin white paper on top of the greenhouse to block some of the Sun's rays.

**Problem:** The evening temperature inside the greenhouse is always much higher than the outside temperature.

**Possible cause:** If you place the greenhouse on a dark surface, such as a brick patio or walkway, the dark materials will absorb heat during the day. That heat will remain trapped under the greenhouse to keep the inside warm in the evening, even when the outside temperature drops.

---

**Change the Variables** You can change the variables and repeat this experiment. For example, you can vary the amount of sunlight reaching the greenhouse by placing one or more layers of thin tracing paper or wax paper over the glass. You can also vary the color of the material under the greenhouse by first placing the greenhouse on a white poster board and then on a black poster board. Does the black poster board absorb more incoming sunlight and make the temperature inside the greenhouse higher? If you place two bricks inside the greenhouse, will they absorb and retain enough heat to keep the greenhouse warm all night? To find out, you would have to take temperature measurements at various times between sundown and sunrise.

When you conduct further experiments, remember to change only one variable at a time or you will not be able to tell which variable affected the results.

## EXPERIMENT 2

### Fossil Fuels: What happens when fossil fuels burn?

Purpose/Hypothesis Fossil fuels, such as oil, coal, and natural gas, are used to warm the world we live in and move the machines that make life easier. However, for every advantage there usually is a disadvantage. That is what this project will demonstrate.

Many fossil fuels are hydrocarbons, which means they contain hydrogen and carbon. When these fossil fuels are burned during combustion, they combine with oxygen and other gases in the air to produce carbon dioxide, water vapor, and other by-products that may harm the environment or act as greenhouse gases. The combustion of fossil fuels is a major contributor to the greenhouse effect.

In this project you will observe how carbon dioxide and water vapor are produced during combustion. You will also look for evidence of free carbon before it combines with oxygen to form carbon dioxide.

Level of Difficulty Moderate. (The experimenter must be mature and responsible when performing this project.)

*Step 4: Carefully hold the rounded end of the spoon 1 inch (2.5 centimeters) above the flame.* GALE GROUP.

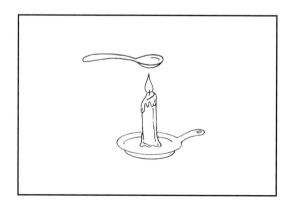

### Materials Needed

- 1 paraffin candle
- matches
- plate or candle holder
- metal spoon
- white index card
- goggles
- leather gloves

Approximate Budget $1 for the candle; other items will likely be found in the home.

Timetable 10 minutes.

## Step-By-Step Instructions

1. Place the candle in the holder or on the plate. Make sure it will not fall over.

2. Remove all nearby flammable materials.

3. Using the matches, light the candle and let it burn for a minute. (Ask for help if needed. An adult *must* be present.)

4. Wearing goggles and gloves, hold the rounded end of the spoon 1 inch (2.5 centimeters) above the flame. Notice if anything accumulates on the spoon. Hold it there 10 seconds or less. Caution! The spoon will get hot.

5. Next, place the spoon directly into the flame for five to 10 seconds and remove. Notice if anything accumulates. Caution! The spoon will be very hot.

6. After the spoon has cooled, use your finger to transfer some of the black residue that has appeared on the spoon onto the index card. The residue is carbon produced by the combustion. Notice that the carbon was formed when the spoon was *inside* the flame. However, when you held the spoon *above* the flame, there was no black residue. A general formula for the combustion of paraffin-type hydrocarbons is illustrated above. During the first stage of combustion, the carbon and hydrogen molecules in the paraffin split apart. So, inside the flame, the carbon is free and has not bonded to the oxygen yet. That is why the carbon collected on the spoon held in the flame. Once the carbon rises out of the flame, it joins with the oxygen in the air and becomes the invisible gas carbon dioxide.

7. Put on the goggles and gloves again and hold the glass upside down so the open end of the glass is even with the top of the candle, and the flame is inside the glass. Use both hands to hold the glass and keep it centered above the flame. Hold it there for 10 seconds or less. Caution! The glass will get hot. Watch for moisture accumulating inside the glass. This is the water vapor produced by the combustion.

---

### How to Experiment Safely

This project *requires* adult permission and supervision. Always use caution when handling matches and candles. Wear goggles, remove loose clothing, and tie back long hair. Do not try this project with any other fuel source. Gasoline, kerosene, propane, lamp oil, and other fuels can be explosive and extremely dangerous.

*Step 6: The general formula for the combustion of paraffin-type hydrocarbons.* GALE GROUP.

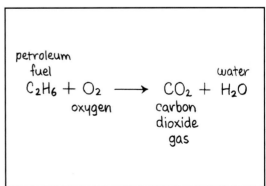

petroleum fuel

water

$$C_2H_6 + O_2 \longrightarrow CO_2 + H_2O$$

oxygen

carbon dioxide gas

## Troubleshooter's Guide

Here is a problem that may arise during this project, a possible cause, and a way to remedy it.

**Problem:** There was black residue on the spoon when held above the flame.

**Possible cause:** The spoon was too close to the candle. Try again, holding the spoon at least an inch above the top of the flame.

**Summary of Results** Make sure you keep a journal of your observations. Pay close attention to what is happening. If you do not give the project your full attention, you can miss events. You can diagram these events in a journal.

**Modify the Experiment** In this experiment, you built a greenhouse and measured the temperature inside and outside over a period of time. You know that carbon dioxide is a greenhouse gas, and studies have shown that levels of carbon dioxide in the atmosphere have been rising. For a more advanced version of this experiment, you can explore how changing the carbon dioxide level will affect temperature.

In modifying this experiment to introduce carbon dioxide, you will need to make two simple greenhouses. You can make the greenhouses from two plastic bottles. Cut the bottoms off and place a thermometer inside each bottle. Place a heat lamp over both the empty bottle and the bottle with the carbon dioxide. You can then add carbon dioxide into one of the bottles. One way to add carbon dioxide is with baking soda and vinegar. Baking soda mixed with vinegar creates a chemical reaction that produces carbon dioxide. Mix the baking soda and vinegar in a small container and immediately set the container inside one of the bottles. Turn on both heat lamps.

Monitor the temperatures of both bottles over several hours and record your results. Compare the temperatures of the carbon dioxide bottle and its control. You can experiment with different concentrations of the baking soda and vinegar. You could also find other sources of carbon dioxide and see if they are more effective in producing a temperature change.

## Design Your Own Experiment

**How to Select a Topic Relating to this Concept** Since the atmosphere acts as a giant greenhouse, sheltering life on Earth from harsh environments in space, the atmosphere is a good starting point for experiments and projects. For example, you might begin with an investigation into the layers of the atmosphere and how they help insulate the earth. You might

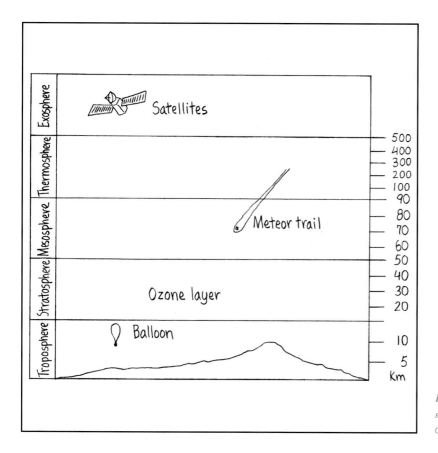

*Layers of the atmosphere surrounding Earth.* GALE GROUP.

also identify which machines or sources of power generate the lowest levels of carbon dioxide and other greenhouse gases.

Check the Further Readings section and talk with your science teacher or school or community media specialist to start gathering information on greenhouse effect questions that interest you. As you consider possible experiments and projects, be sure to discuss them with your science teacher or another knowledgeable adult before trying them. Some of them might be dangerous.

**Steps in the Scientific Method** To do an original experiment, you need to plan carefully and think things through. Otherwise, you might not be sure what question you are answering, what you are or should be measuring, or what your findings prove or disprove.

Here are the steps in designing an experiment:

- State the purpose of—and the underlying question behind—the experiment you propose to do.
- Recognize the variables involved, and select one that will help you answer the question at hand.
- State a testable hypothesis, an educated guess about the answer to your question.
- Decide how to change the variable you selected.
- Decide how to measure your results.

**Recording Data and Summarizing the Results** Your data on the greenhouse effect can be put into charts or graphs or even photographed to enable the information to be shared with others. After the data is collected and analyzed, your final responsibility is to make a conclusion based on your experiment and decide whether your hypothesis was true.

**Related Projects** For atmospheric experiments, it's best to study the layer closest to earth called the troposphere. This layer is where all life exists. For instance, you could design an experiment with plants and insects living in an environment that has an altered atmosphere.

## For More Information

Bilger, Burk. *Global Warming*. New York: Chelsea House Publishers, 1992. Examines the phenomenon of global warming, discussing the greenhouse effect in its positive, life-giving form and again as this mechanism is knocked out of balance.

U.S. Environmental Protection Agency. "Greenhouse Effect." http://www.epa.gov/climatechange/kids/greenhouse.html (accessed on January 17, 2008).

Williams, Jack. *The Weather Book*. New York: Vintage Books, 1997. Includes diagrams and text on the greenhouse effect and other atmosphere-related phenomena.

# 46

# Groundwater Aquifers

The term groundwater sounds as if it refers to an underground lake or river, but relatively little groundwater is found in this form. Groundwater lies below the surface of the land; in fact, it is almost everywhere underground. Mostly it is found in the tiny pores, or spaces, between rocks and particles of soil and in the cracks of larger rocks.

Where does groundwater come from? When rain falls, some of it flows along the surface of the ground into streams and lakes as runoff. Some of the rain evaporates into the atmosphere, some is taken up by plant roots, and some seeps into the ground to become groundwater.

*Aquifers are like big sponges* Underground areas called aquifers collect much of this groundwater. An aquifer is composed of permeable rock, loose material that holds water. Permeable means "having pores that permit a liquid or a gas to pass through." You might think of a groundwater aquifer as a big sponge that soaks up the rain that seeps below the surface.

As water from the surface slowly seeps down, or percolates, through the soil, it eventually hits a solid, or impermeable, layer of rock or soil. The aquifer forms as groundwater collects in the area above this impermeable layer. The water table is the level of the upper surface of the groundwater. If the water table in an area is high, the upper surface of the groundwater is only a short distance below the surface of the ground.

*Confined or unconfined?* Groundwater occurs in two conditions: confined and unconfined. A confined aquifer has a layer of impermeable clay or rock above it, and the water is held under pressure greater than the atmospheric pressure. When a well is drilled into a confined aquifer, it penetrates that impermeable, confining layer, allowing the water to rise under pressure. This is called an artesian well. An unconfined aquifer has no impermeable layer above it and is usually shallower than a confined aquifer.

*How groundwater forms.* GALE GROUP.

*How big is an aquifer?* The size of an aquifer depends on the amount of rainfall and the composition of the underground rock and soil. The world's largest aquifer is in the United States. Called the Ogallala, it spreads under eight western states, from South Dakota to Texas. The Ogallala formed millions of years ago and is still supplying water to cities, businesses, and farms. Unfortunately, people are using water from the Ogallala faster than it can be naturally replenished, and the water table is falling.

*Our most precious resource?* Water is a natural but limited resource. Most of the water on Earth is saltwater; 97% of the world's water supply is located in the oceans. That means that only 3% is freshwater, and two-thirds of that is frozen in the polar icecaps, icebergs, and glaciers. Only the remaining 1% is groundwater or surface water in lakes, ponds, and streams.

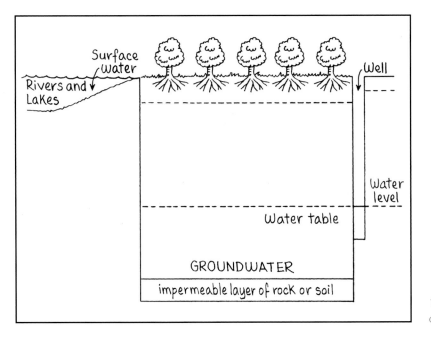

*Where groundwater occurs.*
GALE GROUP.

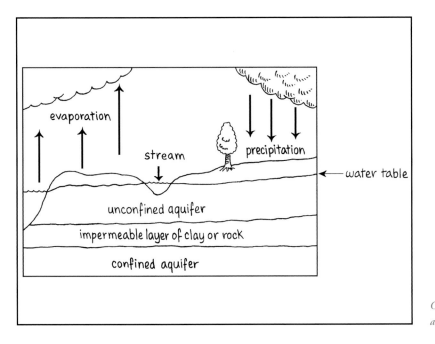

*Confined and unconfined aquifers.* GALE GROUP.

*Where does your drinking water come from?* PHOTO RESEARCHERS INC.

Today, about three-quarters of the cities in the United States depend on groundwater for part or all of their drinking water. Wells also withdraw groundwater to irrigate crops, keep golf courses green, and meet other recreational needs.

When water is pumped out of an aquifer into a well, the water level drops. If rainfall does not replace that water, the aquifer becomes over-drawn. When water is pumped out faster than it is replaced, the ground may sink, creating sinkholes.

*Can aquifers become polluted?* Contamination is another problem. Leaking underground storage tanks may seep petroleum products into groundwater. Inadequate septic systems, sewage treatment plants, fertilizer runoff from farms, salt runoff from highways, and chemicals discharged from factories are other sources of pollution that can make groundwater unsuitable for humans to drink or use.

Pollution can come from specific, identified locations, called point sources, or from scattered areas, called nonpoint sources. Most groundwater pollution comes from nonpoint sources. Once an aquifer is polluted, it may remain that way for years.

Wetlands provide homes for waterfowl and many other animal species. Low-lying wetlands may receive water from an aquifer. If the water is contaminated, it will pollute the wetlands, affecting all the wildlife that depends on these water habitats.

As the human population continues to grow, the demand for fresh, clean water supplies grows too. Careful management and use are essential to maintain the quality of our groundwater and surface water. The following projects will help you understand how aquifers can become contaminated and how dirty water can be cleaned.

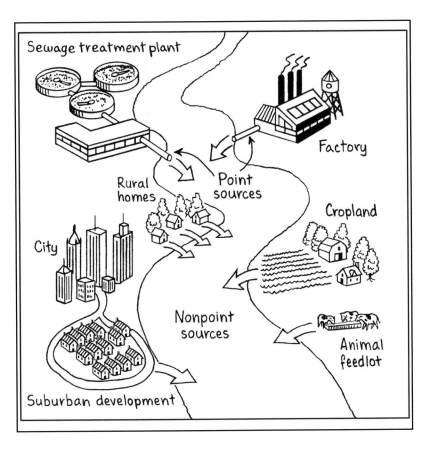

Sewage treatment plant

Factory

Rural homes

Point sources

Cropland

City

Nonpoint sources

Animal feedlot

Suburban development

*Sources of water pollution.*
GALE GROUP.

*Pollution that enters rivers and streams may eventually end up in the groundwater.* PHOTO RESEARCHERS INC.

## PROJECT 1

## Aquifers: How do they become polluted?

**Purpose/Hypothesis** Many communities and homeowners must rely on wells that pump groundwater from aquifers. Unfortunately, groundwater can be contaminated by improper use or disposal of harmful chemicals, such as lawn fertilizers and household cleaners. These chemicals can percolate down through the soil and rock into an aquifer and eventually be drawn into the wells. Such contamination can pose a significant threat to human health.

*Pollution in groundwater aquifers can harm the wildlife in wetlands.* PETER ARNOLD INC.

In this project, you will build a model that shows how water is stored in an aquifer, how groundwater can become contaminated, and how this contamination can end up in a well. You will see that what happens above ground can affect the aquifers below ground—and the drinking water.

**Level of Difficulty** Moderate, because of the time involved.

**Materials Needed**

- 6 x 8-inch (15 x 20-centimeter) clear plastic container at least 6 inches (15 centimeters) deep
- 1 pound (0.45 kilogram) modeling clay
- 2 pounds (0.9 kilograms) play sand
- 2 pounds (0.9 kilograms) aquarium gravel or pebbles, rinsed
- plastic drinking straw
- plastic spray bottle with a clear spray stem
- green felt, 3 x 5 inches (7.6 x 12.7 centimeters)
- 25 cup (59 milliliters) powdered cocoa
- red food coloring
- clean water
- tape

**Approximate Budget** $10 to $20 for the container, sand, clay, spray bottle, and other materials.

## WORDS TO KNOW

**Aeration:** Mixing a gas, like oxygen, with a liquid, like water.

**Aquifer:** Underground layer of sand, gravel, or spongy rock that collects water.

**Artesian well:** A well in which water is forced out under pressure.

**Coagulation:** A process during which solid particles in a liquid begin to stick together.

**Confined aquifer:** An aquifer with a layer of impermeable rock above it where the water is held under pressure.

**Disinfection:** Using chemicals to kill harmful organisms.

**Filtration:** Removing impurities from a liquid with a filter.

**Groundwater:** Water that soaks into the ground and is stored in the small spaces between the rocks and soil.

**Impermeable:** Not allowing substances to pass through.

**Impurities:** Chemicals or other pollutants in water.

**Nonpoint source:** An unidentified source of pollution, which may actually be a number of sources.

**Percolate:** To pass through a permeable substance.

**Permeable:** Having pores that permit a liquid or a gas to pass through.

**Point source:** An identified source of pollution.

**Pore:** An opening or space.

**Runoff:** Water that does not soak into the ground or evaporate, but flows across the surface of the ground.

**Sedimentation:** A process during which gravity pulls particles out of a liquid.

**Surface water:** Water in lakes, rivers, ponds, and streams.

**Unconfined aquifer:** An aquifer under a layer of permeable rock and soil.

**Variable:** Something that can affect the results of an experiment.

**Water table:** The level of the upper surface of groundwater.

**Wetlands:** Areas that are wet or covered with water for at least part of the year.

Timetable 1 to 2 hours.

## Step-by-Step Instructions

1. Tape the straw vertically inside the plastic container along one side, as illustrated. Do not let the bottom end of the straw touch the bottom of the container. This will be the "well."
2. Pour a 1.5-inch (3.8-centimeter) layer of sand on the bottom of the container.

## How to Experiment Safely

Do not drink the water you are using in this project.

3. Pour water into the sand, wetting it completely without creating puddles. The water will be absorbed into the sand, surrounding the particles, much as it is stored in an aquifer.

4. Flatten the clay into a thin layer and cover half the sand with it, pressing the clay into three sides of the container. The clay represents the confining or impermeable layer that keeps water from passing through.

5. Pour a small amount of water onto the clay. Most should remain on top of the clay, with some flowing into the uncovered sand.

6. Cover the whole surface of the sand and clay with the aquarium rocks. On one side, slope the rocks to form a hill and a valley.

7. Fill the container with water until it is nearly even with the top of your hill. See how the water is stored around the rocks in the aquifer. Also notice a surface supply of water (a small lake). This model represents groundwater and surface water, both of which can be used for drinking.

8. Put a few drops of red food coloring into the straw to represent pollution. People often use old wells to dispose of farm chemicals, trash, and used motor oils. The food coloring will color the sand. This demonstrates one way that pollution can spread into and through an aquifer.

9. Place the green felt on the hill. Use a little clay to fasten it to the sides of the container.

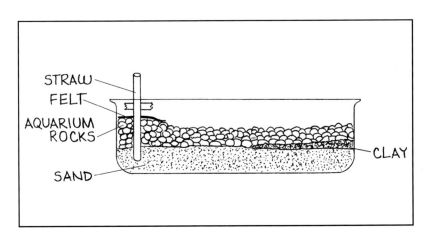

*Steps 1 to 7: How to build an aquifer.* GALE GROUP.

*Experiment Central, 2nd edition*

10. Sprinkle some cocoa on the hill, representing the improper use of materials such as lawn chemicals or fertilizers.

11. Fill the spray bottle with water. Make it rain on the hill and over the aquifer. The cocoa will seep through the felt and wash into the surface water. This is another way that pollution reaches aquifers.

12. Check the area around the straw. The pollution has probably spread farther. Remove the top of the spray bottle and insert the stem into the straw. Depress the trigger to pull up water from the well. Note its appearance. This is the same water that people would drink. It also is contaminated.

### Troubleshooter's Guide

Here is a problem that might arise, a possible cause, and a way to remedy the problem.

**Problem:** The straw is clogged with sand.

**Possible cause:** The straw is too close to the bottom of the container. Make sure you put the straw in first and leave a small space between it and the bottom of the container. Then pour in the sand. If sand still clogs the straw, gently blow through the straw to unclog it.

**Summary of Results** From your model, you can easily see how pollution spread into the surface water and the aquifer, contaminating the water supply. Write a paragraph about what you observed.

## PROJECT 2

## Groundwater: How can it be cleaned?

**Purpose/Hypothesis** Surface water—water in lakes, rivers, and wetlands—often contains impurities that make it look and smell bad. It may also contain bacteria and other organisms that can cause disease. Consequently, this water must be "cleaned" before it can be used. Water treatment plants typically clean water by taking it through these processes:

- aeration, which allows foul-smelling gases to escape and adds oxygen from the air
- coagulation, which causes solid particles to stick together
- sedimentation, which allows gravity to pull the solid particles out of a liquid
- filtration, which removes more impurities with a filter
- disinfection, which uses chemicals to kill harmful organisms

This project will demonstrate the procedures that municipal water plants use to purify water. It's important to maintain a clean water supply,

## How to Experiment Safely

Do not drink the water you are using in this project. Be careful using the scissors when you cut the tops and bottoms off the soda bottles.

as this water often affects the quality of the groundwater used by people who depend on wells.

**Level of Difficulty** Moderate.

**Materials Needed**

- 5 pints (5 liters) of "swamp water" (or add 2.5 cups of dirt or mud to 10.5 pints of water)
- 3 large clear plastic soft-drink bottles: 1 with a cap; 1 with its top removed; 1 with its bottom removed
- 5-quart (1.5-liter) or larger beaker (or another clear plastic soft-drink bottle bottom)
- 2 tablespoons (20 grams) alum (potassium aluminum sulfate; available from biological supply houses or ask your teacher for a source.)
- 5 pounds (0.7 kilograms) fine sand
- 5 pounds (0.7 kilograms) coarse sand
- 1 pound (0.5 kilograms) small pebbles (natural color aquarium rocks, washed)
- large (500 milliliter or larger) beaker or jar
- coffee filter
- rubber band
- stirrer
- scissors

*Step 5: Constructing a water filter.* GALE GROUP.

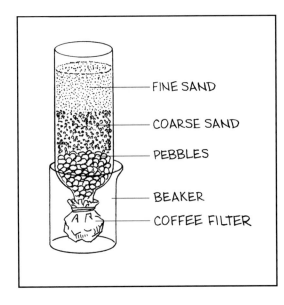

FINE SAND

COARSE SAND

PEBBLES

BEAKER

COFFEE FILTER

**Approximate Budget** $10 for sand, pebbles, and alum.

**Timetable** 1 to 2 hours.

**Step-by-Step Instructions**

1. Pour about 1.5 quart (1.5 liter) of the swamp water into the uncut soft-drink bottle. On a data sheet, describe the look and smell of the water.
2. To aerate the water, place the cap on the bottle and shake it vigorously for 30

seconds. The shaking allows gases trapped in the water to escape and adds oxygen to the water. Then pour the water back and forth between the bottle with the cap and the cut-off bottle ten times. Describe any changes in the water. Pour the aerated water into the large beaker or bottle bottom.

3. To coagulate solid impurities in the water so they can be removed, add the alum crystals to the water. Slowly stir for five minutes.

4. To allow sedimentation, let the water stand undisturbed for 20 minutes. Observe it at five-minute intervals and write your observations about the changes in the water's appearance.

5. Construct a filter from the bottle with its bottom removed. First, attach the coffee filter to the outside of the neck of the bottle with a rubber band. Turn the bottle top upside down and pour in a layer of pebbles. The filter will prevent the pebbles from falling out. Pour the coarse sand on top of the pebbles. Pour the fine sand on top of the coarse sand. Clean the filter by slowly and carefully pouring through 10.5 pints (5 liters), or more, of clean tap water. Try not to disturb the top layer of sand as you pour.

6. To filter the swamp water, wait until a large amount of sediment has settled on the bottom of the bottle of swamp water. Then carefully—without disturbing the sediment—pour the top two-thirds of the swamp water through the filter. Collect the filtered water in a beaker or other container.

7. Compare the smell and appearance of the treated and untreated water.

Note: The final step in water treatment is disinfection by adding chemicals to kill any harmful organisms. Because disinfectants must be handled carefully, this process is not included here. Do remember that the water you have treated is NOT safe to drink.

## Troubleshooter's Guide

Here is a problem that might arise during this project, a possible cause, and a way to remedy the problem.

**Problem:** During sedimentation, the sediments mixed into the water that was being filtered.

**Possible cause:** You might have poured the swamp water too quickly. Pour the contaminated water back into the sedimentation bottle and let it sit undisturbed again. Or pour it through the coffee filter and see if the sediment makes the water flow more slowly. The filter may not take all the sediment out, or it may become clogged with sediment, one of the many problems that occur during the actual water treatment process.

**Summary of Results** Write a report of your observations of the smell and look of the water before and after treatment. Include the amount of time that it took for the sediments to form.

## Design Your Own Experiment

**How to Select a Topic Relating to this Concept** You have seen how water enters an aquifer, how it flows from the aquifer into wetlands, and how it is drawn into wells. Perhaps you wonder how long it takes to replenish the supply of groundwater that is removed from the aquifer. You can use the aquifer you built in Project 1 to design your own experiment to determine how long it takes to replace the water that is removed.

Check the Further Readings section and talk with your science teacher or school or community media specialist to start gathering information on groundwater questions that interest you. As you consider possible experiments, be sure to discuss them with a knowledgeable adult before trying them.

**Steps in the Scientific Method** To do an original experiment, you need to plan carefully and think things through. Otherwise, you might not be sure what question you are answering, what you are or should be measuring, or what your findings prove or disprove.

Here are the steps in designing an experiment:

- State the purpose of—and the underlying question behind—the experiment you propose to do.
- Recognize the variables involved, and select one that will help you answer the question at hand.
- State a testable hypothesis, an educated guess about the answer to your question.
- Decide how to change the variable you selected.
- Decide how to measure your results.

**Recording Data and Summarizing the Results** In the two groundwater projects, the results were not measurable. However, in designing your own experiment, you should decide how to record the data, how to measure much water you draw out, and how to determine how quickly the same amount of water is replenished.

**Related Projects** You can undertake a variety of projects related to groundwater, such as finding out the source(s) of drinking water in your community and what steps are being taken to prevent contamination. You might research the kinds of contaminants found most often in your community's water and the probable sources of these contaminants. You might explore how flooding and drought each affect groundwater and its purity. If possible, compare the smell and appearance of surface water and groundwater—or water that has been treated by the city water division and water from a well. The possibilities just depend on your interests.

## For More Information

Dobson, Clive, and Gregor Gilpin Beck. *Watersheds: A Practical Handbook for Healthy Water.* Buffalo, NY: Firefly Books, 1999. Provides an overview of the fundamentals of ecology and the web of life through the water cycle.

Kellert, Stephen, general editor. *MacMillan Encyclopedia of the Environment.* New York: Simon and Schuster, 1997. Provides information on the water cycle and related topics.

U.S. Environmental Protection Agency Web Site. http://www.epa.gov/seahome/groundwater Provides information on groundwater aquifers and projects and activities that help explain the water cycle and aquifers.

Van Cleave, Janice. *Janice VanCleave's Ecology for Every Kid.* New York: John Wiley & Sons, 1996. Provides projects and information on the water cycle and water pollution.

U.S. Geological Survey. "Ground-water aquifers." *Water Science for Schools.* http://ga.water.usgs.gov/edu/earthgwaquifer.html (accessed January 18, 2008). Provides information on groundwater aquifers and projects and activities that help explain the water cycle and aquifers.

# 47

# Heat

Your feet are bare, and the Sun has been beating down on the sidewalk outside your home all day. You form a hypothesis or educated guess that the sidewalk is cool enough to allow you to walk on it without burning your feet. You decide to test your hypothesis, knowing that if you are wrong, you could be in for some painful moments!

But how does heat from the sidewalk burn your feet? Heat is a form of energy produced by the motion of molecules that make up a substance. The faster the molecules move, the more heat they produce and the higher the temperature of the sidewalk or other substance. Temperature is the measure of the average energy of the molecules in a substance. Heat can travel from one body to another in three ways: by conduction, by convection, and by radiation.

*What is conduction?* Conduction is the flow of heat through a solid. When you walk on a hot sidewalk, the concrete warms—or burns—your feet through conduction. When a warmer substance with quickly moving molecules (the sidewalk) comes into contact with a cooler substance with slowly moving molecules (your bare feet), the faster molecules bump into the slower ones and make them move faster, too.

*The quickly vibrating molecules in the hot sidewalk can transfer their heat energy to your cool feet.* KELLY A. QUIN.

As the slower molecules pick up speed, the cooler substance gets warmer. The warmer substance loses some of its heat energy and gets cooler. Heat energy is the energy produced when two substances that have

*A burner heats the air inside the balloon. As the hot air rises into the cooler atmosphere, the balloon rises, too.* PHOTO RESEARCHERS INC.

different temperatures are combined. The greater the difference in temperatures, the faster both temperatures change.

Some substances conduct or transfer heat better than others. In Experiment 1, you will test five substances to see which is the best conductor of heat.

*What is convection?* The second way heat travels is by convection. Convection is the rising of warm air from an object, such as the surface of Earth. Convection allows heat to travel through both gases and liquids, moving from warmer areas to cooler areas.

Heating the molecules in a gas or liquid makes them move farther apart, so the substance becomes lighter or less dense. The lighter air or liquid rises; it also cools off as heat energy escapes into the surrounding cooler air or liquid. As the molecules cool, they move closer together, and the substance becomes heavier or more dense and falls again.

In Experiment 2, you will use colored water to create convection currents that show how heat moves through a liquid. A convection current is a circular movement of a fluid in response to alternating heating and cooling.

*What is radiation?* Radiation is energy transmitted in the form of electromagnetic waves that travel through the vacuum of space at the speed of light. Infrared radiation consists of wavelengths that are shorter than radio waves but longer than visible light. Infrared radiation takes the form of heat. These heat rays are much like light rays except that we cannot see them.

That hot sidewalk was heated by infrared radiation from the Sun. The Sun's heat did not travel to the sidewalk by conduction or convection because the Sun and sidewalk are separated by the vacuum of space. The transfer of heat by radiation does not require that the hotter and cooler substances touch each other.

Not only the Sun, but all hot objects give out infrared radiation. This radiation gives up its heat energy when it is absorbed by an object, but this energy can also be reflected back toward its source. If that sidewalk had been painted white, it would have reflected the Sun's radiation, just as white clothing does. Why? The color white does not absorb light; it reflects it. Dark colors absorb light—and heat.

*What is heat capacity?* Heat capacity is the measure of how well a substance stores heat. Specific heat capacity is the energy required to raise the temperature of 1 kilogram of a substance by 1 degree Celsius.

*As warm air rises over land, convection causes cool air from the ocean to rush in and take its place. The result is wind.*
PHOTO RESEARCHERS INC.

All substances have the capacity to store heat but at different levels. For example, water has a high specific heat capacity. Water can store a large amount of energy before its temperature will rise. This is important as the high heat capacity of water works to stabilize ocean temperatures and maintain comfortable conditions for marine life. In Experiment 3, you will test three solutions to determine which one has the highest heat capacity.

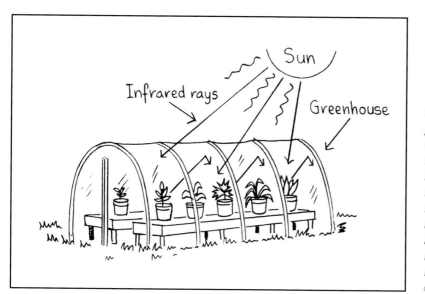

*Sunlight passes through the glass and heats the plants. The warm plants give off infrared radiation, but these rays are longer and cannot pass back through the glass. Trapped inside the greenhouse, the rays heat the air. Pollution in the atmosphere can trap heat close to Earth in the same way. This is called the greenhouse effect.*
GALE GROUP.

## WORDS TO KNOW

**Conduction:** The flow of heat through a solid.

**Control experiment:** A setup that is identical to the experiment but is not affected by the variable that will be changed during the experiment.

**Convection:** The circulatory motion that occurs in a gas or liquid at a nonuniform temperature owing to the variation of its density and the action of gravity.

**Convection current:** A circular movement of a fluid in response to alternating heating and cooling.

**Electromagnetic waves:** Radiation that has properties of both an electric and a magnetic wave and that travels through a vacuum with the speed of light.

**Greenhouse effect:** The warming of Earth's atmosphere due to water vapor, carbon dioxide, and other gases in the atmosphere that trap heat radiated from Earth's surface.

**Heat:** A form of energy produced by the motion of molecules that make up a substance.

**Heat capacity:** The measure of how well a substance stores heat.

**Heat energy:** The energy produced when two substances that have different temperatures are combined.

**Hypothesis:** An idea in the form of a statement that can be tested by observation and/or experiment.

**Infrared radiation:** Electromagnetic radiation of a wavelength shorter than radio waves but longer than visible light that takes the form of heat.

**Radiation:** Energy transmitted in the form of electromagnetic waves or subatomic particles.

**Radio wave:** Longest form of electromagnetic radiation, measuring up to 6 miles (9.6 kilometers) from peak to peak.

**Specific heat capacity:** The energy required to raise the temperature of 1 kilogram of the substance by 1 degree Celsius.

**Temperature:** The measure of the average energy of the molecules in a substance.

**Thermal conductivity:** A number representing a material's ability to conduct heat.

**Variable:** Something that can affect the results of an experiment.

## EXPERIMENT 1

## Conduction: Which solid materials are the best conductors of heat?

Purpose/Hypothesis In this experiment, you will test short lengths of five different materials to compare their ability to conduct heat. Each length will have a dab of wax on one end holding a bead in place. You will heat the opposite end of the lengths with hot water. The time it takes for each bit of wax to melt and release its bead will tell you which material conducted heat the fastest. Before you begin, make an educated guess about the outcome of this experiment based on your knowledge of heat. This educated guess, or prediction, is your hypothesis. A hypothesis should explain these things:

- the topic of the experiment
- the variable you will change
- the variable you will measure
- what you expect to happen

A hypothesis should be brief, specific, and measurable. It must be something you can test through observation. Your experiment will prove or disprove whether your hypothesis is correct. Here is one possible hypothesis for this experiment: "Copper will conduct heat faster than the four other materials; wood will be the slowest conductor."

In this case, the variables you will change are the conducting materials, and the variable you will measure is the time it takes each bit of wax to melt and release its bead. You expect the wax on the copper length to melt first, and the wax on the wood to melt last or not at all.

You will also set up a control experiment to make sure that it is conducted heat from the water and not some other variable that melts the wax. To set up the control experiment, you will create an additional set of the five conducting materials, attach wax and beads to the ends, but not heat them. If the wax melts off the experimental copper length first and the experimental wood length last and if no wax melts off the control materials, you will know your hypothesis is correct.

## What Are the Variables?

Variables are anything that might affect the results of an experiment. Here are the main variables in this experiment:

- the types of conducting materials
- the air temperature during the experiment
- the amount of each conducting material that comes into contact with the water
- the temperature of the water
- the type of wax used
- the amount of wax placed on the end of each conducting material
- the size and type of beads

In other words, the variables in this experiment are everything that might affect the time it takes for each bit of wax to release its bead. If you change more than one variable, you will not be able to tell which variable had the most effect on the rate at which the wax melted.

## How to Experiment Safely

Be sure to ask an adult to help you with this experiment. Handle the matches, lighted candle, and hot water carefully to avoid burns. Keep your clothing away from the flame. Dripping wax can also cause burns.

**Level of Difficulty** Moderate/high, because of safety factors; ask an adult to help you complete this experiment.

## Materials Needed

- 2 4-inch (10-centimeter) lengths of 18-gauge copper wire
- 2 4-inch (10-centimeter) lengths of 18-gauge aluminum wire
- 2 4-inch (10-centimeter) lengths of 18-gauge steel wire
- glass stirrer or solid glass rod
- 13-inch (0.3-centimeter) diameter wooden dowel
- 10 identical beads (glass or plastic)
- candle
- matches
- 2 glass bowls (with straight sides, if possible)
- very hot tap water
- clay
- stop watch or clock with a second hand

**Approximate Budget** $4 for the wire, glass stirrer, dowel, and beads. The other materials should be available in most households.

**Timetable** 30 minutes to set up and conduct the experiment.

*LEFT: Step 1a: Have an adult helper drip one drop of wax on one end of the conducting material.* GALE GROUP.

*RIGHT: Step 1c: Use a piece of clay to attach the conducting material to the side of one bowl. Space the conducting materials evenly around the bowl and anchor them firmly with the clay so they will remain upright.* GALE GROUP.

## Step-by-Step Instructions

1. Use a match to light the candle. Then follow this procedure for each of the five conducting materials:

a. Have your adult helper drip one drop of wax on one end of the conducting material.

b. Quickly push a bead into the drop of wax and make sure it is securely lodged there.

c. Use a piece of clay to attach the conducting material to the side of one bowl, as illustrated. Space the conducting materials evenly around the bowl and anchor them firmly with the clay so they will remain upright. Make sure each material extends the same distance into the bowl.

2. Repeat Step 1 to set up the control experiment in the second glass bowl.

3. Ask the adult to carefully pour about 2 inches (5 centimeters) of very hot tap water into the center of the experimental bowl. As the water level rises, it should touch the lower end of each conducting material. Make sure each material extends the same distance into the water.

4. Immediately start the stop watch. Record on a chart (see illustration) how long it takes for each bead to fall from its conducting material.

5. Observe the beads in your control experiment and record on the chart their position at the end of the experiment.

**Chart of Responses**

| Experimental conductors | Time taken for bead to fall |
|---|---|
| Copper wire | |
| Aluminum wire | |
| Steel wire | |
| Glass rod | |
| Wooden dowel | |

| Control conductors | Position of bead at end of experiment |
|---|---|
| Copper wire | |
| Aluminum wire | |
| Steel wire | |
| Glass rod | |
| Wooden dowel | |

*Steps 4 and 5: Recording chart for Experiment 1.* GALE GROUP.

**Summary of Results** Use the data on your chart to create a line graph of your findings. The graph will indicate the time that lapsed before each bead fell. Then study your chart and graph and decide whether your hypothesis was correct. Did the bead on the experimental copper wire fall first, and the one on the wooden dowel fall last or not at all? Did the beads in the control experiment remain in place? Write a paragraph summarizing your findings and explaining whether they support your hypothesis.

## Troubleshooter's Guide

Here are some problems that may arise during this experiment, some possible causes, and ways to remedy the problems.

**Problem:** The bead on a different conductor fell before the bead on the copper conductor.

**Possible causes:**

1. The hot water might have splashed against the conductors as you poured it, giving some conductors a head start in transferring heat. Try again, pouring slowly.

2. Some conductors may have more wax than the others, affecting the melting speed. Try again, making sure to drip the same amount of wax on all conductors.

**Problem:** A conductor other than the wooden dowel was the last one to release its bead.

**Possible cause:** See possible cause 2 above.

**Problem:** A bead on a control conductor fell off, or most of the beads fell off immediately.

**Possible causes:**

1. The beads are too large or heavy. Try again with smaller, lighter beads.

2. The beads were not firmly attached. Try again, pushing the beads firmly into the wax.

3. The room air temperature is too warm, helping to melt the wax. Move to a cooler location or repeat your experiment on a cooler day.

For your reference, here is a list of the materials in the experiment, plus a few more, with a number that represents their ability to conduct heat, called thermal conductivity. The higher the number, the better the material conducts heat: silver (58.2); copper (55.2); aluminum (29.4); steel (7.2); glass (0.12); wood (0.012); air (0.004); styrofoam (0.0034).

**Change the Variables** You can conduct similar experiments by changing the variables. For example, you can use other conducting materials, such as plastic, iron, or a stick of insulating foam. You can also place a different small object in the wax, such as a metal nail.

Another way to measure conductivity is to use small containers made of different materials, such as a glass jar, an insulated cup, a plastic cup, and a steel can. Put an ice cube in each small container and place them all in a larger container holding a few inches of very hot water. To determine the best conductor, record how long it takes for the ice to melt in each small container.

## EXPERIMENT 2

## Convection: How does heat move through liquids?

**Purpose/Hypothesis** In this experiment, you will put tinted hot water into cold water and tinted cold water into hot water. In both cases, you will observe and record the movement of the water to determine how heat moves through liquids. Your experiment should cause convection currents to develop as heat moves through the water. Before you begin, make an educated guess about the outcome of this experiment based on your knowledge of heat. This educated guess, or prediction, is your hypothesis. A hypothesis should explain these things:

- the topic of the experiment
- the variable you will change
- the variable you will measure
- what you expect to happen

A hypothesis should be brief, specific, and measurable. It must be something you can test through observation. Your experiment will prove or disprove whether your hypothesis is correct. Here is a possible hypothesis for this experiment: "Hot water placed in cold water will rise, and cold water placed in hot water will fall."

In this case, the variable you will change is the temperature of the tinted water placed in the container and the water already in the container, and the variable you will measure is the motion of the tinted water. You expect the cold blue water will sink and the hot red water will rise.

As a control experiment, you will also pour tinted room-temperature water into more room-temperature water to determine if it, too, moves in a certain pattern. During your experiment, if the hot water rises, the cold water falls, and the room-temperature water mixes together in no specific pattern, you will know your hypothesis is correct.

**Level of Difficulty** Easy/moderate.

**Materials Needed**

- 1 small container of very hot water, tinted red with food coloring
- 1 large container of very hot water
- 1 small container of icy cold water, tinted blue
- 1 large container of icy cold water
- 1 small container of room-temperature water, tinted green

## What Are the Variables?

Variables are anything that might affect the results of an experiment. Here are the main variables in this experiment:

- the temperatures of the water in different containers
- the amount of water being dropped into water of a different temperature
- whether the containers of water are stirred or otherwise disturbed

If you change more than one variable, you will not be able to tell which one had the most effect on the movement of the water.

*Step 1: Add 2 drops of the red (hot) water to the container of cold water.* GALE GROUP.

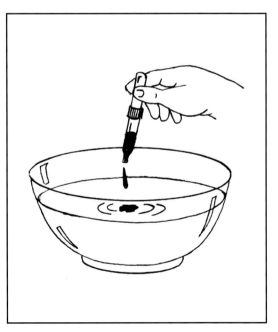

- 1 large container of room-temperature water
- 2 eye droppers

**Approximate Budget** Less than $5 for food coloring and eye droppers.

**Timetable** 20 minutes.

**Step-by-Step Instructions**

1. Using one eye dropper, add 2 drops of the red (hot) water to the large container of cold water. Observe and record the movement of the red water on a chart similar to the one illustrated. DO NOT STIR OR BUMP THE LARGE CONTAINER. Rinse the eye dropper.

2. Using the other eye dropper, add 2 drops of the blue (cold) water to the large container of hot water. Record the movement of the blue water on the chart. AGAIN, DO NOT STIR OR BUMP THE LARGE CONTAINER.

3. As a control experiment, use the rinsed, room-temperature eye dropper to add 2 drops of green (room-temperature) water to

> ## Heat Movement
> Instructions: Draw your large container and use arrows to show direction of the water's movement.
>
> Red (hot) water in cold water:
>
> Blue (cold) water in hot water:
>
> Green (room-temperature) water in room-temperature water:

*Steps 1 to 3: Recording chart for Experiment 2.* GALE GROUP.

the large container of room-temperature water. Record what happens.

**Summary of Results** Study the drawings on your chart and decide whether your hypothesis was correct. Did the hot water rise, the cold water fall, and the room-temperature water mix in no specific pattern? Write a paragraph summarizing your findings and explaining whether they support your hypothesis.

**Change the Variables** Change the way that water of a different temperature is introduced: immerse a glass tube that is open on both ends in a container of very warm (not burning) water colored red. Put your finger over the top of the tube, which should stop the water from flowing out either end. Now immerse the tube in a container of icy cold water. Hold the tube in a vertical position and take your finger off the end of the tube. Observe whether the red water flows out of the top or the bottom of the tube. Try the same experiment with cold, blue water in the tube and very warm water in the large container. From which end of the tube does the blue water flow?

---

## Troubleshooter's Guide

Here are some problems that may arise during this experiment, some possible causes, and ways to remedy the problems.

**Problem:** The tinted hot water (or the tinted cold water) simply spread throughout the water in the experimental large container, in no particular pattern.

**Possible cause:** The difference between the water temperatures was too small. Make sure the cold water is icy and the hot water is very hot. Heat water in a microwave for a minute, if you wish, but ask an adult to help you handle it, using pot holders. Use containers that are microwave-safe.

**Problem:** You could not clearly see the movement of the hot (or cold) water in the large container.

**Possible cause:** The water was not tinted dark enough. Add more food coloring and try again.

---

## EXPERIMENT 3

## Heat Capacity: Which liquids have the highest heat capacity?

Purpose/Hypothesis In this experiment, you will test the heat capacity of three different liquids. You will use water, cream, and olive oil. Water has a relatively high heat capacity. Fats, on the other hand, cannot store a large amount of energy before a temperature rise.

Each liquid will be heated in a hot water bath of 200°F (93°C) and temperature readings will be taken every minute for 10 minutes. You will then cool the liquid in a cold-water bath taking temperature readings every minute for 10 minutes. The time it takes to heat the liquids and the

## What Are the Variables?

Variables are anything that might affect the results of an experiment. Here are the main variables in this experiment:

- the types of liquids tested
- the volume of the liquids tested
- the starting temperature of the liquids
- the temperature of the water baths
- the length of time the liquids are heated

In other words, the variables in this experiment are everything that might affect the temperature of the liquids during the testing period. If you change more than one variable, you will not be able to tell which one had the most effect on the temperature of the liquid tested.

time it takes to cool the liquids will tell you which liquid has the highest heat capacity.

Before you begin, make an educated guess about the outcome of this experiment based on your knowledge of heat. This educated guess, or prediction, is your hypothesis. A hypothesis should explain these things:

- the topic of the experiment
- the variable you will change
- the variable you will measure
- what you expect to happen

A hypothesis should be brief, specific, and measurable. It must be something you can test through observation. Your experiment will prove or disprove whether your hypothesis is correct. Here is a possible hypothesis for this experiment: "The temperature of the cream will increase at a slower rate than the other two liquids."

The variables you will change are the three liquids being tested, and the variable you will measure is the change in temperature of the liquids over a period of 20 minutes.

The control test you will measure against will be the temperature of the three liquids at room temperature.

**Level of Difficulty** Moderate/Difficult, because of safety factors.

*Step 4: To the hot-water bath, add the glass filled with 1-cup of room temperature cream.*
ILLUSTRATION BY TEMAH NELSON.

**Materials Needed**

- 1 medium sized pot for hot-water bath
- 1 medium sized pot for cold-water bath
- 3 glass, heat-resistant measuring cups (or glass mason jars)
- 2 thermometers with a clip that can attach to the side of the water bath
- 1 cup room-temperature water
- 1 cup room-temperature cream
- 1 cup of room-temperature olive oil
- stop watch or clock with a second hand

**Approximate Budget** About $15.

**Timetable** 30 minutes to set up and 60 minutes to conduct the experiment

**Step-by-Step Instructions**

1. Measure out 1 cup of water, cream, and olive oil in separate containers. Set aside until they are at room temperature (about 72°F, 22°C).

2. Have an adult helper bring a medium pot filled half way with water to a temperature of 200° Fahrenheit (93° Celsius). Clip the thermometer to the side of the water bath, making sure it does not touch the sides.

3. Prepare a cold water bath. Fill a medium-sized pot a quarter full of cold water and add several cups of ice.

4. To the hot-water bath, add the glass filled with 1-cup of room temperature cream.

5. Place another thermometer in the cream, clipping it against the glass. Measure the temperature changes at one minute intervals for 10 minutes and record on chart (see illustration).

6. After 10 minutes remove the glass cup of cream with the thermometer from the hot-water bath and place in the cold-water bath. Record the temperature changes at one-minute intervals for 10 minutes.

7. Repeat this procedure, from the hot to the cold water bath, for the water and the olive oil.

**Summary of Results** Graph the results of your temperature reading for all three liquids. The graph will indicate the rate and rise of temperature of each liquid. How does the temperature rise compare to the room temperature? Decide whether your hypothesis was correct. Did the temperature of the cream rise at a slower rate than the water and olive oil? If not, which liquid did rise at the slowest rate? Write a paragraph summarizing your findings and explaining why or why not it supports your hypothesis.

## How to Experiment Safely

Ask an adult to help you with this experiment. Have an adult operate the stove. Handle the hot water bath and hot liquids carefully to avoid burns.

*Step 5: Using this chart, record the temperature changes at one minute intervals for 10 minutes.* ILLUSTRATION BY TEMAH NELSON.

| min. | cream | | water | | olive oil | |
|------|-------|------|-------|------|-------|------|
| | HOT | COLD | HOT | COLD | HOT | COLD |
| 1. | | | | | | |
| 2. | | | | | | |
| 3. | | | | | | |
| 4. | | | | | | |
| 5. | | | | | | |
| 6. | | | | | | |
| 7. | | | | | | |
| 8. | | | | | | |
| 9. | | | | | | |
| 10. | | | | | | |

*Step 6: After 10 minutes remove the glass cup of cream with the thermometer from the hot-water bath and place in the cold-water bath.* ILLUSTRATION BY TEMAH NELSON.

**Change the Variables** You can conduct other heat capacity experiments by finding the heat capacity of different materials. You can use other household liquids or solid materials that change into liquids, such as paraffin wax or calcium chloride (ice melt). If you choose to use a solid material you must first melt or dilute the material so that you can measure the temperature of the material.

## Design Your Own Experiment

**How to Select a Topic Relating to this Concept** You can explore many other aspects of heat movement. For example, you might investigate the relationship between convection and wind, or you could find out how surface area affects the rate of heat conduction. For example, does water boil more quickly if it is in a wide pan or a narrow pan? Does ice melt more quickly if it is crushed into small pieces?

Check the Further Readings section and talk with your science teacher or school or community media specialist to start gathering information on heat questions that interest you. As you consider possible experiments, be sure to discuss them with your science teacher or another knowledgeable adult before trying them. Experimenting with heat is potentially dangerous.

**Steps in the Scientific Method** To do an original experiment, you need to plan carefully and think things through. Otherwise, you might not be sure what question you are answering, what you are or should be measuring, or what your findings prove or disprove.

Here are the steps in designing an experiment:

- State the purpose of—and the underlying question behind—the experiment you propose to do.

- Recognize the variables involved, and select one that will help you answer the question at hand.

- State a testable hypothesis, an educated guess about the answer to your question.

- Decide how to change the variable you selected.

- Decide how to measure your results.

Recording Data and Summarizing the Results In the heat movement experiments, your raw data might include charts, graphs, drawings, and photographs of the changes you observed. If you display your experiment, make clear your beginning question, the variable you changed, the variable you measured, the results, and your conclusions. Explain what materials you used, how long each step took, and other basic information.

Related Projects You can undertake a variety of projects related to the movement of heat. For example, you might explore which kinds of home insulation, insulated cups, or insulated gloves are most efficient at stopping the movement of heat through conduction. When a fireplace burns, how much of the heat escapes up the chimney through convection? Which colors are most efficient at reflecting radiated heat?

## Troubleshooter's Guide

Here are some problems that may arise during this experiment, some possible causes, and ways to remedy the problems.

**Problem: The hot-water bath keeps changing temperature.**

**Possible cause:** The temperature of the stove is too high. Maintain a constant temperature by using a low to medium temperature setting and have cold water available to add to bath to maintain the 200 degrees.

**Problem: All three liquids showed the same results.**

**Possible cause:** The liquids might not have been at room temperature at the beginning of the experiment. Repeat the experiment, allowing the liquids to sit out for at least an hour longer and take the temperature of each of the liquids.

## For More Information

Friedhoffer, Robert. *Molecules and Heat.* New York: Franklin Watts, 1992. Explores scientific concepts involving heat and heat movement by turning them into "magic tricks."

Gardner, Robert, and Eric Kemer. *Science Projects about Temperature and Heat.* Hillside, NJ: Enslow Publishers, 1994. Provides detailed explanations of projects and the concepts they demonstrate.

Gutnik, Martin. *Experiments That Explore the Greenhouse Effect.* Brookfield, CT: Millbrook Press, 1991. Outlines experiments that relate to the movement of heat as it causes the greenhouse effect.

Wood, Robert. *Heat FUNdamentals.* New York: Learning Triangle Press, 1997. Offers more than 25 heat-related activities and brief explanations.

# 48

# Insects

It's easy to think humans are the major animals on our planet, but in reality, we are the minority. There are an estimated 10 quintillion insects alive at any time—that's 10,000,000,000,000,000,000! They live in all different types of places: on water, on the tops of mountains, under rocks, and inside trees. Researchers have identified more than one million different species of insects, which make up about 80 percent of all known species in the world. And experts theorize there are millions more insect species not yet discovered.

The study of insects is called entomology. Understanding how insects live and behave is important because they play such a large role in life on Earth. They pollinate (transfer pollen), break down animal waste, and are a major food source for animals. They also provide humans with products, such as honey and wax. The survival of animals—including people—depend upon these small creatures.

*Taking apart an insect* There is a wide variety of insect shapes and sizes, yet there are certain characteristics all insects share.

1. Six legs: That leaves out the eight-legged spiders and the numerous-legged centipedes and millipedes.

2. An exoskeleton: A strong, hard skin on the outside of their body. The exoskeleton holds the muscles and protects the insect from outside elements. It also prevents the insect from growing once the exoskeleton has fully formed.

3. As insects grow, many need to shed their hard exoskeleton several times. This is called molting. Beneath the exoskeleton a new layer of skin forms. The insect becomes larger, which causes the exoskeleton to split and fall, making way for the new and larger exoskeleton.

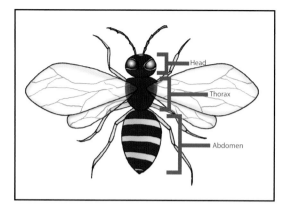

*The three basic body segments all insects have are the head, thorax, and abdomen.* ILLUSTRATION BY TEMAH NELSON.

*Depending upon the insect, they can use antennae to sense smells, movements, and vibration.* ILLUSTRATION BY TEMAH NELSON.

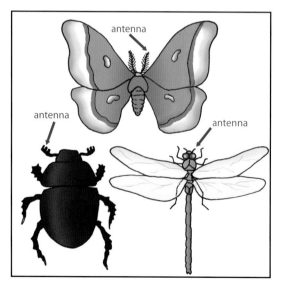

4. Segmented bodies: An insect's body is segmented (separated) into three distinct parts, which are all supported by the exoskeleton.

*The insect segments* The three basic body segments all insects have are the head, thorax, and abdomen. The head is where the insects have their antennae, mouthparts, and eyes. Antennae can be long, as in a grasshopper, or short, as in a fly. Depending upon the insect, they can use an antennae to sense smells, movements, and vibration.

The mouth of an insect depends upon the species. There are a lot of ways insects can eat. Some of the ways they take in food includes sucking, chewing, piercing, lapping, or a combination.

The type of eye an insect has depends upon the insect, but most insects have two compound eyes. Compound eyes are made up of thousands of different individual lens-like units in each eye. Unlike our eyes, they do not rotate or move. Each unit takes in a tiny visual and the brain puts them all together into the image.

The middle segment of the insect body is the thorax. Each part of the thorax holds a pair of legs. If an insect has wings, they are attached to the thorax. The bottom insect segment is the abdomen. The abdomen is where digestion and reproduction take place. An insect also breathes through its abdomen through openings called spiracles.

*Insects on the go* There are a lot of ways an insect can get around. Insects can hop, crawl, jump, fly or some combination. About 300 million years ago, insects became one of the first creatures to fly. Flying allows insects to travel greater distances for food and escape predators quickly. Many insects, such as the grasshopper and bee, have two pairs of wings but only the back pair is used to fly. The front wings are smaller and protect the back pair. Insects such as the butterfly and beetle have linked their sets

*Butterflies have linked their sets of wings together so that the pairs flap together.* ROBERT J. HUFFMAN. FIELD MARK PUBLICATIONS.

of wings together so that the pairs flap together. The fly has a single pair of wings.

For insects that don't fly, and some that do, legs are how they move around. An insect leg is split into distinct sections. In some insects, such as ants, the legs are all about the same size and used mainly for walking. Insects with longer and more powerful back legs use their legs to jump. Grasshoppers and fleas are two types of insects that have powerful jumps.

Some insect legs are designed to dig, cling, or capture food. The praying mantis has a large pair of spiked front legs that it uses to catch prey. Legs can also provide sensory experiences. A fly's feet has tiny taste sensors that let the fly know if it should eat the substance it lands on.

*The busy cycle of life* Insects live relatively short lives of less than a year in general. For example, flies can live about 15 to 30 days and butterflies for about a month or two. But there are a few insects that can live for years. The queen ants of some species can live for over 20 years!

No matter the type of insect or length of time it lives, most insects pass through four life stages: 1) egg; 2) larva or nymph; 3) pupa; and 4) adult. Insects are born from eggs. The second stage, which can also be called other names, is the young immature insect.

A caterpillar is in the larva stage. The caterpillar moves into the pupa stage when it goes through metamorphosis. In this type of metamorphosis (a complete metamorphosis), the insect goes through a distinct change

## WORDS TO KNOW

**Abdomen:** The third segment of an insect body.

**Bioluminescence:** Light produced by living organisms.

**Ecosystem:** An ecological community, including plants, animals and microorganisms, considered together with their environment.

**Entomology:** The study of insects.

**Exoskeleton:** A hard outer covering on animals, which provide protection and structure.

**Hypothesis:** An idea in the form of a statement that can be tested by observation and/or experiment.

**Insect:** A six-legged invertebrate whose body has three segments.

**Invertebrate:** An animal that lacks a backbone or internal skeleton.

**Larvae:** The immature stage between the egg and the pupa; this can also be called nymph.

**Metamorphosis:** The biological process in which an insect transforms from a larva into an adult, changing its appearance.

**Molting:** A process by which an animal sheds its skin or shell.

**Pollinate:** The transfer of pollen from the male reproductive organs to the female reproductive organs of plants.

**Pupa:** The insect stage of development between the larva and adult in insects that go through complete metamorphosis.

**Spiracles:** The openings on an insects side where air enters.

**Thorax:** The middle segment of an insect body; the legs and wings are connected to the thorax.

**Variable:** Something that can affect the results of an experiment.

in appearance and structure. As a pupa, also called chrysalis, the caterpillar does not move or eat. When it emerges into its final adult stage, the caterpillar appears as a butterfly. Insects that look the same as adults and immature insects do not go through a complete metamorphosis. For these insects there is no pupa stage.

Most insects live isolated lives but several groups are known as social insects. Ants, bees, and termites are among the social insects. Most social insects live in large colonies (groups) with distinct division of labors. In ant colonies, the ant nest is started by a queen who lays eggs. Some ants are assigned to defend the colony and others to build the nest. The insects in the colonies communicate with one another through chemical signals.

Insects are a broad and fascinating group of animals. Each group of insects has its own unique characteristics, and you can learn a lot about insects by simply observing them.

## EXPERIMENT 1

### Ant Food: What type of foods is one type of ant attracted to?

Purpose/Hypothesis In this experiment, you will investigate the food that most attracts one kind of ant. There are many types of ants and different ants prefer different foods. Ant diets include sugary substances, seeds, and proteins (in the form of other bugs and dead animals). You can find out the kind of food ants prefer by soaking a sponge in four to five liquid-form foods. By placing the food-soaked sponges in one outside area around the same type of ant you can observe which food attracts the most ants. You can also observe how ants communicate their food find to their fellow ants. The foods you will use include: honey; beef broth; milk; and juice. Water will be the control.

Before you begin, make an educated guess about the outcome of this experiment based on your knowledge of insects and ants. This educated guess, or prediction, is your hypothesis. A hypothesis should explain these things:

- the topic of the experiment
- the variable you will change
- the variable you will measure
- what you expect to happen

A hypothesis should be brief, specific, and measurable. It must be something you can test through observation. Your experiment will prove or disprove your hypothesis. Here is one possible hypothesis for this experiment: "The ants will be attracted primarily to the honey-soaked sponge and then the juice sponge."

In this case, the variable you will change will be the food substance on the sponge, and the variables you will measure will be the relative amount of ants on the sponge over a length of time.

Setting up a control experiment will help you isolate one variable. Only one variable will change between the control and the experimental

### What Are the Variables?

Variables are anything that might affect the results of an experiment. Here are the main variables in this experiment:

- the type of ant
- the item on the sponge
- the size of the sponge
- where the sponge is set in relation to the ants
- the environmental conditions

In other words, the variables in this experiment are everything that might affect the amount of ants attracted to the food on the sponge. If you change more than one variable, you will not be able to tell which variable had the most effect on attracting the ants to the sponge.

## How to Experiment Safely

Do not touch the ants or disturb their living environment; simply observe them. Wash your hands after completing the experiment.

tests, and that variable is the liquid food. For the control, you will soak the sponge in water.

**Level of Difficulty** Moderate.

**Materials Needed**

- sponge
- scissors
- toothpicks with flags (for marking; you can make your own by attaching strips of paper to toothpicks)
- 1 beef bouillon cube or canned beef stock
- milk, about 3 tablespoons
- juice, such as orange juice, about 3 tablespoons
- honey, about 3 tablespoons
- 5 small cups or containers
- spoon
- tongs
- plastic forks
- large plate

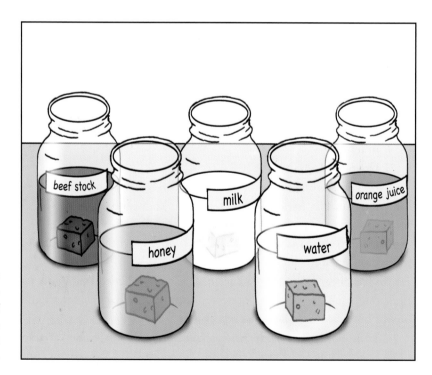

*Step 6: Place one sponge in each container. Allow the sponge to sit for at least 2 minutes and then flip over the sponge.*
ILLUSTRATION BY TEMAH NELSON.

- marking pen
- outside clear area, with primarily one type of ant
- a nice day

**Approximate Budget** $10.

**Timetable** 1 hour.

### Step-by-Step Instructions

1. Use the scissors to cut a sponge into 4 to 5 squares (depending upon if you are testing 4 or 5 food items), about 2 inches square.
2. On each of the flagged toothpicks, mark each of the foods you are using.

*Step 9: Set the sponge squares evenly spaced apart in a circle, with each sponge at least one foot apart from the next.*
ILLUSTRATION BY TEMAH NELSON.

Prepare each of the food items:

1. In container 1, pour about 3 tablespoons of milk.
2. In container 2, pour about 3 tablespoons of honey and stir in several drops of water to thin down the honey.
3. In container 3, add about 3 tablespoons of warm water to the bouillon. Use a spoon to crush and dissolve the cube. If you have beef stock pour about 3 tablespoons of the stock in the container.
4. In container 4, pour about 3 tablespoons of orange juice.
5. In container 5, pour about 3 tablespoons of water.
6. Place one sponge in each container. Allow the sponge to sit for at least two minutes and then flip over the sponge. Wait another two minutes.
7. Use plastic forks or tongs to place the sponge squares on the plate. As you set the sponge on the plate, place its matching marked toothpick in the sponge. If you use a pair of tongs, clean or wipe the tongs after you lift each sponge. Hold each sponge piece for a few seconds over the container until it no longer drips. Set it down, apart from the others, on the large plate. Make sure none of the food sources spread on any of the other sponges.
8. Carry the plate outside to the area where there is mainly one type of ant crawling about.
9. Set the sponge squares evenly spaced apart in a circle, with each sponge at least one foot apart from the next.

10. Wait 20 minutes and note the relative amount of ants on each of the sponges. Does one sponge have a lot more ants than any of the others?

11. Over the next 15 to 30 minutes, observe the ants reaction to each sponge. Also, observe how the ants travel to the sponge they are attracted to. Look for lines of ants or possible ways ants may communicate to one another about the food.

12. When you have finished the experiment, use a plastic fork to throw away the sponges. (You may need to shake the sponges free of ants!)

**Summary of Results** Look over your findings. Was your hypothesis correct? Compare the foods they were not as attracted to? How did the control (water) sponge attract ants as compared to the sponge with milk, or orange juice? Could you see how ants communicated with one another about the food? Write up a summary of your findings.

**Change the Variables** Here are some ways you can vary this experiment:

- Test another type of ant: look around for another size or color of ant.
- Focus on one food, such as the honey, and alter the concentration to determine how concentrated the food needs to be for the ant to sense it.
- Change the foods, using all sweet items or protein sources, and see which attracts the most ants.

## EXPERIMENT 2

### Lightning Bugs: How does the environment affect a firefly's flash?

**Purpose/Hypothesis** There are hundreds of different types of fireflies. These insects, also called lightning bugs, are recognizable by their flashes of light. Fireflies are bioluminescent, meaning they produce light by a chemical reaction within the organism. Fireflies produce a chemical in their abdomen called luciferin. This substance reacts with oxygen and another substance to give off light. How much oxygen the firefly breathes in determines the strength and pattern of the light flashes.

How often the firefly flashes depends upon several factors, including the type of firefly, its sex, and age. The flash of light can also depend upon the temperature, which can affect the amount of oxygen the firefly breathes. In this experiment, you can observe firefly flashes and measure if the rate of flashes changes depending upon the warmth or coolness of the firefly's environment.

You will need to catch a firefly and place it in a large jar. You can time the flashes and note the intensity of the light. You can then place the jar in cold and warm water in order to change the air temperature of the firefly, and again measure the flashes.

To begin the experiment, use what you know about insects and fireflies to make an educated guess about how temperature will affect the bioluminescence. This educated guess, or prediction, is your hypothesis. A hypothesis should explain these things:

- the topic of the experiment
- the variable you will change
- the variable you will measure
- what you expect to happen

A hypothesis should be brief, specific, and measurable. It must be something you can test through observation. Your experiment will prove or disprove whether your hypothesis is correct. Here is one possible hypothesis for this experiment: "The rate of light flashes from the firefly will increase and they will be brighter when it is warmer compared to when it is colder."

## What Are the Variables?

Variables are anything that could affect the results of an experiment. Here are the main variables in this experiment:

- the environment the firefly is in
- the type of firefly
- the time of day
- the vibration of the jar
- the amount of light

## How to Experiment Safely

Have an adult help you use the hammer (or any heavy block) and nail to poke holes in the lid of the jar. Treat the firefly gently, making sure not to leave it in the jar for more than a few hours. When you have finished observing the insect, release it back outside.

*Step 2: Try to catch one of the fireflies in the jar.*

*Step 4: Pour ice and cold water in the plastic container. Set the jar in the container so that it is partly submerged.* ILLUSTRATION BY TEMAH NELSON.

In this case, the variable you will change is the temperature of the firefly's environment, and the variable you will measure is the number and intensity of the its flashes.

**Level of Difficulty** Moderate, due to working with live insects.

**Materials Needed**

- large glass jar with a lid, such as a mason or large mayonnaise jar
- hammer or mallet
- nail
- warm evening
- plastic container
- ice
- clock with a minute hand
- helper (optional)

**Approximate Budget** $0. (Materials should be available in the average household.)

**Timetable** Approximately 30 minutes experimental time; the time to collect fireflies will vary widely and you may want to spread out the three trials over three evenings.

**Step-by-Step Instructions**

1. Have an adult help you use a hammer (or any heavy block) and a nail to poke small holes in the lid of the jar. This will allow air to enter the jar.
2. After the sun goes down, go outside to a dark area. Fireflies live in cities and open grassy areas but it is easier to spot their flashes away from streetlights or bright lights. It also helps to have someone with you when looking for and collecting the firefly. Fireflies are relatively slow fliers and they do not bite. When you see one,

clap your hands over the insect. If you do not have a helper holding the jar, make sure the lid is open before you catch one in your hands.

3. When a firefly is in the closed jar, bring it inside and darken the room so you can clearly see its flashes. Count the frequency of flashes over a period of time, such as two minutes. The exact time does not matter as long as it is the same in all the trials.

4. Pour ice and cold water in the plastic container. Set the jar in the container so that it is partly submerged. Wait about 1 minute and time the flashes again. Note the intensity of the flashes.

5. Replace the cold water in the container with warm water. Wait about a minute. Again, time the number of flashes over the two-minute time period (or what you used in the first trial) and note their intensity.

6. Pour out the warm water. When you have finished observing the firefly, release it back outside.

7. If desired, repeat the entire process for two more fireflies, one at a time. This will strengthen your findings and help you make sure the results are repeatable. Collect the fireflies in the same area so that you will have more chance of collecting the same type of firefly.

## Troubleshooter's Guide

Experiments do not always work out as planned, especially when working with live organisms. Here are some problems that may arise during this experiment and ways to remedy the problems.

- **Problem:** I can't find any fireflies.
- **Possible causes:** Adult fireflies only live about several weeks. When they mature into adults depends upon the area, but it is somewhere in the late spring or summer months. If you do not see any, ask an adult to help you research when they are expected in your area. And when looking for the insects, make sure you are in a dark area and be patient.
- **Problem:** One of the fireflies gave far different results than the other two firefly trials.
- **Possible causes:** There are hundreds of types of fireflies and each produces flashes in a certain pattern. It is possible you caught two different types of fireflies. You might also have collected a firefly that was too old, young, or sick. Repeat the experiment with another firefly. Make sure it is producing a steady rate of light flashes before placing the jar in a cool or warm environment.

**Summary of Results** If you conducted the experiment on more than one firefly, average the frequency of the trials for the room temperature, cool, and warm environment. Was your hypothesis correct? How quickly did the flashes speed up or slow down when the firefly's environment changed? Did the intensity of the flashes change also? Was there a certain pattern to the flashes? Write up a summary of your findings. You may want to include pictures of the firefly, and some possible reasons why the firefly produces light.

Change the Variables One way you can vary this experiment is by looking at other factors that may affect the light a firefly produces. Would vibration or color affect the flash or intensity of a firefly? If you can collect different types of fireflies, you can see the unique lighting patterns in each. In general, male and female fireflies produce light at different frequencies. The male gives off a repeated signal and the female responds. You may want to observe firefly lighting in the wild before deciding on experiments.

## Design Your Own Experiment

How to Select a Topic Relating to this Concept Insects are all around you, living on the sidewalks, in the grass, and often hiding inside homes. As you think about experiments and projects relating to insects, consider what insects you have questions about. Are there insects unique to your area? Think about insect interactions that you have observed. You can also consider when an insect turns into a pest, and how people use insect characteristics to develop pest controls.

Check the Further Readings section and talk with your science teacher to start gathering information on insects and questions that interest you. You may want to speak with people who are knowledgeable about working or dealing with insects. As you consider possible experiments, be sure to discuss them with your science teacher or another knowledgeable adult before trying them. Remember that some insects can be harmful to people and you should research the insect before working with it. Work with someone familiar with the insect and plan how you will care for or handle insects that you collect or purchase.

Steps in the Scientific Method To conduct an original experiment, you need to plan carefully and think things through. Otherwise, you might not be sure what question you are answering, what you are or should be measuring, or what your findings prove or disprove.

Here are the steps in designing an experiment:

- State the purpose of—and the underlying question behind—the experiment you propose to do.

- Recognize the variables involved, and select one that will help you answer the question at hand.

- State a testable hypothesis, an educated guess about the answer to your question.

- Decide how to change the variable you selected.

- Decide how to measure your results.

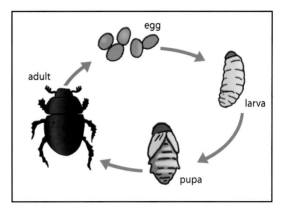

*Insects have four life stages.*
ILLUSTRATION BY TEMAH NELSON.

### Recording Data and Summarizing the Results

The most important part of the experiment is the information gathered from it. Think of how you can share your results with others. Charts, graphs, and diagrams of the progress and results of the experiments are helpful in informing others about an experiment. You may also want to take photographs or draw the insect.

**Related Experiments** You can do many experiments and projects with insects through careful observation. You may want to collect your own insects and observe them over a period of time.

One project that can help you learn about a variety of insects is by identifying the three body segments of different insects. How do the wings, lets, and antennae compare among different insects?

You can also observe the four life cycles of insects. How does the timing of the life cycles compare among different types of insects? Are there certain environmental conditions that speed or slow down the change into one of the life cycles?

You can experiment with how environmental conditions may speed or slow one of the life stages. Insect senses is another possible area of study. You can explore how different types of insects sense food, and threats. You can also experiment with groups of social insects, such as ants. Possible experiments include determining how they communicate with one another and how they build homes.

## For More Information

*Bugbios.* http://www.insects.org/entophiles/index.html (accessed on June 4, 2008). Comprehensive database of photographs and facts about a wide range of insects.

*Butterflies and Moths of North America.* http://www.butterfliesandmoths.org (accessed on June 6, 2008). Searchable database with photographs of butterflies and moths.

"Camouflage." *BBC: Walking with Beasts.* http://www.abc.net.au/beasts/ fossilfun/camouflage/camouflage.swf (accessed on May 11, 2008). An interactive game on animal camouflage.

Doris, Ellen. *Entomology.* New York: Thames and Hudson, 1993. Describes different microorganisms, their functions, and purpose.

Lang, S. *Invisible Bugs and Other Creepy Creatures That Live With You.* New York: Sterling Publishers, 1992. Describes different microorganisms, their functions, and purpose.

Mound, Laurence. *Insect.* London, New York: DK Publishing, 2007.

Parker, Steve. *Ant lions, Wasps, and Other Insects.* Minneapolis: Compass Point Books,, 2006.

"Virtual Insects and a Spider." *3D Insects.* http://www.ento.vt.edu/~sharov/3d/ virtual.html (accessed on June 4, 2008). Movies and information about different insects.

# Budget Index

Chapter name in brackets, followed by experiment name. The numeral before the colon indicates volume; numbers after the colon indicate page number.

## $5–$10

*Experiment Central, 2nd edition*

# Level of Difficulty Index

Chapter name in brackets, followed by experiment name. The numeral before the colon indicates volume; numbers after the colon indicate page number.

## EASY/MODERATE

*Easy/Moderate means that the average student should have little trouble completing the tasks outlined in the project/experiment, and that the time spent on the project is not overly restrictive.*

## MODERATE

*Moderate means that the average student should find tasks outlined in the project/experiment challenging but not difficult, and that the time spent on the project/experiment may be more extensive.*

## MODERATE/DIFFICULT

*Moderate/Difficult means that the average student should find tasks outlined in the project/experiment challenging, and that the time spent on the project/experiment may be more extensive.*

## DIFFICULT

*Difficult means that the average student wil probably find the tasks outlined in the project/experiment mentally and/or physically challenging, and that the time spent on the project/experiment may be more extensive.*

*Experiment Central, 2nd edition*

# Timetable Index

Chapter name in brackets, followed by experiment name. The numeral before the colon indicates volume; numbers after the colon indicate page number.

## 30 TO 45 MINUTES

*Experiment Central, 2nd edition*

## 3 HOURS

*Experiment Central, 2nd edition*

# General Subject Index

The numeral before the colon indicates volume; numbers after the colon indicate page number. **Bold** page numbers indicate main essays. The notation (ill.) after a page number indicates a figure.

**B**

Deoxyribonucleic acid. *See* DNA

Dependent variable, *5:* 1008

Desert

biome, *1:* 103, 104–5, 104 (ill.)

desert biome experiment, *1:* 108–11, 109 (ill.), 110 (ill.), 111 (ill.)

mountains and desert formation experiment, *4:* 741–44, 742 (ill.), 743 (ill.)

Desert plants, *1:* 105, *5:* 898, 899–900, 908, 908 (ill.)

Detergents

action of, *6:* 1260

borax in, *1:* 167

DNA isolation and extraction experiment, *2:* 289–91, 289 (ill.), 290 (ill.)

enzymes in, *2:* 362

eutrophication from, *1:* 55

species differences in DNA experiment, *2:* 291–95, 293 (ill.)

Deveron River, *5:* 956

Dewpoint temperature, *6:* 1285 (ill.), 1286–89, 1287 (ill.), 1288 (ill.)

Diamonds, *2:* 243, 244, 246 (ill.), *4:* 747, 749, 750 (ill.)

Dichlorodiphenyltrichloroethane (DDT), *4:* 846, 847

Dicot plants, *1:* 145–47, 145 (ill.), 146 (ill.), 147 (ill.), 148

Diesel vehicles, *1:* 46

Diet

of bacteria, *1:* 87–88

dietary carbohydrate and fat sources experiment, *4:* 761–64, 763 (ill.), 764 (ill.)

dietary proteins and salt sources experiment, *4:* 764–66, 765 (ill.), 766 (ill.)

how good is my diet experiment, *4:* 766–69, 768 (ill.), 769 (ill.)

vitamins and minerals in, *6:* 1226, 1235 (ill.)

*See also* Food; Nutrition

Diffraction of light, *4:* 660

Diffusion. *See* Osmosis and diffusion

Digestion, *1:* 85, 164, *2:* 359, 360

Digital pH meter, *4:* 860, 860 (ill.)

Dimples, *3:* 554–55, 556–59, 558 (ill.), 559 (ill.)

Dinosaurs, *1:* 85

Dioscorides, *2:* 389

Dirt. *See* Soil

Diseases, *1:* 85–86, 86, 88–90, *3:* 539

Dishwasher detergents. *See* Detergents

Disinfection, *3:* 609–12, 610 (ill.)

**Dissolved oxygen,** *2:* **271–84,** 272 (ill.), 273 (ill.), 274 (ill.)

decay and dissolved oxygen changes experiment, *2:* 274–79, 276 (ill.), 277 (ill.)

design an experiment for, *2:* 282–84

factors effecting levels of, *2:* 271–73

goldfish breathing rate experiment, *2:* 279–84, 281 (ill.), 282 (ill.), 283

Distance, *3:* 501–5, 503 (ill.), *5:* 1047

Distillation, *4:* 724, 725 (ill.)

**DNA (Deoxyribonucleic acid),** *2:* **285–97,** 286 (ill.), 295 (ill.), *3:* 553–54

bacteria, *1:* 86, 87

cell nucleus, *1:* 142–43

design an experiment for, *2:* 295–96

of different species, *2:* 287–88

isolation and extraction experiment, *2:* 289–91, 289 (ill.), 290 (ill.)

mutations, *3:* 555

replication of, *2:* 287, 288 (ill.)

sequencing, *2:* 287–88, 295 (ill.), *3:* 553

species differences in DNA experiment, *2:* 291–95, 293 (ill.)

structure of, *2:* 286–87, 287 (ill.), *3:* 554 (ill.)

DNA fingerprinting, *2:* 296, *3:* 509–10, 510 (ill.), 562

DNA transformation, *2:* 296

Dolphins, *3:* 402

Dominant inheritance, *3:* 554–55

Doppler effect, *6:* 1111, 1112, 1112 (ill.), 1118–20, 1119 (ill.)

Double-acting baking powder, *3:* 464, 470–73, 472 (ill.), 473 (ill.), 474

Double-helix structure, *2:* 286–87, 287 (ill.), *3:* 554 (ill.)

Dried food, *3:* 451, 479, 479 (ill.)

food drying experiment, *3:* 458–61, 458 (ill.), 459 (ill.), 460 (ill.)

process of, *3:* 453

Drinking water, *3:* 604, 605–9, 608 (ill.), 609–12, 610 (ill.)

Drugs, plant-based, *2:* 389–90, 390 (ill.)

*See also* Antibiotics

**I**

**X**

**Y**

**Z**